RECONFIGURING REFUGEES

Reconfiguring Refugees

The US Retreat from Responsibility-Sharing

Alise Coen

NEW YORK UNIVERSITY PRESS
New York

NEW YORK UNIVERSITY PRESS
New York
www.nyupress.org

© 2024 by New York University
All rights reserved

Please contact the Library of Congress for Cataloging-in-Publication data.
ISBN: 9781479827961 (hardback)
ISBN: 9781479827978 (paperback)
ISBN: 9781479828029 (library ebook)
ISBN: 9781479828005 (consumer ebook)

This book is printed on acid-free paper, and its binding materials are chosen for strength and durability. We strive to use environmentally responsible suppliers and materials to the greatest extent possible in publishing our books.

Manufactured in the United States of America

10 9 8 7 6 5 4 3 2 1

Also available as an ebook

CONTENTS

1. Reconfiguring Refugees — 1
2. Bipartisan Logics of Refugee Responsibility-Sharing — 35
3. Nativist Prisms of Cultural Threat — 59
4. Terrorist Infiltrators, Gendered Threat, and the Specter of 9/11 — 85
5. Refugees as Partisan Symbols — 107
6. Enduring and Evolving Identity Narratives — 133

Acknowledgments — 159

Notes — 161

Index — 237

About the Author — 247

1

Reconfiguring Refugees

In November 2015, US presidential candidate Donald Trump warned his followers on Twitter that "Refugees from Syria are now pouring into our great country. Who knows who they are—some could be ISIS. Is our president insane?"[1] The comments coincided with the rise of an intense backlash against US refugee resettlement efforts, particularly focused on Syrian refugees, one year prior to the 2016 general elections. Trump's tweet included several layers of logics justifying US retreats from refugee protection and responsibility-sharing. First, the question of "who" Syrian refugees were as predominantly Muslim migrants "pouring into" and potentially overwhelming an already demographically and ideologically endangered white Christian nation became central to the construction of refugees as threatening the ethos and "greatness" of America. Second, questioning whether "some could be ISIS" justified restricting resettlement on the basis that refugees might be terrorist infiltrators. Third, Syrian refugees became symbols of opposing partisan identities in the context of electoral competition and political polarization in US domestic politics, binding antipathy toward Democrats ("is our president insane?") with opposition to refugee resettlement.

Six years later, following the August 2021 withdrawal of US and NATO forces from Afghanistan, the Biden administration initiated an evacuation and resettlement of Afghans at risk of Taliban persecution. Trump cautioned that "we can only imagine how many thousands of terrorists have been airlifted out of Afghanistan . . . how many terrorists will Joe Biden bring to America?"[2] In an interview with Tucker Carlson on Fox News, former senior Trump adviser Stephen Miller invoked the specter of Syrian refugees to offer a similar warning about Afghans resettled in the United States: "Most of these individuals, when you do a background check, it comes up blank. They're ghosts . . . nobody knows who they are."[3] A cohort of Republican lawmakers circulated corresponding logics opposing the Democratic administration's attempt to "flood our country with refugees from Afghanistan,"[4] permit "the mass entry of foreigners from a known hotbed of terrorism,"[5] and admit "afghan [sic] fighting age men" who "do not belong in our country."[6] The parallels with previous resistance against Syrian refugees were at times made explicit. Sen. Rick Scott (R-FL), for example, likened the Afghan resettlement efforts under Biden to "the same thing that happened with the Obama administration . . . people that are coming here that we don't know enough about."[7]

Questions around how refugee policies become intimately connected with domestic identity narratives are central to this book. Commentators have pointed to Trump's focus on migration as pivotal to his 2016 electoral victory, noting the extent to which he was able to "change the nature of the [Republican] party on immigration."[8] Beliefs in "immigrant threat narratives" became more widespread as political campaigns, candidates, and elected officials repeated and normalized them to mobilize voters.[9] Trump and his supporters arguably found "words that work,"[10] harnessing language around migration to create easily understandable contrasts with political opponents and cuing followers to apply particular metaphors in interpreting refugee policy debates. As millions of Syrians sought refuge from torture, forced disappearance, and mass atrocity crimes, many human rights advocates and liberal Democratic officials compared them to Jewish escapees fleeing Nazi violence during World War II.[11] Relying on discursive processes of racialization—in which racial hierarchies inform everyday meaning and commonsense judgments[12]—Trump and his supporters offered alternative interpretations, configuring displaced Syrians as ISIS fighters and "radical Muslims" plotting an infiltration of "Western" societies. This book shows how such words and metaphors worked beyond short-term electoral strategies, manipulating Self/Other conceptualizations and tethering refugees to local identity-making.

Trump's political ascent and attendant discourse severely impacted refugees. During the Trump presidency, the US refugee resettlement program was decimated and refugee protection principles were undermined in unprecedented ways. Migration scholars have recognized the dramatic cuts to resettlement as a "historic anomaly" in US refugee admissions.[13] Domestic resettlement organizations were defunded and faced growing anti-refugee sentiments.[14] US contributions to global resettlement slots fell by roughly 85 percent, from nearly 85,000 refugee admissions in Fiscal Year (FY) 2016 to less than 12,000 by FY2020.[15] Resettlement offers one of the few legal corridors for protecting displaced persons, and these changes exacerbated the already acute shortage of humanitarian migration pathways.[16] US retreats from refugee protection triggered a domino effect in global delays and denials of protection,[17] including a nearly 50 percent decrease in worldwide resettlement slots.[18] Pressures on refugee-hosting countries in the Global South intensified, and more asylum-seekers died in pursuit of irregular migration routes.[19]

The Trump administration's policy changes were particularly detrimental for Muslim refugees. Between 2016 and 2020, the number of Muslim refugees admitted into the United States fell by 87 percent.[20] These declines were facilitated by Executive Order 13769—commonly referred to as the Travel Ban—which restricted admissions from seven Middle Eastern and North African countries and indefinitely blocked Syrian refugees from entry.[21] In the year following the executive order, Syrian refugee resettlement departures from Jordan declined by 78 percent.[22] Continued declines in Muslim refugee admissions were furthered by the administration's designation of arrivals from eleven countries as "high risk" and therefore subject to "extra screening measures."[23] Many of the populations targeted with these measures were endangered by mass atrocity crimes or were otherwise experiencing severe humanitarian crises.[24] The Trump administration also halted funding to the United Nations Relief and Works Agency for Palestine Refugees (UNRWA), worsening poverty, food insecurity, overcrowding in camps, and lack of access to essential services for millions of Palestinian refugees in Jordan, Lebanon, Syria, Gaza, and the West Bank.[25] This move broke with all previous administrations which had sustained contributions regardless of party or ideology.

The book grapples with the racialized and gendered narratives that have legitimized and made sense of US refugee policies, shedding light on how policies with grave international consequences—including destabilizing regional and global migration dynamics[26] and compounding international trends toward restricting pathways of humanitarian migration[27]—become locally interpreted as necessary and appropriate. While some analysts envisioned a "post-Trump" era following Biden's presidential inauguration in 2021, many elements and effects of Trump's approach lingered.[28] The defunding and downsizing of domestic resettlement agencies and overseas staff continued to impede refugee protection during the first years of the Biden presidency. Increased ceilings for refugee admissions failed to materialize in part due to the slow rebuilding of an eroded resettlement infrastructure.[29] Fiscal Year 2021 entailed the lowest level of formal refugee admissions (just over 11,000) in the history of the US Refugee Admissions Program.[30] Thousands of Syrians who were shut out of resettlement opportunities and pressured to return to Syria continued to face torture, detention, disappearance, sexual violence, and death.[31] The defunding of UNRWA contributed to conditions for a prolonged financial crisis and dire trajectory for Palestinian refugees dependent on international aid.[32]

A major aim of this book is to unpack and understand how the meanings around refugees have been (re)produced, altered, and instrumentalized for political purposes. It calls attention to the role of domestic politics, racialization, and identity narratives in shaping refugee policy and responsibility-sharing. In doing so, it bridges literatures that have scarcely interacted—connecting work on partisan polarization in US politics, for example, with explorations of gendered and racialized imaginaries in International Relations (IR) and interdisciplinary migration and refugee studies scholarship. The book traces the dynamics that enabled an unprecedented breakdown in bipartisan acceptance of refugee resettlement during the 2015–16 US election cycle, showing how nativist, terrorist, and partisan configurations of refugees worked together to justify policy changes and how logics of ethnocultural preservation and Christian victimhood became interwoven with depictions of refugees as threatening infiltrators. It explores how the Syrian "refugee crisis"[33] became linked with partisan identity narratives during the political ascent of Donald Trump in ways that embedded support for and resistance to refugee resettlement within diverging and racialized visions of what America means. The book also situates that moment within a broader trajectory of repeating and ongoing US retreats from refugee protection. As much as the Trump administration's policy shifts signaled disruptions for the refugee regime, they also invoked and accelerated preexisting trends that persisted well after his electoral defeat.

As the opening paragraphs in this chapter suggest, some of the same logics used to undermine Syrian refugee protection during the 2016 election cycle reemerged in 2021 challenges to the resettlement of Afghans. Despite notable levels of bipartisan support for protecting foreign civilian "allies" who served US and NATO forces during the 20-year War in Afghanistan, a cohort of Republican leaders contested Afghans' deservingness of resettlement and contributed to a slowdown in evacuation efforts.[34] Roughly 88,500 Afghan nationals were admitted into the United States via humanitarian parole in the year following the withdrawal—a small portion relative to the hundreds of thousands seeking to escape Taliban persecution and the millions of displaced Afghans hosted by Iran and Pakistan.[35] Those fortunate enough to be resettled subsequently faced precarious temporary protection windows as a small group of Republican senators in the US Congress blocked the 2022 Afghan Adjustment Act.[36] Elements of the racialized narratives that made sense of discriminatory approaches to Syrian and other Muslim refugees under Trump resurfaced around the Afghan "refugee crisis" as domestic political actors continued to recognize such crises as sites for elaborating and sustaining their identities.

For readers unfamiliar with the complexities of terminology associated with refugees and humanitarian migration, the following sections seek to clarify some of those concepts before moving on to the core contentions of the book. These terms are far from static, and their uses continue to evolve through discursive practices as a means of establishing policies and identities. The sections ahead also unpack notions of *refugee responsibility-sharing* and *the refugee regime* to situate the book within these literatures. The chapter proceeds to outline the book's methodology and case-specific approach. It then summarizes the main arguments and contributions to existing work regarding the importance of meaning-making, gendered and racialized identity narratives, and competing partisan visions of national interests in shaping refugee policy. The final section offers an overview of the remaining chapters.

The Language of Humanitarian Migration

In exploring reconfigurations of the refugee label, the book foregrounds how domestic actors employ the language of humanitarian migration for political purposes. Vocabularies of *refugees, asylum-seekers, migrants,* and *illegal immigrants* are contested and open to ongoing (re)interpretations. In addition to operating as fluctuating "administrative categories of identity"[37] that can perpetuate colonial modes of categorizing the world,[38] these terms have become central to partisan rhetoric.[39] They contextualize and decontextualize the people they represent, and are used to validate the provision of protection or the deterrence and removal of people who have crossed borders.[40] While immigration statuses—including refugee status—are social and legal constructs rather than intrinsic traits of individuals, they can shape identities and sense of self.[41] The pages ahead provide an overview of the terminology undergirding the humanitarian protection of migrants—including *refugees*, *asylum-seekers*, and *parolees*—and outline the related concepts of *the refugee regime* and *refugee responsibility-sharing* that are used throughout the book.

Refugees, Asylum-Seekers, and Parolees

Debates around who counts as a refugee are complicated by the myriad usages of the term as an analytical category, a legal status designation, and a colloquial way of referring to people migrating due to various circumstances of adversity.[42] Before considering legal and analytical intricacies, we can begin with some descriptions refugees have used to relay their own experiences. As a self-identified refugee and survivor of the Nigerian-Biafran War, Chris Abani explains the image of the refugee as a person perpetually in flight, "always on the road somewhere, on a boat somewhere, on a plane somewhere, on a train somewhere . . . always traveling, unable to return and unable to truly settle or belong."[43] Dina Nayeri, who fled Iran as a child, describes stories of refugeehood as "stories of uprooting and transformation without guarantees, of remaking the face and the body . . . the annihilation of the self, then an ascent from the grave."[44] Somali-British poet Warsan Shire draws on her experiences around displacement to cast refugeehood in the language of *danger*, *treachery*, and *resilience*—emphasizing in her poem, "Home," that "no one leaves home unless home is the mouth of shark."[45]

With the standardization and codification of international legal instruments after World War II, refugeehood became an identity category that could be formally claimed and conferred.[46] In its narrowest usage within international law based on the Refugee Convention and United Nations Refugee Agency (UNHCR), the term is reserved for individuals who are outside their country of origin and are unable or unwilling to return due to a well-founded fear of being persecuted for reasons of race, religion, nationality, membership in a particular social group, or political opinion.[47] This definition fails to include those who are displaced by the wider range of factors acknowledged by the Critical Refugee Studies Collective—including occupation, empire, militarism, colonialism, conquest, and environmental and climate-related disasters.[48] As such, the legal construct of refugeehood typically excludes millions of people who are driven from their homes for reasons beyond political persecution. As of 2021, for example, roughly 4.4 million Venezuelans were excluded from refugee status under US law because they fled their country to escape violent crime and severe poverty.[49] Protective status is also almost always denied to people fleeing gangs, organized crime, and abuse from police and military agents in El Salvador, Guatemala, and Honduras, as such forms of violence are not classified as traditional "war."[50]

At the end of 2021, the UNHCR reported that of the more than 89 million people forcibly displaced globally due to persecution, conflict, violence, or human rights violations, roughly 27 million were designated as refugees based on the narrow legal definition.[51] The act of "counting" refugees and displaced persons is rarely a value-neutral process, however, and political actors often use such figures to legitimize arguments for containment and control.[52] These numbers also fail to capture the diverse situations and experiences of people who are driven from their homes in search of safety. Drawing on his experiences as a Bosnian refugee, Aleksandar Hemon notes that "each displacement is a tale; each tale unlike any other."[53] Statistics describing refugee flows cannot convey the scope of loss involved in being "violently pushed out from the physical cities and streets where one had long and proud histories,"[54] nor the arduous journeys endured within "the labyrinths of death" navigated by people in pursuit of asylum.[55] They cannot communicate what it means for a refugee to experience "the trauma of losing her country, her family, her property, her security,"[56] or to have "just slipped out from the grip of a nightmare."[57]

The terms refugee and asylum-seeker are often used interchangeably to refer to people who are fleeing violence and persecution, or to broadly describe people who have been forcibly displaced. Some scholars intentionally collapse these terms in challenging the criminalization and denial of protection for asylum-seekers who are not formally registered or recognized as "refugees."[58] The US immigration system distinguishes between these two labels on the basis that overseas refugees may be eligible for resettlement through the US Refugee Admissions Program (USRAP), while asylum-seekers request protection once they are already on or arriving at US territory. With both categories, US law incorporates definitional components of the Refugee Convention oriented around a well-founded fear of persecution. For overseas refugee resettlement, priority has historically been given to individuals referred by the UNHCR, certain designated nongovernmental organization (NGO) partners, or US embassies abroad. Refugees typically go through a lengthy screening process overseen by multiple agencies, including the US Department of State and the Department of Homeland Security (DHS)—a process that, on average, takes between eighteen months and two years.[59] The waiting period is often experienced as a frustrating state of limbo, as many refugees awaiting resettlement are prohibited from working or moving freely.[60]

Understandings of refugees and asylum-seekers are also entangled in politically complex and interdependent webs of meaning. Spontaneous arrivals of asylum claimants along the US southern border with Mexico have long been essentialized as disorderly in "Latino Threat Narratives" emphasizing criminality, invasion, high fertility, and unassimilability.[61] Historical portrayals of migrants from Mexico and Central America as "peons" akin to a feudal slave-labor caste[62] have interacted with discourses depicting a "Hispanic challenge" to American culture.[63] Overseas refugees have more readily been constructed as virtuous symbols of suffering and redemption. As discussed further in chapter 2, US lawmakers previously legitimized resettlement through configurations of refugees as assimilable and bolstering exceptionalist visions of America as "Western," industrious, humanitarian, and self-sufficient.

Because the process of resettlement often entails lengthy screening procedures abroad and results in relatively small numbers of new immigrants, overseas refugees can be perceived as more easily "managed" and "controlled."[64] Yet the pursuit of irregular entry by asylum-seekers along the US southern border has been fueled in part by consistently low levels of formal refugee resettlement from Latin America and the Caribbean. Between 2010 and 2020, only 4 percent of US refugee admissions were from those regions (in comparison with 63 percent and

28 percent, respectively, from Asian and African countries).[65] In both cases—refugees and asylum-seekers—domestic narratives have been crucial in stabilizing policy assumptions, even when those assumptions are largely inaccurate.[66]

Despite the ostensibly more favorable positioning of refugees relative to asylum-seekers, growing emphases on the need for "exhaustive" overseas vetting measures have contributed to assumptions that refugees are inherently dangerous.[67] While the chapters ahead show how frameworks challenging refugee protection have configured those resettled as predominantly Muslim men migrating from the Middle East, such configurations mischaracterize US refugee admissions patterns. Between 2010 and 2020, for instance, nearly half of refugee arrivals with known religious affiliations were Christian (in comparison with roughly one-third who identified as Muslim) and 64 percent were women and children. Some of the top origin countries included Myanmar (21 percent) and Bhutan (13 percent) in southern Asia and the Democratic Republic of Congo (12 percent) in Central Africa.[68] The gaps between such realities of refugee diversity and the stereotypical representations documented throughout the book underscore the distorting power of discourse in influencing interpretations of refugeehood.

The meanings associated with various categories of humanitarian migration in the US context are additionally complicated by the entanglement of *refugees* with humanitarian *parolees*. Parole is an executive authority that enables the ad hoc admission and resettlement of overseas groups for urgent humanitarian reasons. US presidential administrations have often used parole power to exceed annually allotted ceilings for refugees.[69] Parolees are afforded temporary lawful presence and a right to work, which typically expires after two years. Most of the major "refugee" resettlement initiatives in US history—including the resettlement of Hungarian, Cuban, and Vietnamese groups fleeing communism—were largely comprised of humanitarian parolees whose temporary legal statuses were subsequently adjusted by Congress. Thousands of Afghans and Ukrainians resettled during the first two years of the Biden presidency were also predominantly parolees who were widely referred to as "refugees." Journalists and US policymakers have intertwined the refugee and parolee labels for decades such that the two terms are frequently conflated in the discursive landscape of resettlement.

It must be noted here that the distinction of refugees from other categories of migrants tends to reflect an asymmetrical valuing of human life,[70] a problem that speaks to broader debates within IR regarding who counts as an "autonomous, rational, rights-bearing human subject."[71] The distinction is often ill-suited to capture the layered vulnerabilities and mixed motivations of people who cross borders. Underpinning the language of humanitarian migration, we find a refugee/migrant binary that bifurcates people deemed "voluntary" and economically motivated (migrants) from people "forced" to cross borders due to political persecution (refugees)—with the former understood as more easily excludable and the latter perceived as more deserving of admission.[72] Nayeri explains that "every day of her new life, the refugee is asked to differentiate herself from the opportunist, the *economic* migrant."[73] But the drivers of migration are multicausal and not always easily separable into this voluntary/forced dichotomy, as emphasized in work on the role of climate change and environmental degradation in contributing to displacement.[74]

The general trends observed by scholars toward preferences for welcoming overseas refugees (and humanitarian parolees) fleeing war and political persecution over asylum-seekers arriving at the US southern border and other categories of voluntary migrants deemed less deserving of protection makes the disruption in bipartisan acceptance of refugee resettlement examined in this book all the more noteworthy. Of all areas of migration policy, refugee policy should be best positioned to remain resilient regardless of changes in political party and ideology. As the chapters ahead show, this positioning of refugees atop a hierarchy of migrant deservingness is precarious, context-dependent, and subject to shift as the meanings around refugees are revised and reconfigured. In some contexts, the refugee is positioned as an unwanted, inferior, and unrelatable identity, understood as less assimilable into national belonging than that of the voluntary migrant.[75] Relaying experiences of loss and leaving behind loved ones in Nazi internment and concentration camps, Hannah Arendt eschews the refugee label as signifying dependence and misfortune, favoring identification instead as an "immigrant" or "newcomer."[76] The migrant emerges within certain interpretations as a more empowered figure than the refugee on the basis that "unlike economic migrants, refugees have no agency . . . they are so broken, they beg to be remade into the image of the native."[77] Humanitarian regimes at times reinforce such understandings by conceiving of refugees as aid recipients stripped of political context and autonomy.[78]

The Refugee Regime

The book sheds light on how domestic interpretations of refugees intervene in the international refugee regime. Within IR, international regimes encompass the implicit or explicit norms, principles, rules, and procedures that shape behaviors and expectations in a given area of world politics.[79] Specifically, the concept of the "refugee regime" has been used to refer to the norms, principles, procedures, and actors governing refugee protection.[80] Key actors within the refugee regime include the UNHCR, refugee-hosting countries, networks of humanitarian and refugee protection NGOs, and donor countries that contribute to funding and resettlement.[81] A major purpose of the regime is to "ensure refugees receive access to protection," typically via resettlement pathways and asylum claims.[82]

The refugee regime encompasses a bundle of norms—that is, expectations of appropriate behavior—regarding how governments ought to treat refugees and asylum-seekers.[83] These principles are codified in the 1951 Refugee Convention and its 1967 Protocol, and have been reinforced through a number of international legal instruments.[84] Like most human rights–based norms, the majority entail "negative" duties that require states to refrain from particular behaviors.[85] Refugee protection norms include prohibitions on the return of refugees to territories where they might face irreparable harm, torture, or other serious human rights violations (non-refoulement); prohibitions on restricting refugees' freedom of movement (non-detention); prohibitions on penalizing refugees for irregular entry through criminal prosecution, fines, or imprisonment (non-penalization); prohibitions on denial of protection based on race, religion, or national origin (non-discrimination); and expectations to participate in international "burden-sharing" (responsibility-sharing). The principle of "burden-sharing"—discussed further in the sections below—stands out as the only explicitly "positive" duty obligating countries to do something constructive to protect displaced people beyond their borders.

These refugee protection norms vary in their precision and the extent to which they are codified in legal instruments. There is debate over which practices qualify as outright violations of refugee protection norms versus more subtle evasions, which are technically permissible but undermine the spirit of these principles. There is also some disagreement regarding whether protections cover only those who are recognized with formal refugee status—an interpretation favored by many government officials because it limits obligations of protection—or also apply to asylum-seekers whose claims are not yet decided.[86] The UNHCR has emphasized that protections should apply not only to recognized refugees but also to those who "may be refugees" and have not yet had their status officially designated.[87]

The refugee regime has been criticized for myriad shortcomings and protection gaps. One major protection gap involves the separation of Palestinians from other refugee populations. The UNHCR's statute does not cover Palestinian refugees and the Refugee Convention creates a foundation for excluding Palestinians assisted by UNRWA on the basis that its principles "shall not apply" to persons receiving assistance from other UN agencies beyond the UNHCR. Designations of refugee status are typically withheld from Palestinians in ways that prevent their access to "durable solutions" such as resettlement[88] while refusing to acknowledge any right to return to their homes.[89] The protection gap around Palestinian refugees is compounded by their collective statelessness and attendant lack of political rights.[90] Discussions of UNRWA are also typically left out of discussions of the refugee regime, further perpetuating the "invisibilization" of Palestinian refugees.[91]

Many of the protection gaps within the refugee regime are linked with the narrow definition of refugeehood, as previously discussed, oriented primarily toward people crossing international borders due to fear of political persecution. People displaced by converging factors such as climate change, food insecurity, environmental degradation, and human rights violations that fall outside the Refugee Convention's categories of persecution are largely excluded. The refugee regime has failed to evolve to meet the fluctuating "human rights deprivations" driving displacement.[92] More broadly, the regime has been critiqued for reinforcing tensions between the rights of national governments to "arbitrarily exclude strangers" and more universal principles of human rights wherein individuals should have "ethical claims on humanity, beyond the national community."[93] The refugee regime was largely established by and for sovereign states, and their interests in managing and containing cross-border movements continue to be prioritized above the interests and needs of displaced peoples. Within this context, refugees are repeatedly deprived of agency.[94] As the regime comprises a crucial component of the global architecture developed to address humanitarian migration issues, it is important to understand how these shortcomings are exacerbated by inadequate refugee responsibility-sharing among countries.

Refugee Responsibility-Sharing

Based on an understanding that forced migration is inherently transnational in scope,[95] the international refugee regime relies on the principle of "burden-sharing."[96] This concept draws on decades of international migration narratives constructing migration as "a global issue that should be addressed globally"[97] and casts refugee protection as a collective duty of the international community. However, emphases on "burden-sharing" have also exacerbated the extent to which refugees "always feel like a burden" amid journeys of overcoming danger and potential loss of life.[98] They imply that protection duties are a task to be accepted reluctantly, "to be discharged only so as to relieve oneself of the load ... to be avoided via loopholes and excuses and shifted onto others where possible."[99] In seeking to move away from the depiction of refugees as unwanted *burdens*, scholars have increasingly employed "responsibility-sharing" to capture this principle.[100] Beyond the transnational nature of displacement necessitating a multilateral response, the concept of refugee responsibility-sharing draws on normative premises whereby all capable states have a moral responsibility to offer protection.[101] Responsibility-sharing calls attention to how countries ought to contribute and "do their part" in protecting the world's refugees.

Within the refugee regime, the fulfillment of responsibility-sharing is far from straightforward. Refugee resettlement represents an important form of responsibility-sharing, typically providing a more permanent path to protection with greater freedom of movement and political autonomy than what is afforded by refugee encampment contexts in many host countries.[102] Refugee resettlement is not a positive legal right, however, and there are no formal binding obligations on countries to offer resettlement slots.[103] The Refugee Convention provides little guidance on how states ought to allocate legal, financial, and physical responsibilities in responding to displacement.[104] Schemes oriented around capability-based algorithms for responsibility-sharing (e.g., size, population, and wealth) have been proposed,[105] yet appeals to "the spirit of solidarity" and "a more equitable sharing of the burden and responsibility" have often failed to translate into concerted policy actions.[106] In 2020, only around 2 percent of refugees worldwide who were in need of resettlement were successfully relocated to a new country for protection.[107] The UNHCR is frequently caught between advocating for ethical principles around responsibility-sharing and addressing the concerns of donor countries.[108]

Frameworks like the Responsibility to Protect (R2P) have been invoked to argue that countries have obligations to care for refugees and internally displaced persons in mass atrocity situations such as genocide, war crimes, ethnic cleansing, and crimes against humanity.[109] However, R2P similarly lacks clear guidelines regarding how those responsibilities should be distributed. While there is agreement that people have a right to be protected from mass atrocities when their government is struggling or failing to protect them, the duty to ensure such protection falls on no particular country.[110] In the absence of an agreed-upon "moral algorithm for determining fair shares of refugee protection,"[111] the refugee regime is largely animated by responsibility-shifting onto transit countries and countries of first asylum.[112]

While some scholars pointed to the opening of Germany's borders to Syrian asylum-seekers in 2015 under the leadership of Chancellor Angela Merkel as a "model for how a wealthy and capable state should conceive of its responsibilities,"[113] the general trend has been that low- and middle-income countries proximate to the origins of displacement situations host the vast majority (over 85 percent) of the world's refugees.[114] Wealthier donor countries tend to focus primarily on financial contributions to refugee assistance.[115] This has been discussed in terms of a "North-South impasse" in refugee "burden-sharing."[116] The lack of enforcement or accountability mechanisms within the refugee regime exacerbates these inequities. In 2021, countries that accounted for just 1.3 percent of the global Gross Domestic Product (GDP) hosted 40 percent of the world's refugees, while high-income countries hosted only 17 percent.[117]

As calls for greater refugee responsibility-sharing often focus on the Global North, they sometimes envision obligations derived from colonial histories.[118] Asylum might be conceptualized as a form of reparation,[119] and the obligations of Global North countries might be rooted in "the violent subjection of indigenous people that was at times justified with appeals to a duty of hospitality, a duty that these same states refuse to perform."[120] In the case of the United States, responsibility-sharing has additionally been linked with duties of hegemonic leadership in sustaining an international order supportive of human rights.[121] It is important to note such duties are often depicted amid a "purified" historical narrative that downplays past imperial behaviors and racial exclusion.[122]

Calls for more equitable refugee responsibility-sharing might be perceived as cosmopolitan or as moves toward subverting state sovereignty, but we must also acknowledge that they typically narrow the parameters of who is owed protection through reliance on the migrant/refugee binary[123] and reinforce ideals of governance based on discretely defined territorial jurisdictions.[124] Beliefs that states should serve as sites of protection for displaced people and uphold international human rights standards do not translate into a sense of belongingness beyond local jurisdictions or beliefs in the interconnectedness of human life.[125] The architecture of the refugee regime and its encouragement of refugee "burden-sharing" are deeply embedded in global governance structures devised to sustain and reproduce the international state system and whose principal beneficiaries are Global North countries seeking to "contain" movements of refugees.[126]

Wealthier and more powerful countries clearly have the ability to exploit weaknesses in the refugee regime and international law to evade their responsibilities,[127] but they do not always do so in a uniform way. Some governments diligently deploy mechanisms for protecting vulnerable people beyond their borders, while others refuse to make use of their strong resources and capacities to do so.[128] Better understanding is needed regarding how and why local actors vary in the ways they value and interpret refugee protection. US refugee responsibility-sharing prior to 2017 accounted for nearly two-thirds of all refugees resettled worldwide.[129] Interpretations wherein the international community ought to "address humanitarian crises collectively, as part of burden-sharing"[130] were perpetuated not only by international institutions within the refugee regime, but also by domestic political leaders. As will be discussed in chapter 2, both major political parties in the US two-party system have championed notions that "the United States is a leader in providing asylum to refugees worldwide"[131] and reinforced normative foundations wherein refugees constitute a global issue—a "problem which resulted from world conflict"[132]—and thereby generate a "responsibility shared by all democratic nations for resettlement."[133] With the intensification of political polarization, however, the premise that countries have collective duties to protect refugees has become more closely associated with Democrats in US politics.[134] In a 2021 public opinion poll, the notion that "America has a moral obligation to accept refugees facing persecution" was endorsed by 60 percent of self-identified Democrats but only 27 percent of self-identified Republicans.[135]

Scrutinizing the pivotal moment when the United States dramatically retreated from its previous contributions to responsibility-sharing helps us understand the complexity of forces influencing state responses to displacement. The book shows how racialized, partisan, and gendered identity narratives emerged around Syrian refugees during the 2015–16 election cycle in ways that conditioned possibilities for action once Trump was in office, paving paths of support among Republicans and conservatives for major policy shifts in refugee resettlement and the targeting of Muslim refugees via the Travel Ban, enhanced vetting measures, and the defunding of UNRWA. Those narratives enabled Syrian refugees to be declared "detrimental to the interests of the United States"[136] and made sense of unprecedented reductions in annual refugee admissions ceilings over the next four years. Some of those logics and legacies persisted into the Biden administration, manifesting in conservative resistance to Afghan refugee responsibility-sharing and challenges rebuilding the domestic refugee resettlement infrastructure.

Methodology and Case Study: Situating the Book's Approach

This book takes a case-specific approach to explore how racialization, fractures in identity, and disparate visions of national interests at the local level intervene in global refugee responsibility-sharing. It foregrounds the role of (sub)national identity configurations—constructions of Self and Other made and remade through discursive practices—in shaping refugee protection. In particular, it scrutinizes how refugees came to be interpreted through prisms of cultural threat, gendered hierarchy, and partisan polarization during the 2015–16 US election cycle, attending to the modes of expression domestic actors used to make refugee policy shifts conceivable. The sections below outline the book's focus on discourse and meaning-making and on the value of exploring these processes in the context of US refugee protection and responsibility-sharing.

Discourse and Meaning-Making

At the core of the book's approach is a recognition that writing, speaking, and circulating texts and images are political practices that organize, establish, and alter meanings. These practices structure perceptions of reality and make sense of the world.[137] Through repetition and dissemination, they create identities that seem "natural" and "complete."[138] A rich body of work has theorized the dynamics of discourse, identity, and knowledge production.[139] This book augments existing research into how descriptions of policy issues reproduce meaning and reinforce or revise understandings over time.[140] The focus on meaning-making also builds on previous efforts within IR to understand how explicit and implicit assumptions of non-white and non-European/non-American inferiority are reproduced in ways that create hierarchies of inclusion and exclusion.[141] Processes of racializing refugees are dependent on discursive formation, as certain articulations of identity activate and instrumentalize race to distinguish insiders from outsiders.[142]

Alongside scholarship assessing the consequences of refugee policies under the Trump administration,[143] it is important to understand the logics of justification that preceded and enabled such policies. In shaping access to rights and safety, the language deployed around migration often becomes "fate and future."[144] Representations used by political leaders to frame "refugee crises" impact public opinion, the range of policy options deemed appropriate, and the orientation of local communities toward receiving migrant and refugee groups.[145] During the 2015–16 election cycle, US policymakers understood the importance of shaping the underlying narratives structuring debates about refugee responsibility-sharing to constrain political opponents.[146] Their discursive practices had effects beyond electoral and legislative outcomes, including effects on the lived experiences of insecurity and trauma among refugees already resettled in the United States.[147]

The book draws on publicly available sources of discourse[148] among US political leaders and civil society actors to explore how domestic identity narratives influence refugee protection and responsibility-sharing. Studying narratives is valuable for understanding how ways of knowing and representing shape policymaking[149] and how the boundaries of language can be stretched and reimagined to condition perceptions of the world.[150] Narratives are defined by themes—clusters of beliefs and symbols that frame a collective story,[151] an "evolving story of the self" constructed to provide a sense of purpose.[152] Within these stories, how we talk about ourselves in relation to others and to broader sociopolitical contexts becomes central to identity-making.[153] Words create meaning, and identity narratives arrange that meaning in ways that make sense of who we are, what we stand for, and what we are threatened by. Identity narratives create maps of reality, shaping what people believe to be "undoubtedly true"[154] and what premises can be unconsciously taken for granted as "common sense" in navigating the world.[155]

The book utilizes congressional and presidential speeches to examine how narratives are reassembled over time to valorize and critique certain actors and versions of history.[156] Several chapters draw on Republican and Democratic political party platforms. These platforms offer windows into the positioning of refugees within collective constructions of partisan identity across different factions.[157] They also point to shifts in representations of refugees as core party values and priorities evolve over time.[158] Through such texts, we can better grasp how the meanings around refugees fluctuate and become instrumentalized for political purposes within partisan identity narratives. In scrutinizing how refugees came to "be"[159] during the 2015–16 election cycle, the chapters also incorporate media interviews, blogs, websites, campaign ads, and tweets. Trump's ascent coincided with an increasing diffusion of ideas and discourse through online digital networks,[160] and Twitter in particular was described as "the world's most important meaning-making communication platform."[161] In addition to underscoring the importance of framing and elite cues,[162] the tweets and other modes of representation included in the book show how discursive practices continually produce and reproduce identities and generate mutually constitutive notions of insiders and outsiders.[163]

It is important to emphasize that the samples of discourse included are not intended to be entirely representative or exhaustive of meaning-making among domestic actors in the United States. They exemplify the multiple, complex, and evolving layers of interpretations constructed around refugees and offer glimpses into how policymakers harness language to represent the world in ways that condition expectations of what is possible, appropriate, dangerous, and desirable. They call attention to how local actors position certain groups as superior or inferior and as endowed with higher or lower "civilizational attributes" to connote their proximity to Euro-American whiteness[164] and their deservingness of protection. The meanings attached to refugeehood remain in flux and subject to being unsettled and reconfigured. They are never fully "closed" or "complete," but are continuously being rearticulated, reproduced, reinscribed, and reconstituted.[165] Likewise, the moments and events that are analyzed in the book are neither isolated nor self-enclosed, but are part of a "larger relational flow of processes."[166]

It is also important to underscore that refugees are inscribed with particular meanings through multiple, overlapping, and multicausal processes. Representations circulated via media interviews and news reports often involve intervention by journalists through their selection of which quotes by lawmakers or other local leaders to highlight as newsworthy and which labels to use in describing migrants and displaced people. Elected officials often repeat talking points and other information supplied to them by interest groups, and also take cues and borrow language from one another. Members of civil society groups also sometimes take inspiration from political elites and elected officials in devising frames around migration. Public statements offered through tweets, press releases, and speeches might be curated and edited by multiple actors behind the scenes. We must acknowledge and embrace some degree of ambiguity, fuzziness, and "slipperiness"[167] in tracing discursive formations. Discourses need not originate from a singular or cohesive source nor reflect the authentic personal convictions of speakers[168] to establish broader terms of intelligibility whereby certain realities come to be known, accepted, and acted upon. Modes of representation are themselves forms of power,[169] structuring and reworking the bases and boundaries of debates.[170]

Refugee resettlement has been understudied within political science and IR,[171] and the book offers a unique contribution in focusing on the role of US political leaders and elected officials in meaning-making around refugees.[172] Many of the chapters ahead foreground how political elites made refugees identifiable, categorizable, and definable through evolving prisms of interpretation. Resettlement organizations working at the grassroots level observed an increase in negative stereotypes around refugees and the resettlement process "perpetuated by elected officials."[173] Members of the public take cues from what political elites say and do to interpret policy issues and norms, and those cues can be powerful in generating competing perceptions of reality and us/them identities.[174] Elite cues are especially important for local interpretations of refugee protection given that members of the public often lack strong knowledge and understanding regarding the intricacies of refugee policy and resettlement. While some surveys suggest the US public has historically been more opposed to than supportive of refugee resettlement,[175] deeper analysis of public opinion data across time points to public uncertainty regarding refugees and a tendency to approve of the status quo established by policymakers.[176] When questioned about the propagation of immigration threat narratives, journalists have pointed to the importance of "political entrepreneurs" such as elected officials, noting that media outlets and pundits tend to recycle and disseminate policymaker discourse in covering their remarks.[177]

A multiplicity of voices in civil society also constructed, amplified, and echoed frames in ways that contributed to (de)legitimizations of refugee protection. Several of the book's chapters highlight the role of civil society groups in the reproduction of identity narratives and discourses of refugee threat. However, it is important to bear in mind that a far wider range of actors contribute to meaning-making around refugees than those that are the primary focus of this book. These include numerous refugee and humanitarian NGO networks, international agencies, religious organizations, media organizations, veterans, scholars, athletes, artists, former wartime interpreters, filmmakers, and authors.[178] The voices and perspectives of Olympic swimmer Yusra Mardini, psychiatrist and founder of Syria Bright Future Mohammad Abo-Hilal, artist Hasan Abdalla, and poet Amineh Abou Kerech,[179] for example, highlight the roles of Syrian refugees as "both subjects and authors of discourses."[180] Refugees who have recently resettled or established intergenerational roots within their communities influence local constructions around what refugeehood means.[181] While refugees can and do act as collaborators in the creation of narratives about their identities,[182] it is also the case that those who are most disadvantaged by exclusionary practices are often least able to challenge and contest those practices.[183]

The US Context

The book narrows in on the US context. American identity is intimately bound up with migration and displacement. In addition to the common and contested refrain of the United States as a *nation of immigrants* and depictions of the US origin story as one of "high immigration hospitality,"[184] it is inextricably linked with refugeehood—haunted by the "specters of self and previous nations"[185] who arrived, were forcibly brought to the country, or were forcibly displaced by new arrivals amid violence and trauma. At the center of America's nationhood mythology is a "white settler narrative of refugeehood" that positions early Anglo-Protestant settlers as victims of persecution rather than intruders on indigenous lands.[186] This narrative was established on what W.E.B. Du Bois describes as "the racial philosophy upon which America has long been nursed . . . that there are vast and, for all practical purposes, unbridgeable differences between the races."[187] For those configured as white, dislocation could precede a period of adjustment, assimilation, and upward social mobility.[188] America's refugee origin story could thus be selectively translated into an inspiring story of rebirth and redemption.

Despite the significance of refugeehood to American identity, refugee resettlement remains an understudied area of US policymaking. Attention has been paid to immigration in general or to the provision of asylum to individuals already on or arriving at US territories, as well as the treatment, status, and journeys of undocumented migrants and asylum-seekers who enter into the United States irregularly.[189] Policies concentrating on overseas refugee resettlement and US contributions to the international refugee regime have received relatively little consideration by comparison. As previously mentioned, most refugees are hosted by low- and middle-income countries in the Global South, and a growing number of studies have explored refugee and migrant protection in those contexts.[190] Within the small cohort of wealthier countries in the Global North that contributes to refugee responsibility-sharing through resettlement, the United States offers an important case. The US resettlement of more than three million refugees between 1975 and 2016 comprised the largest refugee resettlement endeavor worldwide.[191] Between 1980 and 2016, the United States admitted an average of 80,000 refugees per year,[192] and annual refugee admissions ceilings—established by the president in consultation with Congress—averaged around 100,000.[193] Refugee admissions fluctuated and favored certain groups during these decades (described further in chapter 2), but the United States typically resettled more refugees per year than all other OECD member states combined.[194] Contrary to assumptions of economic reductionism, refugee admissions were expanded even during periods of economic recession.[195] US contributions to the international refugee regime also manifested in funding for both the UNHCR and UNRWA, such that the United States became a primary financial supporter of both agencies.[196]

For these reasons, the United States has been termed "the global hegemon within the refugee regime"[197] and a "world leader on refugee and humanitarian issues."[198] The international infrastructure of refugee protection is heavily dependent on US responsibility-sharing via funding and resettlement quotas.[199] Changes in US humanitarian migration policies can trigger major effects in worldwide resettlement chains, refugee status determination backlogs, and protection dynamics in countries of first asylum[200]—pressuring people in search of safety to pursue more perilous routes.[201] US violations of international norms related to human rights have provided license to other countries to intensify their own abuses and emboldened other governments to resist efforts to be "shamed" for such behaviors.[202] Local interpretations and identity narratives around refugees in the US case are not merely a matter of domestic politics but can have far-reaching consequences in shaping global dynamics of forced migration.

The US case presents a complex and contradictory portrait. Violations of refugee protection principles have simultaneously coexisted with measures of responsibility-sharing. At the same time that US funding and resettlement efforts became crucial to the international refugee regime, they also fell far short of representing an equitable contribution—particularly when considering the refugee hosting and protection responsibilities taken on by countries with less wealth, power, and capacity. Decades of bipartisan consensus surrounding refugee resettlement failed to translate into full compliance with refugee protection norms. Refugee protection principles were selectively applied and interpreted to protect some while denying protection to others.[203] While offering crucial forms of legal solutions to displacement, resettlement has not guaranteed equal treatment or adequate investment in the tools that refugees need to prosper.[204] Particularly for refugees of color, arrival in the United States has often meant grappling with various forms of discrimination and antagonism.[205]

Despite public skepticism and intermittent hostility toward refugees in the decades leading up to the 2016 elections, political elites and civil society groups fashioned a discursive landscape in which refugee resettlement could be understood as bolstering idealized visions of what America means. Beyond serving as strategic tools of foreign policy, refugees were configured in ways that supported domestic identity narratives and transcended partisanship.[206] These configurations are not the focus of most scholarship on refugee policy, but offer important windows into understanding the persistence of refugee resettlement and responsibility-sharing across administrations of differing ideologies and political parties. They helped policymakers justify and legitimize pathways for humanitarian migration that otherwise might not have been available. In exploring how interpretations of refugees during the 2015–16 US election cycle were reconfigured to make sense of shifts away from prior levels of protection, the book advances a broader understanding of how and why refugee policies change.

It is important to outline some limitations associated with the book's case-specific findings. The interplay of US administrative and judicial processes[207] and the "winner-take-all" two-party electoral system fashion distinct dynamics in which identity narratives are reproduced and instrumentalized, and elite cues are particularly potent in shaping polarization.[208] In settings beyond the United States, these dynamics vary.[209] Polities with more diverse parties and proportional representation systems offer a broader universe of partisan identities and institutional power structures that generate different discursive topographies.[210] In other types of regimes, where the government constrains civil society voices and monopolizes public discourse, threat constructions might be geared more toward reifying a singular or more cohesive national identity.[211] In the Canadian context, there are parallels in mythologies embedding resettlement within narratives of benevolent humanitarianism[212] and a similar role for executive discretion in determining annual resettlement contributions,[213] but higher levels of "anti-nationalist" sentiment and conflicting nationalisms forge a different political landscape for configuring refugee identities.[214] In the European context, EU integration processes and notions of "the European project" have shaped distinct milieus of discourse and policy around freedom of movement, asylum, and refugee coordination.[215] Postcolonial conditions also structure nativist and other identity narratives in unique ways.[216]

While calls for responsibility-sharing at times emerge from US foreign policy practices creating or contributing to conditions of harm and displacement abroad, the superpower status of the United States has facilitated the disregard of human rights principles with relatively few consequences.[217] This status also intervenes in both the content of the narratives—such as the exceptionalist and leadership paradigms described in chapter 2—and their potential to influence discourses around refugees in other parts of the world.[218] Government officials and political elites in different countries "learn" from each other's migration rhetoric and tactics,[219] and the United States possesses a notable level of soft power in this regard. Similar discourses in other polities generated characterizations of a "Brazilian Trump" and "Oaxacan Trump,"[220] for example. To the extent that right-wing political parties and leaders draw on nativist frameworks as part of a globalized phenomenon,[221] the US case study points to the value of disaggregating local manifestations of such transnational trends to understand how cultural threat discourses develop, evolve, and reproduce in discrete contexts.

Beyond its case-specific approach to assessing how domestic identity narratives shape refugee protection and responsibility-sharing, the book also points to a global-local nexus in which global processes of meaning-making impact and become part of subnational discourses, and local actors use foreign developments to advance their domestic causes.[222] Globalized discourses elevating "Western civilization" and imprints of colonialism[223] feed into local articulations of nativism. Anti-Muslim and Orientalist ontologies also operate at a global level,[224] with vocabularies of *extremist* and *radical Islam* animating discourses transnationally.[225] Studies of the refugee regime in Europe point to competing transnational/regional normative frameworks pitting human rights and refugee protection against national security and state sovereignty,[226] and constructs of "bogus refugees" have shaped policy debates across Canada, Australia, the United Kingdom, and Western Europe.[227] There are also globalized, transnational discourses perpetuated by institutions within the international refugee regime and other actors emphasizing the need for refugees to be "self-sufficient" and "self-reliant"[228]—themes that emerge in domestic narratives.

Globalized discourses of migrant deterrence and control reinforce local threat configurations.[229] UN Security Council resolutions highlighting the asylum process as "a potential route for terrorists,"[230] transnational networks of police professionals linking immigration with crime,[231] and international frameworks depicting refugees in terms of "crises"[232] have bolstered domestic representations of refugees as state security risks.[233] The language of "unprecedented refugee crisis" circulated by refugee regime actors at the international level arguably overstates the extent to which refugees have increased as a proportion of the overall global population[234] and invokes racialized interpretations of refugee threat as increasingly non-European and non-Western.[235] During the 2015–16 US election cycle, many political elites and civil society actors recycled notions of *unprecedented crisis* in their claims about refugees. Nativist groups capitalized on that "crisis" to advance anti-Muslim, anti-immigrant, and conservative Christian worldviews, and Republican and Democratic lawmakers instrumentalized "refugee crisis" vocabularies in ways that solidified partisan identities and agendas. We must therefore bear in mind that meanings at the international and local levels can be mutually constitutive. Globalized discourses can influence domestic debates, and local frameworks of interpretation can render global norms meaningful.[236]

(Re)configuring Refugees: Main Arguments and Contributions

Given previous decades of US voluntary contributions to resettlement and the refugee regime, how might we understand the dramatic and intentional[237] disruption in responsibility-sharing that began in 2017 as the Trump administration embarked on a series of refugee restrictions? The book departs from most work on refugee policy and the international refugee regime by focusing on the role of domestic identity configurations—constructions of Self and Other made and remade through discursive practices at the national and subnational levels. It argues that major retreats from refugee resettlement following the 2016 elections and the attendant targeting of Muslim refugees were enabled by racialized and gendered logics legitimizing those disruptions as necessary and desirable. The book shows how systems of meaning circulated by political elites and civil society actors positioned refugees as cultural threats, potential terrorists, and symbols of partisan identity. Through repetitions of terms like *political correctness, infiltration, military aged males, males of combat age, Islamic terrorism, radical Islam,* and *radical multiculturalism,* domestic actors harnessed gendered vocabularies of racial difference to appeal to and reinforce parochial identities such that withdrawing from refugee protection "made sense" and could be understood as morally appropriate.

The chapters ahead show how frames for interpreting refugees became bound up with local identity narratives during the 2015–16 election cycle in ways that constrained bipartisan possibilities for defending refugee resettlement. Nativist prisms interpreting refugees as (1) threats to white Christian cultural hegemony combined with iterations of refugees as (2) terrorist infiltrators seeking the destruction of the Western world. In a milieu of intensifying partisan polarization, policy arguments about Syrian refugees and refugee resettlement writ large also cast refugees as (3) symbols of liberal Democratic values related to "multiculturalism" and "globalism." These overlapping conceptualizations of refugees via nativist, terrorist, and partisan configurations drew on gendered binaries and Orientalist ontologies. They co-constituted and mutually reinforced each other, aggregating anxieties surrounding perceived attacks on whiteness, Western-ness, and conservative Christian identity.

It is worth considering how these arguments fit within existing explanations of refugee policy and protection. In the US context, refugee resettlement has often been understood as a function of nationally cohesive foreign policy interests, with emphasis placed on the strategic value of admitting certain refugee and parolee groups.[238] Scholars have also pointed to the efforts of "ethnic lobby groups"[239] and the role of legal and bureaucratic mobilization by refugee advocates[240] in forging consensus across political elites. Civil society actors effectively mobilized in support of admissions for certain groups, while there was insufficient domestic mobilization in opposition to their resettlement.[241] In addition, scholars have pointed to institutional forces, such as the role of presidential power and executive discretion in refugee policymaking and other types of foreign policy decisions.[242] Finally, the low salience of the refugee resettlement program in the past has been highlighted as enabling refugee policy in the United States to remain "somewhat insulated" from anti-immigrant restrictionist politics.[243]

This diverse body of work spanning multiple disciplines is valuable for understanding that refugee policy is multicausal and a range of factors help account for previous decades of US contributions to responsibility-sharing. Little attention has been paid, however, to the role of domestic identity narratives in sustaining bipartisan cooperation over refugee admissions.[244] The commonsensical refrain that refugee resettlement supported "foreign policy interests" during the Cold War was the result of mutually intelligible constructions of refugees among political elites across partisan and ideological identities. As discussed further in chapter 2, Republican and Democratic policymakers co-created and reproduced intersubjective narratives in which selective refugee responsibility-sharing made sense. Republicans and Democrats configured certain refugee groups as lawful, hard-working, "good migrants" capable of integrating and contributing and therefore worthy of protection.[245] These constructs were animated by racial cues signifying proximity to whiteness and compatibility with Westernization. Assimilability was neither objective nor static; rather, certain refugee groups were discursively produced as white or partially white, as assimilable Others who were "almost the same, but not quite."[246]

Beyond the US context, the book carves out paths of investigation that are distinct from the bulk of existing work on refugee protection and responsibility-sharing. Much attention has been paid to normative and legal arguments for devising more equitable and sustainable distributions of refugees, with emphases on the moral obligations of providing asylum.[247] Attention has also focused on the role of international mechanisms in facilitating refugee "burden-sharing" among states, including assessments of state-level commitments to asylum in the context of international norms, public goods, collective action, and multilateral frameworks of cooperation.[248] Studies illustrating the techniques by which wealthy countries have limited refugee and asylum-seeker arrivals on their territories offer instructive perspectives detailing the erosion of refugee protection principles in international politics,[249] and valuable cross-national studies examine how foreign policy, domestic political economy costs, and ethnicity interact to shape worldwide patterns in refugee admissions, returns, and expulsions.[250] While there is much to learn from these accounts, domestic identity configurations are largely absent. Better understanding is needed regarding *how* local systems of meaning inscribe refugee groups as unassimilable or construct them as kindred in ways that influence global resettlement and protection outcomes.

Previous studies have shown that international refugee and migration regimes are intricate, evolving, and overlapping,[251] and that regional processes and repertoires shape the implementation of migration governance.[252] But how does this complex governance architecture interact with domestic social arrangements and diverging visions of national interests and identity at local levels? Global governance scholars acknowledge that normative frameworks and international treaties are impeded when they lack support from domestic actors.[253] Studies concentrating on the impact of domestic bureaucratic and institutional forces have scrutinized variations in state-level refugee dispersal schemes, temporary protection policies, and federalist power structures,[254] and the role of local actors in generating support for refugee protection has received some notice.[255] The role of bordering and identity construction in producing insiders and outsiders is central to refugee protection,[256] yet the thicket of contested and fragmented (sub)national identity is often avoided.[257] This is partly a consequence of the broader devaluing of work in IR deemed too "messy" and "descriptive" and an attendant focus primarily on theory-building and testing—tendencies that have been criticized for enabling the whitewashing of IR's violent and racialized foundations.²⁵⁸

In terms of theorizing refugee protection and responsibility-sharing, the book argues that we must take seriously the power of discourse in shaping refugee policy interpretations and outcomes. We also need to better account for domestic identity narratives within countries when considering state contributions to international regimes, "burden-sharing," and compliance with international norms. In the context of relatively weak international norms and enforcement mechanisms characterizing the refugee regime,²⁵⁹ the book presses IR and migration scholars to unpack "national identities" and "national interests" to understand shifts in state policies and adherence to (or departure from) refugee protection principles. This approach has implications for the wider study of norms in global politics, suggesting more attention be paid to how contested, fragmented, and racialized visions of identities and interests *within* states intervene in norm internalization and implementation.²⁶⁰ As the explorations of domestic identity forces in the chapters ahead show, interpretations of refugeehood and what constitutes an appropriate response to refugee "crises" can become heavily bound up with diverging interpretations of national identity and contestation over which interests are in need of defense and preservation.

The book asserts that US retreats from global refugee responsibility-sharing can be understood in part as a manifestation of fragmented and cross-cutting local identities bound up with gendered binaries and assumptions of racial difference. Exploring how such domestic boundary-drawing and meaning-making processes intervene in refugee protection disrupts parsimonious portraits of refugee policy outcomes as guided primarily by a cohesive national interest or national identity. But this disruption can be productive for efforts within IR to move beyond "methodological nationalism"²⁶¹ by opening up the "black box" of the state and examining how conceptualizations of national identity are manufactured, hegemonized, and reproduced.²⁶² Notions of "liberal democratic states" with ostensibly unified national identities and interests that subsequently drive refugee policy and "burden-sharing" outcomes²⁶³ obscure more causally complex dynamics beneath the surface. Boundaries of belonging that (de)legitimate refugee policies are created, disseminated, and altered along uneven splinters of local identities. The chapters ahead show how support for refugee resettlement became conceptualized as antithetical to conservative Christian and Republican visions of America, for example, while being championed as integral to America's core values and interests in more liberal religious and Democratic frameworks. While previous work has explored how migrant groups become interpreted as threatening,[264] attending to these competing interpretations in an environment of growing partisan polarization advances understanding on how certain refugee policy and protection outcomes become thinkable and possible.

Conventional wisdoms within IR tend to juxtapose "liberal states"— characterized by "self-identities [that] include the promotion of values such as human rights, political freedoms and freedom from persecution"[265]—with "illiberal states" disruptive of these principles.[266] Erosions of international human rights norms (including refugee and asylum protection principles) have been linked with trends of "liberal states" behaving "illiberally."[267] The book urges us to probe more deeply beyond liberal/illiberal typologies of states to consider how contestation and fragmentation among ideological, partisan, and other domestic identities mediate governmental approaches to human rights and migration. Scholars have explored how "states" constitute refugees as markers of national sovereignty in ways that challenge international human rights and refugee law,[268] but we must also consider how certain groups *within* states construct different meanings around sovereignty and position refugees in those diverging interpretations.

Refugee policies do not fit neatly within the domestic/international dichotomy underpinning state-centric conceptualizations of world politics.[269] The disciplinary boundaries established between IR and American politics within political science[270] have constrained understandings of US refugee protection and responsibility-sharing. The book offers a unique approach in attempting to work across these divides and explore how forces within domestic politics shape aspects of global refugee governance. It encourages us to more forcefully question the extent to which "states share a 'we' identity,"[271] enabling a fuller picture of how and why norm implementation and refugee protection change over time by considering local contestation over refugee meanings. It also contributes to existing work suggesting that political elites play a crucial role in identity-making and polarization.[272] Through the repetition and circulation of particular images and vocabularies, they help interpret and adapt what refugeehood means. In this process, they reproduce certain social identities and respond to opposing partisan narratives. The following chapters illustrate how Republican and Democratic policymakers used refugee image-building to curate diverging visions of what was at stake in preserving "America" and tethered those understandings to partisan and ideological identities. These systems of meaning were co-dependent and relational—preempting, countering, and constituting the arguments of political opponents. This focus underscores the need to better grapple with how competing ideologies and antagonistic visions of national interests impact international human rights principles.[273]

Finally, the book foregrounds the importance of domestic discursive processes in perpetuating a "global color line"[274] in international relations and refugee protection. In tracing representations of refugees and logics justifying and (de)legitimating responsibility-sharing over time, the book contributes to broader understandings of how racialization unfolds in political rhetoric in ways that limit social inclusion and belonging.[275] Depictions of refugees as unassimilable and as potential terrorist infiltrators can be situated within previously studied assumptions around racial difference and Western superiority in global politics.[276] Debates over when and how protection is owed to foreign civilians are informed by social constructions of gendered and racist hierarchies that extend beyond individual bigotry or prejudice.[277] Exploring how Syrian and other Muslim refugees were positioned as culturally threatening during the 2015–16 US election cycle speaks to wider explorations of how whiteness is continuously "reinvented" and how certain groups become enfranchised and disenfranchised from racial belonging with attendant perceptions of being "deserving" or "undeserving" of rights and protections.[278]

Overview of the Book

The remainder of the book traces the evolving meanings and imagery attached to refugees in domestic identity narratives and considers the consequences of these representations for refugee protection and US responsibility-sharing. Chapter 2 explores how intersubjective constructions of foreign policy values and interests among political elites facilitated relatively high levels of refugee resettlement, skewed to favor certain groups, for decades prior to the 2016 elections. Throughout the Cold War, these constructions drew on mirror image logics, contrasting American ideals with communist enemies, as well as themes of providential exceptionalism. The chapter shows how Republicans and Democrats co-created and reproduced narratives in which refugee resettlement bolstered visions of America's superiority, global leadership, and Safe Haven status. These logics persisted after the Cold War ended, with refugees reconfigured as symbols of America's commitment to human rights. Refugee protection was discursively constructed to justify interventionist foreign policy and perpetuate visions of humanitarian hegemony while largely diverting attention away from US violations of human rights. Chapter 2 also highlights how representations of refugees amplified racialized ideas of what it means to be American—to be *Western, industrious, self-sufficient*—in ways that cued whiteness and were mutually intelligible across partisan identities.

Next, the book explores how bipartisan logics of support for refugee resettlement unraveled during the 2015–16 election cycle. Chapter 3 focuses on nativist narratives that combined defensive nationalism with anti-Muslim, anti-immigrant, and conservative Christian logics to help justify US retreats from refugee responsibility-sharing. The chapter defines nativism and Orientalism and establishes their importance in interpretations of domestic identity. Civil society actors and political elites capitalized on the Syrian "refugee crisis" to reinforce a sense of racialized cultural crisis, positioning Syrian and other Muslim refugees as unassimilable outsiders. Configurations converged around notions of *Muslim infiltration, radical multiculturalism,* and *Christian victimhood* to construct refugees as threatening to the preservation of white Christian cultural hegemony. These configurations bolstered ethnocultural identity narratives and competitive victimhood to legitimate US withdrawals from the refugee regime. The nativist prisms examined in the chapter also provided logics for delegitimizing global governance, the United Nations, and non-discrimination principles.

Nativist frameworks of meaning were intertwined with images depicting refugees as potential terrorists. Chapter 4 shows how configurations of Syrian and other Muslim refugees as dual threats of terrorist and civilizational infiltration helped forge opposition to refugee resettlement while eliding the role of decades of US foreign policy actions that contributed to conditions of harm and displacement. The shadow of the 9/11 attacks and "War on Terror" loomed large in rhetorical maneuvers linking refugees with *radical Islamic terrorism* and Orientalist conceptualizations of the Middle East as a threatening and *non-Western* space. The November 2015 Paris attacks amplified the specter of 9/11 and crystallized previous Republican efforts to graft ISIS infiltration frames onto refugee resettlement. These constructions often unfolded in gendered ways that masculinized the threat of refugee admissions. Democrats, too, co-created gendered logics, defending refugee responsibility-sharing on the basis that most Syrians admitted were women and children and therefore did not pose security risks. Drawing on legislative debates over H.R. 4038 (the SAFE Act), other bills introduced in Congress to restrict refugee admissions, and discourse circulated by governors and presidential candidates, the chapter shows how these prisms became bound up with identity narratives.

The representations of refugees explored in chapters 3 and 4 extend and innovate long genealogies of threat construction rooted in the defense of whiteness and colonial frameworks of Western civilization. Beyond those deeply rooted trajectories, the tethering of refugees to antagonistic partisan and ideological identity narratives is crucial for understanding the breakdown in bipartisan justifications of refugee protection and responsibility-sharing. While literatures on partisanship and polarization are rarely engaged by IR scholars or scholars of migration and refugee studies, chapter 5 engages this work to help explain the instrumentalization of refugees as symbols of opposing policy values in the US two-party system. Drawing on political party platforms, congressional rhetoric, gubernatorial statements, and other sources of discourse, the chapter delineates how competing intersubjective communities of Republicans and Democrats conceived of the "refugee crisis" in disparate ways linked with diverging accounts of what America means. In Republican narratives, refugees were situated within gendered and racialized mirror image logics wherein Republicans were masculinized cultural warriors and strong defenders of the in-group—implicitly coded as white and explicitly demarcated as Christian—while Democrats were feminized as weak, submissive, and defined in terms of pro-Muslim/anti-Christian binaries. In Democratic narratives, embracing refugee resettlement bolstered claims on compassion and inclusion along with liberal visions of safeguarding America's Statue of Liberty ethos.

Taken together, these chapters show how affixing the Syrian "refugee crisis" to domestic identity narratives during the 2015–16 election cycle altered the politics of refugee resettlement, closing off possibilities of support for refugee protection and responsibility-sharing among Republican policymakers in new ways. Political elites and civil society actors adopted discourse supporting or opposing refugee admissions in ways that replicated and innovated what constitutes liberal versus conservative and Democrat versus Republican, what an authentically Christian worldview entails, and what America means. Chapter 6 considers the durability of these configurations, assessing their persistence after 2016 as well as moments when bipartisan logics of support for refugee resettlement reemerged. The chapter also spotlights the endurance and evolution of meaning-making surrounding refugees during the 2019–20 election cycle. As the COVID-19 pandemic further diminished global refugee responsibility-sharing, it enabled opponents of refugee resettlement to augment multilayered threat configurations and link refugees with the spread of the coronavirus. Chapter 6 additionally reflects on the perseverance of domestic identity narratives in shaping refugee protection following the transition to the Biden administration in 2021. Discriminatory approaches were not vanquished with the conclusion of the Trump presidency or the end of the Travel Ban but endured in more subtle manifestations of racial hierarchy. Ukrainians were more widely welcomed and offered greater measures of protection than displaced people of other nationalities as the racialized symbols and identities associated with *refugees* shifted. Finally, chapter 6 briefly looks ahead to what might be anticipated in the future of US refugee policy.

2

Bipartisan Logics of Refugee Responsibility-Sharing

Before delving into retreats from refugee protection and responsibility-sharing associated with the 2016 elections, it is important to understand how intersubjective constructions of refugees and identity narratives among political elites had previously facilitated US contributions to the refugee regime. Throughout the Cold War, the 1990s, and the 2000s, the UNHCR depended on the United States for both funding and resettlement assistance.[1] Refugee responsibility-sharing spanned Democratic and Republican administrations, and some of the most vocal advocates for refugees included Republican lawmakers.[2] Paradigms of past US refugee policymaking often elevate anticommunist foreign policy interests, but refugee resettlement endured long after the Cold War ended. Even after the September 11 attacks, the refugee resettlement program continued to be lauded as "a bipartisan success story."[3] Amid the intensification of immigration deterrence and heightened emphasis on border security,[4] it remains unclear how policymakers justified maintaining US contributions to refugee resettlement in ways that resonated across partisan identities. In exploring the legitimation of refugee admissions for decades prior to the 2016 elections, this chapter addresses that question and provides important context regarding the continuity and discontinuity of discourses around refugee resettlement and the "breaks in representational practices"[5] which emerged over time.

To begin, it is necessary to foreground how racialized narratives oriented around providential exceptionalism manifested in notions of America as a Safe Haven and "leader" of the international refugee regime. These narratives persisted in shaping interpretations of refugee responsibility-sharing during and after the Cold War. Republicans and Democrats co-created and reproduced webs of meaning in which refugees bolstered America's superiority and divinely ordained mission in the world. The chapter will then explore how refugees were positioned within mirror image logics contrasting American values with communist enemies. In addition to fueling anticommunist rivalries, refugee depictions amplified racialized visions of what it means to be American—to be *Western, industrious, self-sufficient*—in ways that cued whiteness.

Next, we turn to the construction of refugees as diversionary symbols of America's commitment to human rights. After the Cold War ended, mirror image juxtapositions shifted toward the repressiveness of failed states and Islamic extremism. These logics reinforced America's special status and responsibilities as a global role model, justifying interventionist foreign policy while largely diverting attention away from US violations of human rights. Lawmakers from both parties instrumentalized refugee resettlement to portray the United States as a humanitarian hegemon. Policymakers often reproduced the bifurcation between overseas refugee admissions and domestic immigration and asylum-seeker arrivals in support of those narratives. The final section of the chapter shows how that bifurcation increasingly broke down during the second term of the Obama administration.

Previous work links earlier climates of bipartisan "consensus" and cooperation surrounding US refugee policy to geostrategic foreign policy interests, bureaucratic and legal mobilization by refugee advocates, lobbying efforts among certain ethnic groups and diasporic communities, and the insulation of refugee resettlement from more contentious realms of immigration politics.[6] The interaction of these forces converged with romanticized images of refugees as "freedom seekers" and "freedom fighters."[7] By examining the evolving meanings attached to refugees over time, we can better understand the power of discursive and identity dynamics within the complex causal story of US refugee protection and responsibility-sharing. In delineating how refugee configurations were anchored in shared colonial fantasies of what America means that transcended partisanship, this chapter sets a valuable stage for comprehending the reconfigurations of meaning and unraveling of bipartisan logics of support described in subsequent chapters.

Refugees and Exceptionalist Mythologies

Throughout the Cold War, the 1990s, and the War on Terror (WOT),[8] Republicans and Democrats configured refugees within exceptionalist mythologies, generating intersubjective lenses for interpreting US refugee protection and responsibility-sharing. While definitions of American exceptionalism vary, the concept of providential exceptionalism captures the "iconography of the city on the hill" in imaginations of America as "a chosen nation, one upon which Providence has bestowed unique blessings of liberty," and one that carries unique obligations and responsibilities.[9] Providential exceptionalism is deeply rooted within American identity narratives.[10] George Washington linked America's "unexampled prosperity" to "circumstances which peculiarly mark our situation with indications of the Divine beneficence toward us"—blessings that carried a special "duty" and "great obligations."[11] Exceptionalist narratives positioned America as a "salvation" of the world[12] and an "asylum for mankind."[13] These constructs incorporated storylines of a "manifest destiny" to civilize barbarous others.[14] They helped sustain a sense of American superiority and infused the welcoming of migrants with "patriotic significance"[15] while diverting attention away from US culpability in the displacement of native inhabitants and those forcibly brought to the country as slaves.

Providential exceptionalism has proven malleable in articulations of threat and welcoming. Visions of Americans as a chosen people fleeing religious bondage in Europe and building a new Promised Land—a "New Jerusalem"—were sometimes deployed to craft nativist frameworks of cultural threat.[16] During implementations of restrictive national origins quotas, interpretations of America's "providential mission" were harmonized with beliefs that its ethnocultural and racial composition "should never change."[17] At other times, providential exceptionalism was oriented around more inclusive notions of hospitality.[18] Faith-based civil society groups helped assemble images of a divinely ordained Safe Haven, depicting migrants as "children of God" who should be welcomed in accordance with the "moral and spiritual principles of our founding fathers."[19] Policymakers also intertwined providential exceptionalism with portraits of caretaking. President George W. Bush asserted that immigrants "make our country more, not less, American," describing Americans as "called to do great things" and drawing on the Christian parable of the Good Samaritan helping a stranger: "Abandonment and abuse are not acts of God, they are failures of love . . . when we see that wounded traveler on the road to Jericho, we will not pass to the other side."[20]

Safe Haven mythologies reinforced the providential role of the United States to serve as a global refuge. These mythologies were animated by a sense of righteousness, supremacy, and moral responsibility.[21] The Republican Party platform of 1956, for instance, justified providing "asylum for thousands of refugees, expellees and displaced persons" in the context of America's special duties—"our responsibility for world leadership." Serving as "a haven for the oppressed" was constructed as an American "tradition."[22] Similarly, in 1960, Republicans outlined the importance of "fulfilling our obligation as a haven for the oppressed."[23] Within these frameworks, refugee admissions were not merely tools of anticommunist foreign policy maneuvers but supported specific visions of what America represented in the world. Refugees could be "absorbed and granted citizenship in the settler colonial state" in ways that enabled US policymakers to elide and counter critiques of colonial violence and indigenous dispossession.[24]

In his speech at the 1980 Republican National Convention, Ronald Reagan positioned America as a *refuge*: "Can we doubt that only a Divine Providence placed this land, this island of freedom, here as a refuge for all those people in the world who yearn to breathe freely?" The messianic fervor of the idea of *Divine Providence* elevated America as a singular beacon of liberty in the world, an *island of freedom*. Reagan fused providential exceptionalism with anticommunist cues around "Jews and Christians enduring persecution beyond the Iron Curtain,"[25] denigrating communist enemies while reproducing decades of discourses in US foreign policy linking notions of freedom and "freedom-loving" peoples with white racial identity.[26] Refugee admissions were selective and skewed to favor certain groups. Cubans, Jews and Christians fleeing the Soviet Union, and particular cohorts of Vietnamese, for example, were prioritized over Haitians, Salvadorans, and Guatemalans.[27]

The recognition of refugee status and granting of resettlement were withheld from many whose identities called into question narratives of providential exceptionalism and white supremacy. Haitians, for instance, had long been configured as threatening Euro-American "civilization" on the basis that the Haitian Revolution was an assertion of Black political autonomy that undermined the foundations of slavery and global racial hierarchy.[28] Central Americans racialized as Afro-Latinx or Indigenous were frequently depicted as hyper-reproductive, gender nonconforming, or threatening the racial-colonial origins of US state-building.[29] In contrast, those who received recognition as refugees were often inscribed by political elites and advocacy groups as aligning with the core values that make America sacred and distinct—including representations of US democracy as founded upon an Anglo-Saxon inheritance and "blood of freedom"[30] and understandings of communism as "Christianity's archenemy."[31] Such representations diverted attention away from America's origins as a slaveholding republic that forcibly displaced Native Americans.[32] Refugees sometimes actively contributed to the positioning of their identities within narratives of American exceptionalism, describing themselves as having "found freedom in the land of open arms, which opens the great gates of life."[33]

The Refugee Act of 1980 engendered a fuller harmonization of US domestic policy with international legal standards. It established a baseline expectation that the United States would resettle 50,000 refugees, raising the previous admissions ceiling from 17,400—which had been repeatedly exceeded through presidential uses of parole authority and attorney general exercises of emergency admissions. The legislation emerged from a combination of forces, including desires among lawmakers to reassert congressional control over refugee admissions and "a growing sense of responsibility" for coordinating the departures of refugees from communist countries in Southeast Asia.[34] The Republican governor of Iowa, Robert Ray, played a crucial role in the passage of the Refugee Act—which moved through Congress with strong bipartisan support—and in generating increases in federal spending on resettlement. Gov. Ray focused on America's "moral obligations" toward Vietnamese allies[35] and promoted interpretations of refugees from Asia as "model minorities" possessing a strong work ethic and values that supported fiscal conservativism.[36]

The Democratic Party platform praised the Refugee Act as "the first comprehensive reform of this nation's refugee policies in over 25 years" and framed this accomplishment within Safe Haven imagery: "America's roots are found in the immigrants and refugees who have come to our shores to build new lives in a new world."[37] The emphasis on *new lives* and a *new world* bolstered narratives of white settler refugeehood, erasing the presence of indigenous peoples and the violence used to displace them. The 1980 Republican Party platform painted similar visions of

America: "The traditional hospitality of the American people ... remains the strongest in the world. Republicans are proud that our people have opened their arms and hearts to strangers from abroad and we favor an immigration and refugee policy which is consistent with this tradition."[38] Refugees were inscribed as symbols of American *hospitality* that whitewashed America's imperial past and inhospitality to those deemed racially inferior. As annual refugee admissions peaked at a high that surpassed 207,000,[39] welcoming refugees was portrayed in both party platforms as foundational to America's origin story, in the *roots* and *traditions* of what makes America great. These bipartisan narratives helped facilitate a collective amnesia around the racism and oppression involved in the establishment of the United States.

Between FY1983 and FY1988, annual refugee admissions hovered between 61,000 and 76,000—much lower than the initial levels of the decade but still above the Refugee Act baseline of 50,000. Admissions from parts of Asia and the Soviet Union were consistently favored.[40] The Republican Party Platform of 1984 represented refugees amid praise for "the spiritual and intellectual genius of the American people" and the "freedom that inspires and guides the American Dream."[41] Shared visions of the United States as "chosen" and bound by "a special responsibility to engage the international system"[42] continued to shape justifications for refugee protection and responsibility-sharing after the Cold War as Republicans and Democrats reproduced logics of providential exceptionalism in shifting contexts. President Clinton reminded Americans that "people on every continent can look to us and see the reflection of their own great potential," quoting biblical scripture to position the United States as "the repairer of the breach, the restorer of paths to dwell in ... America is far more than a place. It is an idea, the most powerful idea in the history of nations."[43]

Political elites from both major parties used refugees to curate a founding mythology wherein the United States had always been a hospitable site of asylum. In advocating for the Refugee Protection Act of 1999, Sen. Sam Brownback (R-KS)—a deeply conservative figure in the Republican Party—reminded his colleagues about "the refugee Pilgrims" who helped establish the United States. The senator cited George Washington urging Americans in 1795 to "render this country more and more a safe and propitious asylum for the unfortunates of other countries." Brownback also quoted Thomas Jefferson's 1801 annual message: "Shall oppressed humanity find no asylum on this globe?"[44] In praising President George W. Bush's refugee admissions efforts in 2002, Sen. Jim Bunning (R-KY)—one of the Senate's most conservative members—declared: "One fact we as Americans must never forget is that our forefathers were also political and religious refugees in search of a better life."[45]

These depictions of America's Founding Fathers as inclusive and embracing of others omitted nativist aspects of the origin story, including Jefferson's reference to indigenous peoples in the same 1801 annual message as "savages of the wilderness."[46] Alexander Hamilton's characterizations of immigrants in terms of a "Grecian horse" and John Adams's representation of foreigners in the context of "insidious intrigues"[47] were also sidestepped in cultivations of the Safe Haven narrative. Highlighting an enduring commitment to refugees enabled policymakers to produce unblemished portraits of America's superiority and cast the United States as a "moral protagonist" in international relations.[48] Policies of discrimination and forced removal, denials of protection, and other violations of human rights were minimized or treated as aberrations in logics representing America as fulfilling its destiny as a place of asylum.

Following the escalation of conflict in Iraq in 2006, members of Congress approved a resettlement program for Iraqi interpreters configured as "allies" who aided the US mission in the Iraq War.[49] Applauding a 2008 "bipartisan" refugee protection bill, Rep. Jim McDermott (D-WA) perpetuated mutually intelligible constructions of such refugees as testaments to America's special status as an oasis of *liberty* in a world of *persecution* and *injustice*: "I think the torch of the Statue of Liberty might just be burning a little brighter today because we are soon going to send to the President a bill that helps the most vulnerable on our shores, refugees coming to America fleeing persecution, injustice, torture and even the threat of death." While US refugee admissions included increasing proportions of refugees from Myanmar (formerly Burma) and Bhutan, as well as from African countries such as Somalia, Sudan, and Eritrea, the congressman emphasized "Jews from the former Soviet Union, Kurds from Iraq, [and] Hmong fighters from Vietnam" in his description.[50] These frameworks helped legitimize continued contributions to the refugee regime,[51] while at the same time downplaying the role of

US foreign policy in contributing to harm, displacement, and "nation-destroying" processes within some of those contexts.[52] These frameworks also diverted attention away from the surveillance, harassment, imprisonment, and deportation of those who failed to be recognized as refugees despite their service to US personnel overseas and the risks they faced as a result.[53]

Leading the Refugee Regime

Lawmakers from both parties constructed the United States as the central driving force behind the creation and sustainment of the international human rights and refugee regimes, aligning US "leadership" in these realms with exceptionalist visions of America's role in the world. Frameworks legitimizing refugee protection and resettlement emphasized that the United States had "always taken the lead on resettling refugees"[54] and "led the effort to establish universally recognized fundamental rights."[55] In 1990, as George H. W. Bush authorized an increase in the refugee admissions ceiling to 131,000[56] and issued a presidential proclamation establishing October 30 as "Refugee Day," the Republican president affirmed "tremendous pride in our leading efforts to assist refugees."[57] Refugee advocacy groups amplified and perpetuated these leadership logics over time, appealing to America's status as "the world leader in recognizing the moral obligation to resettle refugees"[58] and linking "America's international leadership" in refugee responsibility-sharing with a "proud legacy of welcoming refugees."[59]

These narratives elevated partial truths. The United States did play a major role in the development of the institutional architecture surrounding refugee protection and human rights and in resettling European displacees after World War II.[60] President Truman situated immigration and refugee policy within "a global context" in terms of America's "responsibilities of leadership,"[61] and President Eisenhower made sense of US refugee admissions as part of a "contest for world leadership."[62] But the United States also rejected the nascent international refugee regime by refusing to sign the 1951 Refugee Convention[63] and initially undermined the UNHCR's capacity to protect refugees by depriving it of funds.[64] Leadership narratives placing the United States at the center of human rights and refugee regimes overlook the impediments to refugee protection created by the US government and neglect the importance of other actors.[65] These narratives also minimize the shortcomings of the refugee regime (discussed further in chapter 1), eliding its Eurocentric and colonial foundations, power asymmetries, protection gaps, and exclusion of marginalized voices.[66]

In submitting the Refugee Convention's 1967 Protocol to the US Senate, President Johnson asserted that its ratification would uphold "our traditional role of leadership" in refugee protection.[67] The Protocol perpetuated many of the original Convention's flaws. The refugee regime continued to lack accountability mechanisms for ensuring state compliance with refugee protection principles or equitable responsibility-sharing. These dysfunctions, along with repeated US violations of refugee protection norms, are part of the US leadership outcome. During a 1987 conference on human rights and refugees, the director of the US Committee for Refugees spoke to the paradox wherein the international refugee protection system depended on US financial support and resettlement contributions, yet simultaneously was undermined by the US interdiction, detention, and deportation of people with reasonable cases for protection.[68]

Leadership narratives sidestepped these contradictions, reconstructing the past and establishing a storyline wherein the international system depended on US hegemony. The 2000 Republican Party platform pledged to uphold "America's longstanding practice of aiding the innocent victims of political repression" and to "lead other countries in responding similarly."[69] During his inaugural address, newly elected President George W. Bush framed America's leadership as an obligation: "If our country does not lead the cause of freedom, it will not be led . . . where there is suffering, there is duty."[70] Throughout the 2000s, lawmakers from both parties circulated logics casting America's leadership as a *duty* and its refugee resettlement program as a standard for other countries—"an example for other nations to follow"[71] and "a commitment for other nations to emulate."[72] Political elites undoubtedly harnessed these narratives for strategic purposes to further policy objectives facilitating US dominance in international relations, but in the process they also reinforced the extent to which these frameworks became constitutive of national identity and evolving stories of the Self.

As annual refugee admissions plummeted in the two years following the 9/11 attacks and federal and state funding for resettlement dwindled,[73] some lawmakers used the leadership narrative to justify the establishment of the Bipartisan Congressional Refugee Caucus. Republican Representatives Chris Smith (R-NJ) and Ileana Ros-Lehtinen (R-FL) joined Democratic Representatives John Conyers (D-MI) and Zoe Lofgren (D-CA) to co-chair the caucus in 2003, describing its purpose as "dedicated to affirming the United States' leadership and commitment to the protection, humanitarian needs, and compassionate treatment of refugees and persons in refugee-like situations throughout the world."[74] Later that year, lawmakers from both parties co-authored a letter to the Bush administration calling for a return to higher levels of refugee responsibility-sharing to "honor our nation's longstanding tradition of providing a safe haven for refugees around the world."[75] Refugee resettlement did not rebound to the levels of the 1990s, but the restoration of 52,000 admissions in 2004 represented nearly a doubling of post-9/11 levels.[76] While the previously mentioned 1980 Refugee Act established an annual admissions ceiling of 50,000 as a baseline, understandings of what constituted adequate or "normal" levels of US responsibility-sharing via refugee resettlement were nebulous and evolving.

Leadership narratives and Safe Haven mythologies continued to feature prominently in bipartisan configurations of refugee protection during the Obama administration. Lawmakers from both parties championed assertions that "the United States has resettled more refugees on an annual basis than the rest of the world combined"[77] and represents the "global leader in the protection of refugees . . . the single largest refugee resettlement country in the world . . . the single largest donor to the Office of the United Nations High Commissioner for Refugees."[78] The notion that "America has provided more assistance to refugees seeking protection than any other country" was tethered to its origins as "a safe haven with a history of aiding those seeking protection from persecution, violence, and war."[79] The 2012 Republican Party platform echoed praise for "our country's historic tradition of welcoming refugees,"[80] and President Obama reaffirmed that "all nations ought to share in our collective responsibilities" of refugee protection.[81] Roughly 70,000 refugees were resettled annually across both terms of the Obama administration, facilitating a common "representation of normality" regarding refugee responsibility-sharing.[82]

It is important to note that the absence of explicit or equitable refugee responsibility-sharing parameters within the international refugee regime contributed to idealizations of US leadership. On a per capita basis, countries such as Australia, Norway, Canada, and Sweden have arguably acted as "leaders" in contributing to resettlement,[83] at times exceeding the United States in absolute resettlement numbers for certain refugee groups.[84] Moreover, as previously discussed, Global South countries have long hosted the overwhelming majority of worldwide refugees, sheltering people from geographically proximate displacement situations for indefinite lengths of time as the United States maintained highly controlled and selective admissions.[85] The protracted refugee situation of Afghans living in Pakistan and Iran since the 1970s offers one example. Despite culpability in the conditions shaping their displacement, the United States has historically withheld resettlement from Afghan refugees, focusing instead on humanitarian aid and repatriation.[86] US leadership narratives elide such realities, omitting the crucial contributions of other countries to global refugee responsibility-sharing.

Mirror Image Identity Logics and Racial Whiteness

Anticommunist foreign policy interests are often treated as the overarching impetus for US contributions to refugee resettlement during the second half of the twentieth century. Anticommunist logics undoubtedly influenced asylum and admissions patterns.[87] Yet reducing those processes to geostrategic interests misses the role of discursive and identity components. Refugee resettlement was viewed as an anticommunist foreign policy tool because it was actively constructed and reproduced as such by political elites.[88] Associations between refugees and anticommunism were made and remade by lawmakers from both political parties within exceptionalist mythologies and mirror image frameworks that intersected with constructions of racial whiteness. Selective admissions of refugees and justifications of those admissions during the Cold War reproduced selective interpretations of what America means, crafting attendant qualifications for who counts as an insider deserving of protection.[89]

President-elect Eisenhower advocated for admitting more refugees and "escapees" from Europe in the context of a competition "between the Communist idea and the American ideal"—a competition in which "we are on the side of freedom ... we are on the side of humanity," while "the Communists are on the side of slavery, the side of inhumanity."[90] Anticommunist foreign policy was structured over decades through such identity language, with refugees placed at the center of juxtapositions between American *freedom/humanity* and communist *slavery/inhumanity*.[91] Republican Party platforms in the 1980s legitimized refugee protection and responsibility-sharing through repetitions describing refugees as "suffering people" fleeing "brutal acts" of Communist governments[92] and "oppressed people in search of freedom."[93] Refugees were configured to simultaneously affirm the *brutality* of the enemy and America's special status as a beacon of *freedom* for the *oppressed*. Lawmakers from both parties positioned refugees as "Cold War trophies," personifying American superiority and stories of Self wherein "we are the good guys, we take people who are fleeing from the bad guys."[94]

At the same time that policymakers instrumentalized refugee resettlement to build up heroic self-images of Americans as the good guys, refugee admissions were increasingly restricted. Throughout the first half of the 1980s, annual ceilings were steadily lowered from over 200,000 for FY1981 to 67,000 for FY1986.[95] This trend reflected growing pockets of restrictionist inclinations toward immigration among both Democrats and Republicans spilling over to impact refugee policy.[96] The 1984 Republican Party platform commended President Reagan for "encouraging other countries to assume greater refugee responsibilities," emphasizing "the refugee problem is global and requires the cooperation of all democratic nations."[97] Refugees fleeing communist governments in Southeast Asia and Europe continued to be favored for admission.

Anticommunist vocabularies oriented around Westernness and freedom intersected with interpretations of racial whiteness. Certain refugee groups were represented as more deserving of inclusion and protection. Hungarian refugees experienced a level of generosity and possibility based on their connections to "the free world."[98] Russian, Polish, Ukrainian, and "Baltic peoples" were depicted as "peoples culturally most closely in contact with the West" who "share our outlook" and belonging within "the community of free nations."[99] Exceptionalist mythologies of America oriented around individualism, religiosity, and a superior work ethic were reinforced through discursive constructions of refugees embedded in cues of whiteness. Latvian, Lithuanian, and Estonian refugees were depicted as sharing American ethos regarding "independence, diligence, and spirituality" and "developing industries [in which] the stores all looked prosperous."[100] Beyond being victims of communist enemies and pawns of geostrategic rivalries, these refugee groups were represented as non-threatening through their alignment with visions of America as *independent, spiritual, industrious*—imagery associated with the blossoming of white Christian nationalism and libertarianism during the Cold War.[101]

Earlier groups of "white elite Cuban" refugees were favored over later arrivals of "Afro-Cubans,"[102] in part because the US government sponsored a public relations campaign bridging their anticommunist values with socially and racially desirable qualities of "good immigrants" who could be perceived as white.[103] In contrast, constructions of US foreign policy worked in tandem with anti-Black racism to cast Haitians as "poor," "ignorant," and as "economic migrants" undeserving of refugee protection.[104] Positive portrayals of refugees from Asia emphasized proximity to whiteness by drawing on the circulation of "model minority" myths.[105] These stereotypes emphasized "persistence in overcoming extreme hardships and discrimination to achieve success . . . with 'their own almost totally unaided effort' and 'no help from anyone else.'"[106] The elevation of self-sufficiency in such frameworks resonated with narratives of agrarian American whiteness idealizing hard work and self-reliance.[107] Anticommunism was intertwined with racialized language to recast migrants of Asian descent from "an excludable, undesirable, racial pariah group to a model minority . . . held up to other American minority groups as exemplars of racial respectability."[108]

Logics were perpetuated "whereby the 'right' Asians could be rescued and enter the United States."[109] Vietnamese, Chinese, and Korean refugee and migrant groups were partially whitened through depictions of economic productivity and self-sufficiency vis-à-vis "family businesses" and "can-do" attitudes.[110] They were configured as symbols of the triumph of capitalism.[111] Such depictions aligned with the discourse of the Reagan administration and the Republican Party platforms of the 1980s, which guided messages of welcoming and hospitality narrowly toward those who make a "positive contribution to America"[112] and "bring to America their ideals and industry."[113] While Republicans emphasized the importance of personal responsibility and self-sufficiency more than Democrats,[114] lawmakers from both parties justified support for refugee admissions within a "metanarrative of democratic capitalism."[115] Representing refugees as fleeing oppression *over there* and subsequently becoming industrious and self-sufficient *here* strengthened ontologies of America as a land of opportunity in which hard work, determination, and personal responsibility could culminate in achieving the American Dream. As members of the public and some legislative voices cast refugee resettlement in nativist prisms of "too many Orientals,"[116] configurations emphasizing industriousness and productivity partially whitened refugee resettlement and made sense of selective admissions within representations of America as a "modernizing" force.[117]

Religious identity cues around refugees further supported mirror image logics contrasting America's divine purpose with the "godless creed" of communism.[118] Faith-based logics resonated in a discursive environment increasingly shaped by the evangelical political movement.[119] In arguing for US support of Nicaraguan refugees—who benefited from a period of preferential treatment relative to other Central American groups[120]—Rep. Bob Livingston (R-LA) read aloud a letter appealing to Americans' "Christian faith" and describing the brutality committed against Nicaraguan refugees and "Evangelical pastors . . . only alive by the grace of God . . . saved by God's divine salvation."[121] The Christian identities of some Vietnamese refugee groups also facilitated their representations as "Westernized" and as reinforcing rather than threatening America's providential role.[122] Refugee resettlement was often portrayed as an ecumenical effort framed in the language of religious service,[123] and the prevalence of faith-based organizations in integration services bolstered notions of religion transforming *foreigners* into *Americans*.[124]

Cold War identity configurations of refugees endured long after the strategic conditions of anticommunist foreign policy changed. Republican lawmakers encouraging refugee protection and responsibility-sharing in the 2000s continued to speak about "Hmong tribesmen who fought on the side of the United States" and "victims of communist dictatorships."[125] Refugees were described as "Jews fleeing religious persecution in the former Soviet Union," Cubans, and "Hmong people from the highlands of Laos who served on the side of the United States military during the Vietnam War."[126] In 2004, half of all refugees admitted into the United States were from Somalia, Cuba, and Laos.[127] Emphasis on the latter two countries of origin (Cuba and Laos) in justifications of resettlement reproduced images of America as a Safe Haven for "the 'good' victims of communism."[128] The "stickiness" of anticommunist lenses throughout the 1990s and 2000s sustained preferential programs for refugees at the same time that Congress passed punitive legislation criminalizing other types of migrants.[129] Legitimations of refugee resettlement perpetuated mirror image frameworks crafted decades earlier, reflecting an enduring power for identity constructs in making sense of refugee policy.

Religious identity logics, too, persisted in justifications of refugee protection and responsibility-sharing throughout the 2000s, particularly among Republican lawmakers. Support for resettlement was positioned within "a wide range of faith-based and community groups,"[130] stitching refugees into tapestries of America oriented around *faith* and *community*. Logics wherein "refugees are alive only because of a faith in God and an unshakable will to survive"[131] enabled interpretations of refugee protection that supported conservative evangelical worldviews. Refugees were configured in ways that reinforced the messianic, service-oriented spirit of providential exceptionalism. Sen. Orrin Hatch (R-UT) linked "helping refugees" with supporting "our country's religious denominations to continue uninterrupted in their call to serve," highlighting the role of faith-based groups in assimilating refugees to "adjust to a new way of life."[132] These logics offered a corrective to nativist arguments. Rather than refugees transforming American culture, refugees could be understood as objects of transformation assimilated and adjusted in accordance with American ideals and traditions. Such interpretations left unchallenged the assumption that rapid integration and assimilation are desirable objectives, eliding the harmful effects of these processes on migrants and refugees.[133]

Human Rights and Humanitarian Hegemony

In the latter portion of the Cold War, President Carter centered human rights as a new "cornerstone" of US foreign policy, partially dislodging the dominance of the anticommunist containment paradigm.[134] While initially elevated by a Democratic administration, Republican lawmakers also amplified and prioritized human rights concerns. In 1983, Representatives John Edward Porter (R-IL) and Tom Lantos (D-CA) established the bipartisan Congressional Human Rights Caucus/Commission (CHRC), "dedicated to the defense of all rights codified in the United Nations Universal Declaration of Human Rights."[135] The CHRC kept liberal and conservative members of Congress attuned to the plight of Soviet Jews and sustained pressure on the Reagan administration to increase Soviet Jewish emigration and refugee admissions.[136] The Reagan administration pursued a "conservative human rights policy" that balanced decreases in overall refugee admissions with continued commitments to resettling certain groups.[137] In the final year of the Reagan presidency (FY1988), the annual ceiling was raised from 70,000 to 87,500 and refugee admissions increased from more than 64,000 to more than 76,000.[138]

Advocacy on behalf of specific refugee groups increasingly incorporated appeals to international human rights instruments, citing "refugee law and protection standards" that conveyed a sense of global legitimacy as they were "adopted by the international community."[139] In addition to providing "an anticommunist rallying cry"[140] and rhetorical tool for critiquing communist and autocratic regimes,[141] human rights frameworks structured logics of appropriateness wherein humanitarian efforts were connected with American exceptionalism and "the civilizing mission of Empire."[142] In the post–Cold War context, the meanings attached to human rights became linked with visions of a "new world in the making."[143] Justifications of policy on the basis of supporting and promoting human rights intensified in the 1990s as the United States ratified a series of international human rights treaties.[144] Annual refugee admissions were increased to fluctuate between 107,000–132,000 during the Republican presidency of George H. W. Bush (FY1989–1992), and remained over 100,000 in the first two years of the Clinton administration.[145]

Amid widespread coverage of mass atrocity crimes unfolding in Rwanda and in Bosnia and Herzegovina, humanitarian missions proliferated and a "humanitarian agenda" inscribed images of US foreign policy.[146] While President Clinton embraced a "prevention through deterrence" approach to domestic arrivals of asylum-seekers and migrants along the US southern border with Mexico,[147] he positioned the resettlement of Bosnian refugees within a framework of "what America's mission in this world is." Bosnian refugees were used to symbolize the moral righteousness of US foreign policy: "We stood up for peace in Bosnia. Remember the skeletal prisoners, the mass graves, the campaign to rape and torture, the endless lines of refugees."[148] Clinton described Bosnian refugees resettled in the United States as "the human faces of the war" in the context of signing a presidential proclamation declaring December 10, 1995 as Human Rights Day: "I'm glad they're here. I'm honored to have such fine people strengthening the fabric of America."[149] Perceptions of Bosnian refugees as "white," "Western," and "European"[150] facilitated their praise. Tethered to visions of America's mission as a defender of peace and human rights, such configurations helped secure narratives of providential exceptionalism amid shifting normative environments wherein human rights were becoming an important standard of legitimacy.[151]

Within a growing humanitarian marketplace, global human rights advocacy campaigns sought funding and publicity.[152] The extent to which an "international language" of human rights[153] influenced domestic justifications of refugee protection and responsibility-sharing points to the role of global norms and discourses in shaping what policymakers know and expect.[154] Refugee protection legislation combined human rights and democracy promotion as pillars of US foreign policy. Co-sponsored by a roughly equal number of Democrats and Republicans, the Human Rights, Refugee, and Other Foreign Relations Provisions Act of 1996 was praised as "a consensus bill" that was "supported by a broad range of human rights organizations"—including liberal-leaning groups like the Hebrew Immigrant Aid Society as well as conservative groups like the Christian Coalition and Family Research Council.[155] The bill extended admissions of refugees from former Soviet countries and Baltic states who were persecuted as religious minorities (particularly for participation in Catholic or Orthodox churches), allowed for parole status to be granted to groups from former Soviet countries, Baltic states, Vietnam, Laos, and Cambodia, and required reporting about refugee protection within countries receiving foreign assistance.[156]

Annual refugee admissions hovered between 70,000 and 85,000 throughout the second term of the Clinton presidency (FY1996–2000).[157] Lawmakers presented refugee resettlement as "a strong humanitarian element in our foreign policy"[158] that facilitated "a strong American presence abroad."[159] Refugees were instrumentalized within these bipartisan frameworks to applaud the continued projection of US power and hegemony while portraying it as benign and humanitarian. Spotlighting refugee resettlement distracted from the numerous double standards animating US policies regarding human rights.[160] Celebrations of welcoming refugees from African countries as "emblematic of a post–Cold War US commitment to human rights untainted by geopolitical ambition"[161] enabled diversions away from US culpability in contributing to conditions of harm abroad and deliberate inhibitions of Black political power domestically.[162]

The number of refugees resettled from African countries doubled during the 1990s, with Somalia and Sudan as prominent countries of origin.[163] Discourse surrounding the resettlement of Sudanese "Lost Boys" often positioned them as "good migrants," as "vessels waiting to be filled by US material culture," and elevated exceptionalist frameworks oriented around individualism, self-sufficiency, and America as a "Promised Land."[164] Lawmakers highlighted the infrastructure in place to help refugees become "self-sufficient" and to "make a new life for themselves, rather than becoming dependent on the Government."[165] Discussions of "newly arrived Somali children" were accompanied by reassurances of "assimilation" and "skills training" programs.[166] Emphases on assimilation perpetuated colonial desires for a "reformed, recognizable Other,"[167] obscuring the coexistence of overlapping migrant identities that transcend "homeland-hostland borders."[168] Continued emphases on resettled refugees being reborn through a new life also carried forward narratives wherein the humanitarian mission of US foreign policy eclipsed its militarism and settler colonialism.[169]

Congress began recognizing World Refugee Day each June starting in 2001, with Democrats and Republicans commending US contributions to global refugee responsibility-sharing in annual resolutions. The refugee resettlement program was linked with foreign policy and human rights, celebrated on the basis that "it advances our foreign policy objectives by protecting human rights."[170] Following 9/11, Bush-appointed Immigration and Naturalization Service (INS) Commissioner James Ziglar emphasized that the attacks were "caused by evil, not immigration ... we cannot judge immigrants by the actions of terrorists."[171] As previously discussed, changes associated with the creation of the Department of Homeland Security prompted a sharp decline in admissions, to less than 30,000 for FY2002–2003. The 9/11 attacks arguably offered an opportunity for refugee responsibility-sharing to be indefinitely suspended, but resettlement started to rise again by 2004. Members of Congress—including Republicans—encouraged "expediting refugee admittance"[172] and returning to "historical averages."[173] The Bipartisan Congressional Refugee Caucus refocused attention on "the plight that refugees face and the urgent need for the United States to provide assistance to them."[174]

Refugees were configured in ways that buttressed the War on Terror (WOT) and legitimized interventionism in Afghanistan and Iraq. Situated within prisms of "failing states," refugees were depicted in relation to "a breakdown of institutions and governance . . . conditions where warlordism, terrorism and chronic instability flourish."[175] Legislation linking refugees to the possibilities of a "failed state in Iraq" supported justifications of US military expenditures and nation-building projects.[176] As annual refugee admissions fluctuated between 41,000 and 60,000 during the second term of the Bush administration (FY2005–2008),[177] refugees were instrumentalized as tools to condemn human rights abuses in foreign countries such as Vietnam, Myanmar/Burma, North Korea, and Sudan, and to promote democracy, freedom, and human rights abroad. The suffering of refugees was affixed to human rights abuses happening elsewhere, in geographically distant locales that could be condemned as repressive and backward—as manifestations of "men in *other* places" using violence.[178]

Refugees were embedded in prisms of saving "women and girls" in Muslim-majority countries like Afghanistan and Iraq—though relatively few Afghan refugees were admitted.[179] These configurations augmented broader constructions of America as a savior and a rescuer, a humanitarian hegemon aiming to "make the fruits of democracy thrive."[180] Policymakers linked refugees with "democracy-building programs" and public diplomacy efforts in "countries with predominantly Muslim populations."[181] Notions of "helping refugees" were tethered not only to US democracy promotion but also to combatting terrorism.[182] Woven into discussions of a mission to drive out "hatred and intolerance,"[183] refugees were portrayed as victims of the enemy—Islamic extremism. From women and girls fleeing "the Taliban's reign of terror"[184] to Christians fleeing "the National Islamic Front,"[185] these portraits reinforced the moral virtues of post-9/11 US foreign policy and the WOT.

In his 2003 State of the Union address, President George W. Bush referenced Iraqi refugees to help legitimize the Iraq War and toppling of Saddam Hussein's regime:

> The dictator who is assembling the world's most dangerous weapons has already used them on whole villages, leaving thousands of his own citizens dead, blind, or disfigured. Iraqi refugees tell us how forced confessions are obtained, by torturing children while their parents are made to watch ... If war is forced upon us, we will fight in a just cause and by just means.[186]

Using Iraqi refugees as symbols of a just cause diverted attention from the myriad ways that US policy actions in the Middle East violated human rights and created conditions of harm.[187] Lawmakers spoke about refugee protection in ways that propelled visions of US foreign policy as a benevolent force that "fosters democratic and transparent governments, promotes human rights and helps millions of people in need."[188] Refugees were configured as signifiers of America's "compassion abroad."[189]

It is important to note that discussions of refugees sometimes prompted confrontations with culpability. During the second term of the Bush administration, calls for greater Iraqi refugee responsibility-sharing were linked with concerns about "abandoning" displaced Iraqis "whose lives are threatened because they had the courage to serve as translators, drivers, and provide other services to the United States."[190] The notion of a special duty to protect Iraqi refugees emerged in assertions that "America owes an immense debt of gratitude to these Iraqis, and we have a special responsibility to help them."[191] Such logics contributed to major increases in Iraqi refugee resettlement after 2007.[192] Similar recognitions of special responsibilities rooted in culpability manifested in discussions of Vietnamese,[193] Nicaraguan,[194] and Kosovar refugees.[195]

Yet refugees were also positioned in redemptive frameworks downplaying or minimizing past policies of harm, as shown with the instrumentalization of refugees from Iraq and Afghanistan to legitimize the WOT, the use of Bosnian refugees to idealize America as a defender of peace and human rights, and the construction of refugees from Southeast Asia as specters of rescue and righteousness in the Vietnam War.[196] Portrayals of refugees tended to downplay US roles in imperialist violence and occupation,[197] propelling visions of America as a humanitarian hegemon. Configured as testaments to "the principles of freedom and democracy our nation lives by,"[198] refugees often diverted attention from the harmful effects of US policies. Refugees were symbols of human rights abuses taking place in geographically distant "failed states," reinforcing racialized conceptions of world order[199] and directing the gaze away from denials of protection to asylum-seekers and migrants arriving on US territory.[200] The sustainment of this narrative relied in part on a bifurcation of refugees from other types of migrants.

Bifurcation and Breakdown

The 1980 Refugee Act formalized a legal basis for separating refugees from other types of migrants. Over time, the refugee path to humanitarian protection became increasingly distinct from asylum. In the decade following the end of the Cold War, policymakers "redefined asylum-seekers as unauthorized migrants, conceptually separating them from refugees waiting in camps to be resettled" such that asylum policy was no longer insulated from domestic immigration politics.[201] Whereas refugees applied for protection from outside the borders of the United States (through the United Nations and US embassies overseas) and already had legal status upon their entry, asylum applications were submitted once someone was on US territory or arriving at the border via a port of entry. The asylum-seeker's state of "legal limbo" became similar to that of undocumented immigrants,[202] reflecting a deliberate trend to realign asylum-seekers with "illegal immigrants."[203]

The bifurcation of refugees from other types of migrants was produced and reproduced through elite discourse. The Democratic and Republican Party platforms of the 1980s largely distinguished refugee policy as an "international" and "global" issue from policies toward "undocumented" and "illegal" aliens arriving on US territory. Refugees were often disentangled from domestic immigration or portrayed in line with the good/legal immigrant—"those in foreign lands patiently waiting for legal entry."[204] Democrats joined Republicans in targeting irregular migrants in the 1990s,[205] emphasizing, "we cannot tolerate illegal immigration."[206] Vietnamese refugees throughout the 1980s and early 1990s were resettled as part of an Orderly Departure Program. Framing refugee responsibility-sharing as orderly enabled policymakers to commit to refugee assistance and the "vigorous administration of refugee programs"[207] while simultaneously championing themes of border control and law and order. The lengthy admissions and screening process for overseas refugees aligned with constructions of America as "a nation of laws."[208]

As the domestic landscape became increasingly animated by immigration contestation during the 2000s,[209] immigration policy emerged as a key issue used by elected officials and political candidates to mobilize segments of the population and discourse over migration "crises" intensified in television news coverage, online networks, and talk radio.[210] Refugees remained mostly shielded from restrictionist rhetoric in the immigration debate.[211] Refugee resettlement was constructed to be "a crucial part of our foreign and humanitarian policy."[212] Lawmakers argued that refugees be treated as "distinct groups" that do not compete for admission with other types of immigrants,[213] emphasizing that they enter and reside in the United States "legally" and "for humanitarian reasons."[214] Those admitted through resettlement were "genuine refugees,"[215] whose deservingness of protection should be unsullied by the politics of illegal immigration.[216] The UNHCR also perpetuated distinctions between refugees and other types of migrants during the 2000s as part of its advocacy approach.[217]

The bifurcation of refugees as "good immigrants" and refugee policy as "foreign policy" visibly broke down during the second term of the Obama administration. The convergence of Republican and Democratic platforms regarding "illegal immigration" unraveled as polarization trends deepened, pressing the two parties toward vocalizing increasingly distinct policy positions.[218] Members of Congress often act as critical "policy entrepreneurs" and coalition-builders,[219] and the Tea Party movement infused the Republican Party with national and subnational legislators championing more restrictionist and nativist perspectives who were uninterested in bipartisan cooperation.[220] Amid these changes, some Democrats shifted toward a greater emphasis on the vulnerability of irregular migrants and their need for protection despite lacking legal documentation—describing the arrivals of "migrant children" from Central America in 2014 in terms of a "refugee crisis" wherein "their request for asylum is justified."[221]

A particularly important moment for the entanglement of refugeehood with immigration contestation came with discussion surrounding H.R. 5230 (Secure the Southwest Border Supplemental Appropriations Act of 2014). The bill was backed by Republicans and passed the House in a partisan vote, with only one Democrat voting in favor.[222] Democratic opposition to the bill and advocacy for the protection of unaccompanied children was linked with a "responsibility to care for refugees."[223] References to "vulnerable children and refugees" were combined with condemnations of Republicans for legislative moves that "dishonor America" and show a "rejection of our values."[224] Democratic language merged "the influx of refugees from Central America" with border and immigration vocabularies,[225] arguing that it is "morally deficient . . . as we demand other countries around the world take in refugees who are facing dangerous circumstances, that what our answer is, No, not here. Not in our backyard."[226]

Conceptualizing refugees as *in our backyard* recalled 1980s liberal and Democratic opposition to the Reagan administration's policies toward Central America.[227] Such frameworks challenged configurations of refugees in terms of distant suffering in faraway lands and confronted prior decades of anticommunist imagery. Rep. Joaquin Castro (D-TX) deliberately called attention to an evolution in interpretations of refugeehood: "The question that we must answer now is: What does it mean to be a refugee in the twenty-first century? Just as we offered that status to Cubans fleeing Castro, to those from the Soviet Union, to the Vietnamese, just as our adversaries have changed . . . I would argue that so, too, have our refugees changed, and we must recognize that."[228] This change around the meaning of refugees as encompassing asylum-seekers arriving at the US-Mexico border was not mutually intelligible across partisan identities. It was bound up with Democratic policy proposals such as Deferred Action for Childhood Arrivals (DACA) and the expansion of protections for asylum-seekers entering the country irregularly—policy proposals that were largely rejected by Republicans. These more explicitly partisan articulations in 2014 pressed against the foundations of intersubjective bipartisan understandings of what it means to be a refugee, dynamics that would soon intensify with the 2015–16 election cycle.

Conclusions

Throughout the Cold War, the 1990s, and the 2000s, refugee responsibility-sharing levels fluctuated in response to a combination of domestic and international forces. Refugee admissions were often selective and skewed to favor certain groups. The United States nonetheless made important contributions to resettlement, and the international refugee regime depended on those contributions. In legitimizing refugee protection, both Democrats and Republicans configured refugees through racialized foreign policy lenses connected with providential exceptionalism, Safe Haven mythologies, global "leadership" narratives, mirror image identity logics, and prisms oriented around human rights and humanitarianism. These meanings were continuously made and remade, and affirmations of the refugee resettlement program were harmonized with moves by both parties toward the deterrence and restriction of other categories of migrants.

Beyond strategic foreign policy calculations, the chapter has shown that identity and discourse were powerful in making sense of refugee protection and responsibility-sharing. Certain refugee groups were constructed as possessing "the right cultural values"[229] in ways that validated visions of America as industrious and self-sufficient, as "Westernizing" and "modernizing" while at the same time rooted in religiosity and tradition. These frameworks endured and adapted to legitimize refugee resettlement amid shifting normative and geopolitical contexts. In a domestic identity terrain where "Conservative Democrats" and "Liberal Republicans" were fairly common,[230] refugees were not heavily associated with partisan identity but were often imbued with intersubjective imaginations of providential exceptionalism and humanitarian hegemony. Republicans and Democrats instrumentalized refugees to condemn human rights abuses in other countries, placing the root causes of instability and displacement "at the door of post-colonial societies and states."[231] Policymakers, among others, embedded refugees within shared stories about the "good heartedness of Americans."[232] These narratives often justified continued projections of power and interventionism in ways that evaded accountability regarding the consequences of US foreign policy actions[233] and the colonial structures encoded in migration and refugee regimes.[234]

3

Nativist Prisms of Cultural Threat

In warning his Twitter followers in 2015 that "Refugees from Syria are now pouring into our great country," presidential candidate Trump demonstrated a rhetorical technique common among immigration restrictionists—the use of marine framing metaphors. Marine framing techniques dehumanize refugees through language of floods, tides, flows, and waves *pouring in* and drowning an imagined cultural ethos.[1] Trump's tweet further invoked ominous imagery by adding, "Who knows who they are?."[2] Emphases on *who* Syrian refugees are as predominantly Muslim and non-"Western" migrants poised to overwhelm a demographically and ideologically precarious white Christian nation were central to cultural threat narratives legitimizing US retreats from refugee responsibility-sharing. Positioning refugees as unknown and unknowable reinforced notions of Otherness and enabled possibilities of reversed victimhood wherein allegedly vulnerable victims of persecution (refugees) could be cast as invasive aggressors.

During the 2015–16 election cycle, Syrian and other Muslim refugees were represented as cultural threats via nativist prisms. Drawing on ethnocultural understandings of national belonging, nativist systems of meanings fuse defensive nationalism with interpretations of immigrants and internal minorities as threatening on the basis of their perceived foreignness. Nativist frameworks played a crucial role in making sense of policy moves to restrict refugee admissions by casting Syrian and other Muslim refugees as unassimilable outsiders. An important element of domestic opposition to refugee responsibility-sharing was premised on concerns about racial, religious, and civilizational transformation—*cultural* threats that no amount of thorough security vetting or arguments about refugees' economic productivity could address.[3] Regardless of whether refugees could be proven terrorists or ISIS sympathizers, their identities were irrevocably threatening within nativist narratives emphasizing themes of Muslim infiltration, immigrant invasion, and white Christian victimhood.

To begin, we must define nativism and establish its importance in domestic identity narratives. Understandings of Syrian and other Muslim refugees as culturally ominous and outside the parameters of national belonging helped legitimate US withdrawals from the international refugee regime. The chapter moves on to discuss the role of nativist and Orientalist frames in (re)producing logics of opposition to refugee responsibility-sharing, describing three prisms wherein refugees emerged as culturally threatening during the 2015–16 election cycle. Political elites and civil society groups used anti-Muslim, anti-immigrant, and conservative Christian discursive prisms to cast the "refugee crisis" in terms of cultural crisis, positioning refugees within systems of meaning that bolstered ethnocultural identity narratives and competitive victimhood.

Nativist Prisms and Refugee Responsibility-Sharing

Work on nativism offers valuable paths for grappling with racialized cultural threat configurations. Nativism entails opposition to migrants and internal minorities on the basis of their "foreign connections,"[4] and is linked with "the desire to restrict, exclude, or attack immigrants."[5] In evolving combinations of ethnocentrism and nationalism, nativism emerges from the integration of "unfavorable reactions to the personal and cultural traits" of particular ethnic, racial, or religious groups with "a hostile and fearful nationalism."[6] Nativism thus entails the bridging of ethnocentric, racist, or religious antipathies with cultural threat perception.

Nativism is crucial for understanding how national and subnational identity processes intervene in refugee protection. Inherently tied to notions of national belonging and Otherness, nativism juxtaposes those deemed to be culturally *native*, *true*, or *real* members of the national group with some subversive *foreign* or *alien* enemy interpreted as threatening the group's values, identity, and survival. In the case of the United States, nativist logics defend an "American way of life" from encroaching attack by cultural outsiders—groups understood as Other on the basis of racial and/or religious difference. As Du Bois observes, racial prejudice often takes shape in claims of cultural and civilizational defense.[7] The concept of civilization itself has been "tightly tied to whiteness" for centuries within international relations[8] and within the narratives of US political elites.[9] "Refugee crises" provide opportunities for nativist actors to articulate and capitalize on a sense of cultural and civilizational crisis, heightening the salience of policy debates about refugee resettlement and arguments encouraging ethnocultural "re-homogenization."[10]

Justifications of retreats from refugee protection during the 2015–16 election cycle reverberated within a long history of exclusionary conceptualizations of American national belonging.[11] Scholars of US immigration have pointed to "cyclical patterns of anti-immigrant hostility that emerge with increasing intensity from one period to the next."[12] Ethnocultural visions of what America means historically positioned white, Northern European, and Protestant Christian individuals as the *true* Americans who fully "count" as part of the national group.[13] Nativist discourses inscribed American identity in terms of Euro-Nordic superiority, linking whiteness with industriousness and freedom.[14] Indigenous peoples were positioned outside racial and religious belonging as "heathens" and "wild Indians"[15] whose presence threatened white settlers' assumed ownership of the continent.[16] In nineteenth-century iterations of nativism, Irish and Italian Catholic migrants were targeted over concerns about idolatry and conspiracies to replace the King James Bible with Catholic teachings.[17] Nativist groups promoted the Chinese Exclusion Act of 1882 and the National Origins Act of 1924 on the basis of preserving America as a "white nation" during moments of fluidity in the domestic racial order.[18]

Nativist narratives instrumentalize moments of cultural crisis as catalysts for promoting policies aimed at ethnocultural preservation and re-homogenization. In contemporary nativist plotlines we find the traces of past discourses and representational practices. During World War II, subversive representations of "the Refugee Invasion" promulgated notions of a "Jewish conspiracy" to destroy American society.[19] Orientalist systems of meaning supported nativist logics by exaggerating and distorting a dichotomy between the "West"/Europe and the "East"/Islam.[20] These interpretations justified exclusionary immigration and naturalization policies while anxieties about preserving a white Christian polity transcended shifting historical, economic, and foreign policy circumstances.[21]

Understandings of whiteness and ethnocultural belonging also evolved and interacted disparately with these anxieties depending on context.[22]

Notions of contemporary cultural crisis arise in part from the eclipse of a "bygone era" when white Christian demographic and power structures were undeniably dominant.[23] During the 2015–16 election cycle, nativist logics situated debates over refugee resettlement within cultural crisis narratives oriented around Muslim infiltration, immigrant invasion, and Christian victimization. The following sections explain how political elites and civil society groups used these prisms to configure Syrian and other Muslim refugees as culturally threatening. Disseminated by conservative members of Congress and an elaborate, well-organized, and well-funded network of nativist groups with a strong online presence,[24] these frameworks promoted opposition to refugee protection through the defense of an imagined community fortified by Orientalist and ethnocultural boundaries of belonging and rhetorical strategies of reversed victimhood.

Orientalism and Muslim Infiltration

Orientalist interpretations have long modulated perceptions of the Middle East, Islam, and proximity to whiteness. While Syrians and Palestinians were legally classified as "Caucasian" by US immigration authorities in the late 1800s, they were soon thereafter distanced from whiteness and racially recategorized as "Mongoloid" amid the growing nativism of the early 1900s.[25] Members of Congress suggested Syrians "belonged to a distinct race other than the white race," and were "the degenerate progeny of the Asiatic hoards."[26] In challenging the eligibility of Syrians to naturalize, US judges and other policy actors construed whiteness as European descent, suggesting Syrians may be scientifically white (Caucasian) but not the *right kind* of white "who, from tradition, teaching, and environment, would be predisposed toward our form of government, and thus readily assimilate."[27] Despite possibilities of self-perceived whiteness and technical inclusion within US legal classifications, these examples reiterate the limits and ephemerality of whiteness vis-à-vis full inclusion in American national belonging.[28]

Often labeled as "Asiatics" and grouped with Turks, Iranians, Chinese, Japanese, Filipinos, and Jews as "Orientals,"[29] Syrians were embedded in essentializing frameworks based on assumptions of "basic, unchanging natural conditions of cultural difference."[30] Rooted in imperialist discourses, these systems of meaning depicted "the Orient"—including composites of Islam, Arabs, and the Middle East—as something to be feared and controlled by "Western" societies.[31] In the US context, these interpretations evolved into a distinctly American Orientalism molded through early representations of Muslims and Arabs that were circulated by American missionaries, tourists, and merchants.[32] Throughout the Cold War and beyond, American Orientalism dehumanized Arabs and Muslims as violent and irrational "disrupters."[33] Depictions of Muslims and Arabs as dangerous and unassimilable were reproduced through decades of American popular culture and political rhetoric.[34]

Enduring Orientalist understandings of the Middle East and Islam shaped configurations of Syrian refugees to reinforce notions of unassimilable foreignness. Orientalism ascribes conditional agency to Muslim societies such that they are "unable to auto-generate or self-develop" into modernity,[35] buttressing notions that migrants from the Middle East are limited in adjusting to new cultural environments. Nativist narratives constituted Syrian refugee identities as problematic along both religious (Muslim) and racial (Arab) dimensions,[36] with some exceptions for Syrian Christians perceived to be "whitened" on the basis of Christian identity.[37] Threat perceptions are inflated by racial difference,[38] and the positioning of Syrian refugees on racial and religious continuums of belongingness rendered them unassimilable into an "American way of life." Orientalist instincts made sense of Syrian refugees as invasive non-"Western" arrivals that ought to be feared and controlled. Refugee policy shifts provided a means to reassert cultural control, to re-homogenize and restore the nation, and thereby to defend and take back the sociocultural order from would-be Muslim usurpers.

Within Orientalist systems of meaning, Islam is typically represented as "a violent political ideology" and characterized as monolithic, irrational, inferior, incapable of adapting to modernity, and lacking shared values with other major religions.[39] These attributes featured prominently in anti-Muslim discursive formations mobilized by lawmakers and civil society groups during the 2015–16 election cycle. Important anti-Muslim nativist groups included the American Freedom Law Center (AFLC), the Center for Security Policy (CSP), and ACT for America. These groups previously mobilized protests, lawsuits, and grassroots activism against mosque construction projects, and also developed and promoted anti-Sharia legislation across the United States. Such campaigns shaped a discursive topography in which the cultural threats posed by Syrian and Muslim refugees could be constituted as commonsensical. The anti-Sharia campaign, for example, helped construe Muslim religious principles as alien and lacking commonality with other religious systems, despite strong parallels with Jewish halakhah.[40] In arguing for bans on the use of Islamic law as *foreign* law in US courts to protect the American legal system and way of life from Islamic legal traditions,[41] anti-Muslim nativist groups paved the way for justifying bans on refugees along similar logics. Rhetoric warning of a conspiracy to replace US constitutional and educational principles with Sharia helped promulgate notions of Muslim "infiltration."

In 2016, the CSP published *Mosques in America: A Guide to Accountable Permit Hearings and Continuing Citizen Oversight*. The book was promoted as a "how-to manual for patriotic Americans who are ready to counter the leading edge of Islamic supremacism," geared toward "helping those seeking to protect our freedoms against all enemies, foreign and domestic."[42] Emphasis on protecting *patriotic Americans* from *enemies* reiterates the centrality of Self/Other juxtapositions and defensive nationalism in nativist logics. The CSP worked to develop standardized language for anti-Syrian refugee measures at the local level to help counties introduce municipal laws restricting resettlement.[43] Trump cited research from the CSP during his presidential campaign to justify proposals for "a total and complete shutdown of Muslims entering the United States,"[44] highlighting the collaboration of nativist organizations and political elites in co-creating and propagating such narratives.

Arguing for restrictions on Syrian refugees and Muslim immigration writ large, Rep. Louie Gohmert (R-TX) similarly cited the CSP, quoting the organization's Threat Information Office director to underscore the dangers of "so-called Syrian refugees." Linking arguments against refugee resettlement with opposition to *political correctness*, Gohmert cast Muslim migrants as culturally destructive and undeserving of protection from discrimination:

Unfortunately, polls these days are showing that there is a massive number and a massive percentage of people who have already immigrated into the United States who are Muslim that say that they owe their allegiance more to sharia than to our Constitution. I know that people constantly say we should not discriminate, and certainly we should not . . . But if somebody is committing a crime, has committed a crime, wants to destroy our way of life, bring down our government, destroy Western civilization, it is okay to discriminate against those people because what they have done or want to do is called a crime. If they want to bring down our Constitution and have it submissive to sharia law, the appropriate term for that is treason . . . If someone wants to immigrate into this country . . . it is important to find out, before we give American citizenship to people, whether or not they can take the oath as a citizen honestly, truthfully, with no hesitation.[45]

Rep. Gohmert references *massive numbers* and *percentages* to infer that high-volume Muslim migration might overwhelm the nation. He links migrants with *committing crime*, contravening empirical evidence suggesting a negative or null impact of immigration and refugee resettlement on US crime rates.[46] He also deploys the rhetorical commonplace of *Western civilization*[47] to position Muslim identity outside the parameters of group belonging and outside the protections of the US Constitution, reproducing racialized logics wherein the Constitution and its principles of political equality are reserved for "civilized" insiders.[48] Such invocations of Western civilization also tend to erase histories of Arab and Muslim communities in Western philosophy, culture, and science,[49] while marginalizing the myriad Eastern components and origins of "the West."[50] The interconnections among European/Western and postcolonial/non-Western are rendered invisible,[51] and Muslim refugees are rendered innately culturally ominous.

Rep. Gohmert's depiction of Muslim immigrants as potentially disloyal to the Constitution aligned with the anti-Muslim talking points promoted by the CSP in its campaign against Sharia.[52] As *Muslim* migrants, Syrian refugees were constituted as treasonous, jeopardizing the American *way of life* and Western civilization writ large. The defensive positioning of the in-group's way of life relies on a classification of the Other as "irreparably deviant—as another species, really, not at all like ourselves."[53] The notion that *it is okay to discriminate* against Muslim migrants based on a perceived collective affinity for Sharia provides a powerful counternarrative against human rights non-discrimination principles, whereby migration and asylum should not be restricted on the basis of characteristics such as race, religion, or nationality.[54]

ACT for America (ACT) also played an important role in developing and disseminating anti-Muslim nativist frames to mobilize opposition to refugees. ACT is classified by the Southern Poverty Law Center as an anti-Muslim hate group that "pushes wild anti-Muslim conspiracy theories, denigrates American Muslims, and deliberately conflates mainstream and radical Islam."[55] ACT described itself as a grassroots organization that "recruits, trains, and mobilizes citizens . . . to help protect and preserve American culture and to keep this nation safe."[56] Other ACT materials specified the protection of "the Western values upon which our nation was built."[57] The organization's founder, Brigitte Gabriel, is the author of *Rise: In Defense of Judeo-Christian Values and Freedom*, which motivates readers to "unite with other patriots who wish to preserve our endangered Judeo-Christian values."[58]

During the 2015–16 election cycle, ACT devoted a section of its website to refugee resettlement. It asserted that "allowing vast numbers of refugees from failed states such as Syria, Somalia, Yemen, and Afghanistan will place our nation at risk," with the admission of such refugees into "western countries" resulting in rape and crime while providing ISIS with "cover to infiltrate the West."[59] Refugees from the Middle East, North Africa, and Central Asia were linked with inferior *failed states*—vocabulary rooted in racialized conceptualizations of world politics[60]—and contrasted with the superiority of "our nation." The infiltration of the Western Self by non-Western Others cued Orientalist assumptions and anxieties surrounding the decline of white Christian hegemony. This framing provided an important counter-logic to arguments for refugee resettlement oriented around preventing civilian harm in the countries specified (Syria, Somalia, Yemen, and Afghanistan)—all four of which were highlighted by the Global Centre for the Responsibility to Protect as populations at risk of mass atrocity crimes.[61]

ACT encouraged citizens to join its Refugee Awareness Coalition, a subgroup dedicated to local community activism opposing refugee resettlement. ACT representatives were vocal in shaping national as well as local debates about refugees, circulating nativist narratives via their website, Facebook page, refugee resettlement working group, speaking events, conferences, and interviews on the Fox News television network.[62] In response to resettlement efforts in Montana, an ACT representative traveled to the state to speak at a community forum where residents were fearful of Syrian refugees being resettled in their area. The representative emphasized that "Islam means submission" and affirmed local concerns that Muslims "want to convert us or they want to kill us."[63] Similarly, ACT's founder traveled to Twin Falls, Idaho to speak to more than 200 residents at the local high school auditorium, explaining that refugee resettlement was "part of a larger plot to infiltrate and take over the West" and encouraging community members to "wake up," write to their lawmakers, and vote.[64] The use of terms such as *infiltrate, take over, submission, convert,* and *kill* created a sense of urgency in opposing Muslim refugee admissions, and the refugee resettlement program was construed as a vehicle of cultural and existential threat. These rhetorical maneuvers perpetuated Orientalist assumptions of Muslim homogeneity and "a reduction of Islamic cultural and juristic systems to objects that can be named, comprehended, and finally dismissed entirely in western terms."[65]

While the CSP and ACT for America sought to resist myriad dimensions of perceived Muslim infiltration threats, Refugee Resettlement Watch (RRW) was distinguished by its focus on opposition to Muslim refugees. RRW was founded by self-described blogger and activist Ann Corcoran, who worried that refugees who had settled near her home in rural Maryland represented "part of a larger movement to infiltrate America and promote Islam."[66] RRW bolstered infiltration fears by highlighting "startling" statistics regarding the number of Muslim refugees resettled in the United States:

> Non-profit groups bring to the US on average each year 15,000 (FY90–FY03) Muslim refugees from the Middle East, Africa, the Balkans, etc. . . . There needs to be a national debate about how many refugees and other immigrants we take and from what cultures they come from. Frankly, we have made a grievous error in taking the Muslim refugees . . . who have no intention of becoming Americans. They are here to change America.[67]

Refugee arrival statistics from non-"Western" regions helped establish imagery of foreign forces inundating the cultural landscape. Muslim refugees were homogenized as unassimilable, lacking the ability or desire to become Americans. Suggestions of insidious intentions to *change America* cued conspiratorial visions. Amid the threat of impending Islamic takeover, cultural preservation was rendered more urgent than principles of human rights or refugee protection.

RRW's popularity enabled Corcoran to become an influential figure among anti-Muslim and anti-immigrant groups. Her arguments were circulated via her RRW blog, the RRW Facebook page, the websites of other groups opposing refugee resettlement, interviews on Fox News, and speaking engagements.[68] Corcoran embraced the notion that her work was anti-Muslim, declaring, "Maybe there should be a bumper sticker—*Proud Islamophobe on board!*"[69] RRW tracked Syrian refugee resettlement efforts across the United States to encourage grassroots opposition among "concerned citizens." In spotlighting efforts to resettle Syrian refugees in Reno, Nevada, for example, RRW provided a link to an article on far-right political news outlet Breitbart warning of a "400 percent increase" in Syrian refugee resettlement within the state[70] and urged Reno citizens to "question what was coming to their community" in the hopes that "maybe some will speak up now."[71] Syrian refugees were otherized as an unknowable force *coming into* American communities and dehumanized as *what* rather than *who*. Opposing refugee resettlement meant speaking up in the face of imminent cultural crisis.

Combining defensive nationalism with anti-Muslim conspiracism, many RRW posts emphasized the Muslim identities of refugees and envisioned citizens opposing their resettlement as "pockets of resistance." Posts were tagged under "Changing America," "Changing the Way We Live," and "Community Destabilization." RRW discourse also utilized reversed victimhood to counter non-discrimination principles:

> Forget the idea that resettling refugees from the third world to your Midwestern town is driven by compassion for the poor and downtrodden. It is driven by greed and money as big companies reap the rewards . . . Then if you say a word about how your community is socially, culturally, and economically disturbed, you are called a racist, a hater, a xenophobe and

so on . . . You, the average American, who liked your town just as it was and who wants jobs for your own kids and grandkids, are vilified and attacked.[72]

The audience was racialized as white via code words like *average American* and *your Midwestern town*. There was a nostalgic longing for the preservation of white Christian hegemony symbolized in the town *as it was* before *refugees from the third world* undermined ethnocultural homogeneity.[73] Victimhood was reversed from the refugee—often conceived of by proponents of resettlement as a sympathetic survivor of grave suffering—to the white, Midwestern prototypical member of the national group (the average American) who suffers the experiences of being *vilified* and *attacked*. This logic echoes Rep. Gohmert's previously discussed justification of discrimination against Muslim refugees. *Racist, hater*, and *xenophobe* were constituted as false accusations, if not reasonable responses, in the wake of severe *social* and *cultural* dangers.

These configurations of refugee threat dispelled logics of moral responsibility and compassion, transplanting notions of victimhood and protection. In contrast to arguments among refugee advocates emphasizing displaced Syrians as sufferers of plight and persecution, nativist narratives cast Syrian and other Muslim refugees as invasive, unassimilable, and destructive aggressors *infiltrating* their "Western" host country. In systems of meaning oriented around the religiously foreign identities of refugees, it was the "average American"—white, Midwestern, and presumably Christian (or at least "Judeo-Christian")—who was most vulnerable and therefore in greatest need of defense as Muslim outsiders poured into and potentially engulfed the nation.

Multiculturalism and Immigrant Invasion

Anti-Muslim and Orientalist ideas worked in tandem with resistance to "multiculturalism"—the notion that immigrants should have a right to preserve customs and traditions associated with their home country or heritage[74]—amid a perceived immigrant "invasion"[75] to constitute refugees as culturally threatening. Within an anti-immigrant prism constructing immigration in general as problematic, Syrian refugees were linked with mass incursions of foreigners overwhelming the national ethos and defying assimilation. Language invoking the dangers of *open borders, multiculturalism, illegal aliens,* and *mass migration* embedded refugee resettlement in nativist frames of cultural difference[76] that previously animated debates over immigrants and asylum-seekers along the southern border.[77]

The focus on multiculturalism to bolster anti-immigrant logics traces back to discourses circulated prior to the 2016 elections. In 2004, Samuel Huntington linked the erosion of Anglo-Protestant values in American identity to the rise of a "doctrine" and "cult" of multiculturalism.[78] During a congressional debate over immigration the same year, Rep. Tom Tancredo (R-CO) described a philosophy of "radical multiculturalism" that had "seeped into the absolute soul of our society" such that migrants "keep their separate language and cultural and even political affiliation with the country from which they came." Rep. Tancredo further tethered multiculturalism to immigrants "coming here not wanting to be Americans."[79] Rep. Steve King (R-IA) reiterated the nexus between multiculturalism, non-assimilation, and the erosion of American identity, arguing against "this multiculturalism that is infused into every level of our curriculum, every level of our lives, and [that] rejects a greater American civilization." The congressman contrasted the new "cult of multiculturalism" in the United States with older generations of European immigrants who held "a philosophy of buying into this culture and this civilization," such as his own German immigrant grandmother who refused to speak German after the family's arrival because "we came here to be Americans."[80]

This journey back to 2004 provides a window into the endurance and evolution of identity narratives in structuring representations of migrants. Disseminated by conservative political elites and immigration restriction activists, Huntington's arguments about cultural assimilation became "paradigmatic of the way many Anglo-Americans view Latinos," such that notions of *invasion, porous borders,* and *illegality* accompanied the mainstreaming of cultural debates over immigration in US politics.[81] These logics were extended to configure Syrian refugees as similarly unassimilable—as non-white and non-"Western" and therefore fomenting cultural crisis, or what Rep. King described as "cultural suicide by demographic transformation."[82] The congressman later tweeted, "we can't restore our civilization with somebody else's babies." When interviewed about this statement, King explained, "I'm a champion for Western civilization."[83]

These configurations linked authentic assimilation into American belonging and civilization with white European immigrants of the past. Assimilation logics laden with Anglo-conformity and one-way "acculturation"[84] were contrasted with invocations of multiculturalism as enabling non-white and non-"Western" immigrants of the present to facilitate cultural destruction by producing *somebody else's babies*. Notions of re-homogenizing and restoring civilization reflected defensive and nostalgic "re" vocabulary (reclaim, restore, renew, revive), signifying "an outgunned minority struggling valiantly against outside powers."[85]

Such logics manifested in the rhetoric of US policymakers during congressional debates over Syrian refugee resettlement. Arguing against resettlement, Sen. Dan Coats (R-IN) suggested that displaced Syrians do not want to assimilate and would be better served by the creation of regional safe havens within the Middle East. Drawing parallels to the alleged advantages of safe havens created in the 1990s, Coats compared Syrian refugees with individuals displaced during the Balkans crisis who "didn't want to try to take on a different language and have to learn different skills in order to assimilate in other countries any more than we would want to move our people out to another country if we were in that situation."[86] The senator invoked visions of ethnocultural homogeneity in prompting the audience to imagine the difficulty of *our people* being forced to move and learn different languages, excluding millions of multilingual and naturalized US citizens possessing those experiences from full belongingness within the national group. Such refrains reproduce a "permanent foreignness" for Americans with immigrant backgrounds, reflecting the subtle discursive processes by which migrant groups are rendered "perpetual outsiders."[87]

The comparison of Syrian refugees with displacees in the Balkans not *wanting* to assimilate borrowed framing techniques characteristic of the threat narratives targeting southern border crossers from Mexico and Central America, wherein "Latinos do not want to speak English" and "do not want to integrate socially and culturally."[88] Sen. Coats also juxtaposed European immigrants of the past with "overwhelming" refugee flows from Iraq and Syria:

> My mother is an immigrant. I am the son of an immigrant. She came here as a young child with her sisters and brothers the legal way. My mother and father learned the language and worked hard so that we could get a good education and assimilate into the United States. But now we simply don't have the capability... today we have a major national security issue combined with the ability to assimilate refugees from other countries.[89]

Contrasting his white, European (Western) immigrant ancestors[90] who *came the legal way* and were capable of cultural integration with *refugees from other countries* who purportedly lack the same capacity for assimilation, the senator positioned Iraqi and Syrian refugees as more foreign, more distant in proximity to whiteness, and more culturally threatening. The senator's description of his European ancestors as willing to "work hard" to attain productive inclusion in the nation reinforced intertwined notions of the "good immigrant" and Protestant work ethic in American exceptionalism.[91] The senator's exclusion of Syrian and Iraqi refugees from this good, assimilable category of migrants supportive of exceptionalist mythologies reminds us that whiteness is neither fixed nor objective, but continuously (re)constituted as a "style of embodiment" and a way of claiming and inhabiting space.[92] It is noteworthy that Sen. Coats was later selected to serve as the Director of National Intelligence during the Trump administration.

Themes of cultural transformation and invasion by unassimilable immigrants align with nativist perceptions that the group's identity and core values are under attack.[93] Nativist visions of America tend to imagine prototypical (white European) group members with a strong work ethic and desire to preserve individual freedoms. However loosely articulated values of freedom may be within this narrative, they are nonetheless understood as "Western" and therefore superior. In criticizing the European response to refugees from the Middle East and North Africa, Rep. Fortenberry (R-NE) lamented, "the great cities of Europe were secure places of cultural strength," but have since become endangered by "reckless open border policies and naïve assumptions about the potential for multicultural conversion to Western economic and political freedoms." Underscoring the failures of multiculturalism, Fortenberry urged European leaders to take "proper pride in the ideals that bind and animate wider Western civilization."[94]

Refugees from the Middle East were reified as non-Western and therefore in need of conversion into identities which value freedoms. Nostalgia for the former cultural power of a more homogenously "Western" and less diverse Europe invoked parallel anxieties surrounding transformations of American racial and religious demographics. The congressman did not explicitly draw on racial inferiority arguments but relied instead on cultural difference logics. Cultural difference frames often "blur into constructed racial and ethnic differences," enabling a kind of racism that "presents itself as anti-racist" and rooted in "colorblind ideology."[95] Syrians and other refugees from the Middle East were represented as incompatible with the ideals of the white "Western" in-group due to perceived cultural flaws (the inability to subscribe to "economic and political freedoms"). In other parts of his speech, Rep. Fortenberry described the Middle East in vocabularies of *barbaric onslaught, conflict, catastrophe, metastasizing, turbulent,* and *the collapse of the nation-state order*[96]—underscoring the entanglement of nativist frameworks with Orientalist ontologies of the region. Fortenberry's invocation of "open borders" cued connections to broader immigration invasion logics.

Within the anti-immigrant prism, retreats from refugee protection were legitimized by grafting notions of cultural disruption posed by *mass migration* from Mexico and Central America onto images of Syrian refugees. Congressional debates summoned paradigms of Latino invasion and "Hispanization,"[97] highlighting alleged "cultural liabilities" in terms of falling "at the very bottom of the skill ladder,"[98] "lacking ambition," and threatening "modernization and progress."[99] Conservative lawmakers transposed such deficiencies onto Syrian refugees, with Sen. Jeff Sessions (R-AL) contending, "most are low-skilled and frequently lack any formal education and many—most don't speak English." Sessions further aligned his resistance to Syrian refugee admissions with majorities of American voters who believe "projected growth in immigration should be curbed," embedding opposition to refugee resettlement within restrictionist approaches to immigration in general.[100]

Associations of Syrian refugees with frameworks of Latino invasion were enabled implicitly by discourse linking Syrian refugees with *illegal aliens* and explicitly by direct references to migrants from Mexico, Central America, and the southern border. Speaking against the Obama administration's proposal to resettle 10,000 Syrian refugees, Rep. Marsha Blackburn (R-TN) argued: "It is important to note that the Office of Refugee Resettlement . . . has been resettling thousands of illegal aliens that are coming across our southern border . . . We know that there are more than Mexicans and Central Americans coming across that southern border, and we know that once they are here, the ORR has no way of tracking them and keeping up with them."[101] Different categories and pathways of migration were blurred such that refugee resettlement was interpreted as facilitating unlawful immigration. The bifurcation of overseas refugees from southern border crossers (described in chapter 2) was absent. Syrian refugees were categorized with Mexicans and Central Americans as part of an uncontrollable incursion of "illegal" border crossers.

Anti-immigrant civil society actors mobilized resistance to refugee resettlement through similar systems of meaning. The Federation for American Immigration Reform (FAIR) and the Center for Immigration Studies (CIS) were both established in connection with the work of John Tanton, described by the Southern Poverty Law Center as a nativist and white nationalist.[102] Tanton's initiatives helped cultivate a "web of nativist leaders and organizations" in the 1990s, creating an institutional infrastructure for "supporters of racialized immigration policy."[103] In arguing for greater restrictions on all forms of immigration into the United States, these groups reinforced logics critical of multiculturalist agendas. FAIR included a quote from Rep. Tancredo about the dangers of "radical multiculturalism" on its website,[104] and the CIS warned of the need to "curb radical multiculturalism."[105] RRW similarly drew on this framing, lamenting that "unfortunately, political correctness and a worshipful attitude toward multiculturalism have blinded us."[106]

FAIR and CIS representatives testified before Congress as expert witnesses,[107] underscoring the role of nativist groups in providing "privileged expertise" to rationalize immigration policy changes.[108] These groups also circulated nativist narratives through their websites, media interviews, public events, Facebook pages, and blogs. A 2016 FAIR blog post emphasized the burden placed on "the American people who are forced to house these so-called refugees," arguing for a halt to the acceptance of Syrians "whose background checks, motivations, and ability to assimilate are questionable."[109] FAIR conflated refugees with the "mass resettlement of migrants," emphasizing: "the consequences of not assimilating millions of immigrants and their children, who do not share Western cultural values, threaten our way of life."[110]

In 2015, FAIR President Dan Stein issued a statement in support of Trump's proposal for a "shutdown" of Muslim immigration into the United States:

> Americans can no longer trust the government's vetting process and its ability to screen out those susceptible to beliefs *and* actions inconsistent with life in a modern, Western-style democracy . . . Failure to come to grips with this reality has the potential to radically alter the American way of life and undermine our national freedoms . . . every nation has the right to exclude people when the manifestation of their religious, political, or ideological beliefs threaten public safety or is fundamentally at odds with the values and freedoms set forth in our Constitution.[111]

In addition to recycling Orientalist juxtapositions of a *Western, modern,* and *democratic* America with an archaic non-Western Muslim Other, this framing prioritized the need to defend the "American way of life." Stein offered a justification for violating non-discrimination principles ("the right to exclude") aligning with Rep. Gohmert's aforementioned logic that "it is okay to discriminate" against Muslim migrants: discrimination and exclusion were acceptable, even necessary, on the basis of ethnocultural preservation. This convergence of anti-immigrant and anti-Muslim nativism made sense of policies that halted or suspended the entry of refugees.

Anti-immigrant civil society groups also depicted refugees as undeserving of protection through dispelling notions of Syrian suffering:

> By allowing a mass migration of refugees, particularly those from places where religious or political violence is endemic, we open ourselves up to possible threats . . . we aren't able to distinguish legitimate refugees from terrorists . . . Not all people who are fleeing dangerous situations are innocent victims . . . many—especially in places like Syria—are simply on the losing end of bloody ethnic and religious conflicts. They may be fleeing for their lives, but had the outcome of these conflicts been different, they might be committing atrocities and it might be the other guys

fleeing. The challenge of our refugee policy is, amid the complete chaos in the sending countries, to be able to sort out the innocents from those who may have ulterior motives.[112]

Positioning refugees within vocabularies of *mass migration*, FAIR embedded refugee resettlement within a broader immigration invasion paradigm. The language of "legitimate refugees" distorted international legal principles by suggesting there are "illegitimate refugees." Those who have participated in war crimes and violations of international human rights law, including the crime of terrorism, are already excluded from protection as a refugee.[113] FAIR countered portraits of vulnerability and victimhood circulated among human rights and refugee advocates by questioning refugee innocence, pointing to "ulterior motives," and suggesting scenarios in which refugees were the ones "committing atrocities." These discursive moves were reinforced by emphasis on refugee origin countries as *places where religious or political violence is endemic, places like Syria*, places defined by *bloody conflicts* and *complete chaos*—descriptions aligning with Orientalist representations of the Middle East and Islam.

Elevating the cultural threat of refugee resettlement, CIS clarified that addressing concerns regarding insufficient vetting for terrorist threat would not suffice to quell the paramount problem of unassimilability:

> Even if background checks on refugees were flawless, importing a substantial Muslim population to the United States risks the growth of the same kind of unassimilated, radicalized segment of the Muslim community with which Europe is now struggling . . . It is depressing that some people who grew up in the West could so violently reject our societies, but that is what has happened. For a not-inconsequential number of Muslims in Western Europe, assimilation has failed. Can we really be sure it won't fail here?[114]

Anti-immigrant and anti-Muslim logics were interwoven to amplify the dangers of Muslim migrants. Even those raised in "Western" countries were cast outside the boundaries of belonging as *unassimilated, radicalized, violent* Others juxtaposed with *our societies, here, in the West*. Regardless of legal residence and territorial place of birth,

Muslim refugee identities were configured as perpetually foreign and non-Western.

Competitive Victimhood and Conservative Christian Logics

In addition to anti-Muslim and anti-immigrant prisms, conservative Christian logics facilitated interpretations of refugee responsibility-sharing as an existential cultural threat. The notion of a *White Christian America* has served as a "cultural touchstone" in the United States, providing "a shared aesthetic, a historical framework, and a moral vocabulary" institutionalized through churches, hospitals, civic organizations, and through policies upholding slavery and segregation.[115] Segments of the "religious right" increasingly aligned with anti-immigrant networks during the 2000s, devising arguments against immigration oriented around themes of preserving family and cultural values.[116] During the 2015–16 election cycle, refugee admissions were located within a broader attack on an endangered conservative Christian identity. Conservative Christian groups and political elites promulgated narratives casting American Christians as vulnerable victims facing discrimination and crisis in a rapidly changing demographic and cultural landscape.

Discursive strategies framing the dominant ethnoreligious power group as the principal victim have been studied in relation to "competitive victimhood," wherein the in-group amplifies its own victimhood, portrays itself as the underdog, and claims it has suffered more harm than the out-group that is threatening its moral identity.[117] This section shows how Evangelicals for Biblical Immigration (EBI), the Christian Coalition (CC), the Family Research Council (FRC), and some members of Congress fused nativism with competitive victimhood in conservative Christian identity narratives to legitimize retreats from refugee protection and responsibility-sharing.

EBI described itself as an "ad hoc movement" and forum for "those seeking the whole counsel of Scripture about immigration," as opposed to "pro-amnesty evangelicals [who] are selectively quoting Scripture."[118] In advocating for a "biblical" approach to immigration, the group combined nativist logics with scriptural references and prompted audiences to interpret immigration and refugee issues in the context of an endangered Christian nation. The book of Nehemiah in the Old Testament was used as a scriptural reference point, with Nehemiah's calls to refortify the city of Jerusalem—"Come, let us rebuild the wall" (2:17)—aligning with Trump's 2016 campaign slogan to "build the wall" along the US southern border with Mexico. The story of Nehemiah was also used to bolster victimhood and revival narratives by comparing the crumbling of Jerusalem's walls with the erosion of "the spiritual walls of the nation," such that "the ground has shifted beneath our feet . . . the evangelical church is now considered the enemy," and steps must be taken to "rebuild America."[119]

EBI combined appeals to conservative Christian identity with anti-Muslim and Christian victimization frames. An EBI Facebook post emphasized that "94% of refugees are Muslim" and further argued that:

> God loves us all. But Obama does not seem bothered by the persecution and even genocide of Christians in the world. Yet he goes to great expense (with our money) to bring Islamic "refugees" to hundreds of our American cities, hugely funding so-called "Christian Voluntary Agencies" (not voluntary but highly paid) to do it . . . imagine the EPA freak-out if a non-assimilating snail dart were brought into a pond.[120]

Competitive victimhood positioned Christians as the true victims in need of protection through language of *persecution* and *genocide*. The use of quotation marks around "refugees" questioned the authenticity of the refugee label vis-à-vis Muslims. Networks of faith-based refugee resettlement organizations were delegitimized as "so-called" Christian voluntary agencies, suggesting their support of refugees was neither genuinely Christian nor charitable. Muslim refugees were compared to "non-assimilating snail darts" in an ecological metaphor intended to highlight the hypocrisy of the Obama administration welcoming unwanted intruders (Muslim refugees) into American cities while insisting on strict environmental regulations for ponds. Within this metaphor, Muslim refugees were configured as unassimilable and inhuman, likened to an invasive species that "enters a relatively undisturbed site and assumes dominance, displacing existing species completely."[121]

Competitive victimhood was also prevalent in frameworks deployed by the Christian Coalition. Co-founded by televangelist Pat Robertson, the CC has wielded significant political power in US conservatism as an important player within the "Christian Right."[122] The CC presented itself as "one of the largest conservative grassroots political organizations in America ... made up of pro-family Americans who care deeply about ensuring that government serves to strengthen and preserve, rather than threaten, our families and our values." Nativist logics of cultural strengthening and preservation reverberated within a conservative Christian lens wherein traditional family values were perceived as threatened in the wake of "anti-Christian bigotry."[123] In line with themes of nostalgia animating Trump's 2016 campaign promise to "Make America Great Again," the group promoted its efforts to restore America as a Christian nation with the slogan, "Let's Take America Back."[124]

In a post on its website titled "Refugee or Infiltrator," CC rhetoric made sense of opposition to Syrian and other Muslim refugees through an emphasis on Christians as the principal victims in greatest need of asylum:

> The refugee-migrant issue is compounded by the most vulnerable people of all, the Christians, who are truly fleeing physical brutality and loss of home and property. Moreover, they continue to be physically abused by Muslims while they are fleeing and seeking asylum ... With the knowledge that Christians are the least likely to commit crimes, most countries are partial to opening their borders first to Christians. So now many Muslims, including those with nefarious intentions, are claiming to be Christians in order to enter countries on the backs of innocent people.[125]

Christians were constructed as *the most vulnerable* and *truly* deserving of human rights protections, while Muslims were cast as *abusers* fraudulently appropriating Christian identity to appear innocent to unsuspecting host countries. Christian refugees were constituted as members of the in-group, virtuous and law-abiding, and therefore more desirable and worthy in terms of providing migration pathways. In contrast, the closing of borders to Muslim refugees was rendered appropriate given their abuse of Christians and status as potential infiltrators intent on doing harm.

The Family Research Council circulated similar logics justifying halts to Syrian refugee resettlement. As an influential conservative think tank, the FRC has promoted legislation centered on the preservation of traditional Christian values and maintained an active presence across a wide range of media, press releases, policy statements, amicus briefs, and Values Voter summits.[126] The group described itself as seeking to "advance faith, family, and freedom" in US policy and culture "from a Christian worldview."[127] During the 2015–16 election cycle, the FRC encouraged retreats from Syrian refugee responsibility-sharing within the logic of Christian victimhood. The refugee resettlement program was delegitimized as reflecting a "disgraceful pattern of prejudice" against Christians since "98.6%" of Syrians granted asylum in the United States were Sunni Muslims, despite Christians being "the ones in the direst need of help."[128] Competitive victimhood positioned the suffering of Christians as more urgent and construed their underrepresentation in resettlement statistics as a discriminatory pattern of prejudice, sidestepping the complexities of the Assad regime's alliances with Christians and other non-Sunni religious minorities in the Syrian conflict.[129]

The FRC also sought to counter arguments promoted by faith-based refugee advocates emphasizing that Christian morality and religious teachings necessitated refugee responsibility-sharing:

> In a rush of goodwill, Christians are anxious to reach out and help those in need. Obviously, those are good intentions—loving the sojourner, as Deuteronomy talks about—but they aren't the only consideration. There's this false narrative . . . that insists there are only two options in the refugee crisis: give Syrians unfettered access to America or leave orphans and widows dying in the street. That's just not true . . . We could provide humanitarian support directly to displaced people currently in refugee camps . . . And what's more compassionate than taking military action to defeat ISIS? Most people want to stay in their homelands of Iraq and Syria, but they're unable to because ISIS has been allowed to grow . . . "Is it unchristian to not want radical jihadists shooting people in our communities?" Kevin DeYoung [of The Gospel Coalition] asked. "The answer is not as easy as fear versus compassion. Christian charity means loving the safety of the neighbor next door at least as much as loving the safe passage of the neighbor far away."[130]

Opposition to Syrian refugee resettlement was justified within a logic of Christian "compassion" and "charity" wherein shifting efforts away from resettlement was better for both refugees ("the neighbor far away") and the American "neighbor next door." This framing offered reassurance that increased US military operations against ISIS and aid to refugee encampments within the Middle East were sufficient for upholding biblical instructions to "love the sojourner." Retreats from refugee resettlement were constituted as fully compatible with Christian religious identity and values of "helping those in need." An author from the Gospel Coalition was also quoted as problematizing the premise that Christian ethics require helping distant strangers when those strangers are "radical jihadists." These discursive maneuvers offered formidable counter-logics to refugee responsibility-sharing while reaffirming conservative Christian identity and vulnerability.

Political elites also perpetuated Christian victimhood frames in congressional debates over refugee policy. Sen. Ted Cruz (R-TX)—one of the more prominent Republican presidential candidates in 2016—argued in favor of legislation halting the resettlement of Syrian refugees with the exception of Syrian Christians, which he conceptualized as "persecuted minorities facing genocide."[131] In constituting Syrian refugee resettlement as a "grave threat" to the country, Rep. Brian Babin (R-TX) not only reproduced the persecution of Christians but also presented the United Nations as complicit in Christian suffering:

> The UN connection could explain why so many non-Christian refugees are chosen to be brought into the United States while persecuted Christians in Syria, Iraq, Egypt, and other nations there have a very hard time getting within sight of the Statue of Liberty. In fact, the glaring shortcoming of the UN refugee program is that it falls short of helping one of the most persecuted groups around the world, and that is Christians . . . It was reported this past April that 12 Christian migrants trying to get to Europe by boat were simply thrown overboard by fellow Muslim migrants and drowned. Most are afraid to go to the UN refugee camps and fear the actions taken by some of their more radicalized Muslim neighbors within the camps.[132]

The congressman's discrediting of the principal refugee protection institution as negligent toward "persecuted Christians" tarnished the international refugee regime more broadly as a discriminatory infrastructure.

These logics resonated with conservative Christian "understandings of 'the international' as a fundamentally anti-Christian space."[133] Christians were cast as "one of the most persecuted groups around the world," obscuring the legacies of Christian hegemony in international power structures and the expansion of Christianity as a global religion.[134] Anecdotes of violence against Christian migrants perpetrated by Muslim migrants elevated Christian suffering while contesting Muslim refugees' deservingness of protection. Christians afraid of UN refugee camps and "radicalized Muslims" in the Middle East offered identity proxies for conservative Christian Americans who feared that global governance and Islam were disrupting their local value systems and cultural power.

Conclusion

Nativist narratives impeded refugee protection by structuring interpretations of Syrian and other Muslim refugee groups as perpetually and dangerously foreign, justifying US retreats from refugee resettlement as necessary and appropriate measures to safeguard racialized visions of an American way of life. Refugees were configured as threatening cultural and civilizational preservation and nostalgic portraits of American greatness—modes of representation rooted in the defense of a social order oriented around white Christian hegemony. Nativist rebuttals of refugee protection facilitated the targeting of Syrian and other Muslim refugees, constructing migration from non-white and non-Christian spaces as encroachments on the ethnocultural status quo. In showing how anti-Muslim, anti-immigrant, and conservative Christian discursive prisms bolstered nativist and Orientalist configurations of refugees during the 2015–16 election cycle, the chapter advances our understanding of how refugees are constituted as "being more or less assimilable" in different contexts and identity narratives.[135] The assimilability of refugee groups is neither objective nor static, but shaped by shifting constructions and reconstructions of racial meanings.[136] Political elites and civil society groups distanced Syrian and other Muslim refugees from whiteness, racializing them through threatening and undeserving characteristics[137] and reproducing ethnocultural understandings of what America means grounded in white Christian supremacy.

Reinforcing interpretations of refugees as "intruders" who come from "an obscure and incomprehensible world,"[138] vocabularies of religious (Christian) and civilizational (Western) superiority were powerfully combined with motifs of defensive nationalism to rework conceptualizations of refugee protection commonly promoted by international refugee regime actors such as the UN and local faith-based resettlement groups. Rather than constituting a moral or humanitarian imperative, refugee responsibility-sharing was depicted as a vehicle of Muslim infiltration, immigrant invasion, and Christian victimization. These frameworks conceived of precarious American in-groups reproduced as prototypically white, Western, and (Judeo-) Christian. The "refugee crisis" became intertwined with nativist interpretations of subnational identity crises, shaping the conditions in which "the gatekeepers to safety" doubt and reject refugee claims of persecution.[139]

Aligning with observations that conservative nationalist and religious forces have targeted the principles underpinning international human rights regimes[140] and shifted from indirect expressions of discrimination against Muslims to more openly hostile anti-Muslim discourses,[141] the nativist prisms examined in this chapter provided logics of appropriateness for delegitimizing global governance, international institutions, non-discrimination principles, and refugee responsibility-sharing. The UN in particular was rendered suspect for its false victimhood portraits depicting Muslim refugees as deserving of protection and for its complicity in a discriminatory resettlement system "prejudiced" against Christians. Non-discrimination principles foundational to international human rights and refugee protection norms were either negated by logics in which "it is okay to discriminate" against Muslim outsiders or reversed in rhetorical strategies positioning Christians (and Westerners) as the true victims in need of protection from abuse and discrimination. Within these frameworks, notions of racial difference articulated as cultural preservation justified discrimination. Members of the in-group—*Christians, Westerners, average Americans,* and *neighbors next door* who live in *Midwestern towns* (implicitly coded as white)—were constituted as more vulnerable and worthy of protection than "so-called refugees" whose flights from persecution were contested or nullified by threats of cultural transformation.

While the nativist configurations of Syrian and other Muslim refugees assessed in this chapter were tied to domestic identity narratives, it is important to acknowledge the interaction between subnational and transnational identity dynamics. Online networks have played a particularly central role in establishing virtual cross-national linkages that draw on shared frameworks of white nationalism, immigration restriction, and anti-Muslim platforms.[142] Social media sites have been harnessed to facilitate transnational constructions of a collective white identity—the "universal white man"—juxtaposed with culturally threatening "Muslim" and "migrant" Others.[143] Grappling with how nativist systems of meaning made sense of US refugee policies offers important vistas into local manifestations of a globalized phenomenon in which "white working class" identity narratives target refugees and migrants of color through logics of being victimized and "left behind."[144] More broadly, it calls attention to how race and racism continue to structure US policy and contemporary world politics, with nativist articulations of cultural difference and cultural hierarchy preserving racist tropes while ostensibly replacing the biological racism of earlier discourses.[145]

4

Terrorist Infiltrators, Gendered Threat, and the Specter of 9/11

In November 2015, Tennessee State Representative and chairman of the Tennessee House Republican Caucus Glen Casada proposed using the US National Guard to round up and remove recently arrived Syrian refugees, stating, "When we let them in, we are letting terrorists in."[1] That same week in Virginia, Roanoke Mayor David Bowers—a Democrat—requested that all local agencies in his jurisdiction halt assistance to Syrian refugees on the basis that "President Franklin D. Roosevelt felt compelled to sequester Japanese foreign nationals after the bombing of Pearl Harbor, and it appears that the threat of harm to America from ISIS now is just as real and serious as that from our enemies then."[2] This discourse emerged on the heels of the November 13 Paris attacks, in which ISIS claimed responsibility for killing 130 people in a series of coordinated bombings and shootings in France. The Paris attacks represented a crucial juncture in the reconfiguration of refugees as terrorist threats. As the Paris attacks became equated with 9/11, debates over refugee resettlement became bound up with civilizational identity and War on Terror (WOT) prisms.

One week after the attacks, members of Congress in the House of Representatives debated and passed H.R. 4038—the American Security Against Foreign Enemies (SAFE) Act—proposing additional security certifications from the FBI, Department of Homeland Security, and Director of National Intelligence that would effectively "halt" or "pause" all refugee admissions from Syria and Iraq. While the SAFE Act ultimately stagnated in the Senate and therefore failed to become federal law, the logics circulated in its justification solidified the nexus between refugees and terrorist infiltration. These logics conceived of refugees within Orientalist ontologies, gendered binaries, civilizational battles, and allusions to 9/11—conditioning systems of meaning to make sense of policy moves such as the suspension of refugee admissions (later implemented as part of the 2017 Travel Ban). These frameworks were also promulgated amid a 2015 gubernatorial effort across thirty-one states seeking to block Syrian refugee resettlement in local jurisdictions.

Legislative debates over the SAFE Act and discourse circulated by governors, presidential candidates, and additional political elites during the 2015–16 election cycle represented Syrian and other Muslim refugees as dual threats of terrorist and cultural/civilizational infiltration through similar logics that animated WOT discourses following the September 11 attacks. Such maneuvers were an important component in the multicausal processes legitimizing US retreats from the international refugee regime. Representations of refugees as would-be attackers—*refugees-turned-jihadis*—reproduced several familiar themes in the discursive scaffolding of the WOT. These interrelated and co-constitutive themes manifested in several ways. First, configurations of Syrian and other Muslim refugees reified Orientalist frameworks envisioning the Middle East as innately violent and anti-American, obscuring culpability-based logics for refugee protection. Second, gendered binaries essentializing Syrian refugee men as potential combatants perpetuated masculinized notions of terrorist threat while largely preserving WOT proclivities oriented around "saving" Muslim women. Third, constructions of an attack on "Western civilization" reinforced nativist narratives linking refugees with cultural transformation. Finally, debates over refugee resettlement conflated the Paris attacks with 9/11 as a civilizational identity symbol and traumatic reminder of threat from an omnipresent terrorist (Islamic) Other.

Discursive Legacies of the War on Terror

The September 11, 2001 attacks on the World Trade Center and Pentagon have been conceptualized as a "crack in time" that fundamentally altered perceptions of foreign policy[3] and understandings of Muslim and American identities.[4] President George W. Bush declared a "War on Terror" that would not end "until every terrorist group of global reach has been found, stopped and defeated." Bush characterized the enemy in terms of "Islamic extremism," "radical networks," and desires to "kill Christians and Jews," describing a war between "the civilized world" and an amorphous *them* who "plot evil" and seek to destroy "our way of life."[5]

Impulses to link Muslims, the Middle East, and Central Asia with security threats were already prevalent in American imaginations prior to 2001, but the discursive landscape of the WOT enabled innovations and intensifications of such linkages.[6] Notions of border control, national security, and anti-terrorism became intimately intertwined,[7] and repetitions of "Islamic extremism" and "radical Islam" fashioned frameworks of meaning lacking nuanced context regarding Islam.[8]

WOT prisms relied on civilizational discourse to make sense of violent state actions, conjuring up notions of a dehumanized, irrational enemy that only responds to force—themes that share continuity with European colonial projects.[9] An attack on "the West" was conceived as an attack on the civilized world, reproducing "Western Civilization" as exemplary and the United States as its guardian. Inverting the tangible power asymmetries of global politics, WOT logics necessitated the defense of a "terrorized, traumatized Western liberal subject."[10] These logics were instrumentalized throughout the 2000s via the extension and renewal of the USA PATRIOT Act, the establishment of the National Security-Entry-Exit Registration System (NSEERS) targeting men of Arab and Muslim backgrounds, the use of Guantanamo Bay as an extraterritorial detention and interrogation site, the CIA's drone warfare program, and other policies oriented around the threats of "militant/extremist Islam" and "jihadist" terrorism.[11]

The WOT logics that legitimated US policy actions in the wake of 9/11 reappeared during the 2015–16 election cycle to help justify US retreats from refugee protection. Several hallmarks of WOT discourse were particularly foundational to the configuration of refugees as potential terrorists. First, Orientalist ontologies conceived of the Middle East as a space of innate violence, instability, and inferiority. Second, gendered prisms of threat coded all Muslim/Middle Eastern adult males as militants while depicting Muslim women as passive and oppressed victims in need of being "saved." Third, depictions of America as the vanguard of white Christian civilization bolstered notions that "the West" was under attack. Finally, the Paris attacks were constituted as a kind of 9/11 that symbolized the terrorized and traumatized West and elevated the threat of Islamic terrorism as the primary lens for assessing refugee resettlement. These themes worked in tandem to make sense of major shifts in US refugee policy.

Orientalist Ontologies of the Middle East

As discussed in chapter 3, Orientalism—also termed neo-Orientalism in the post-9/11 context[12]—refers to a framework for understanding the Middle East, Central Asia, Arab states, and areas associated with Islam as "distinctly different and therefore subordinate" vis-à-vis "the West."[13] Orientalism suggests "the West spreads democracy, while Islam spawns terrorism,"[14] and conceives of spaces associated with Islam and the Middle East as undifferentiated and dangerous. In addition to erasing realities of diverse and complex cultural matrices, Orientalist lenses downplay the culpability of external forces such as colonialism and US foreign policy in creating conditions of harm and fail to historicize deeper causes of conflict and displacement.[15]

In debates over refugee admissions, this one-dimensional view of regional and religious identity contributed to the conflation of Syrian, Middle Eastern, and Muslim refugees. Republican presidential candidates Ben Carson and Rand Paul both generalized about refugees from the Middle East in justifying US retreats from refugee resettlement. Carson spoke of *that region* (the Middle East) in terms of *jihadist infiltration*: "If we're going to be bringing 200,000 people over here from that region—if I were one of the leaders of the global jihadist movement and I didn't infiltrate that group of people with my people, that would be almost malpractice." Paul similarly cautioned against "tens of thousands of people coming from the Middle East" on the basis that "many of them actually wish us harm."[16] Both statements otherized refugees within constructions of the Middle East as an undifferentiated space of ominous connections to jihadist terrorism and desires to do harm. The vulnerable in-group, *us*, was positioned as precarious against daunting statistical figures—200,000 or tens of thousands—of *them*.

Syrian refugees were configured as exceptionally dangerous because of their ties to the Middle East. In arguing for S. 2284 (Syrian Refugee Verification and Safety Act), a Senate bill halting Syrian refugee admissions, Sen. David Vitter (R-LA) pointed to "the real dangers of taking in thousands upon thousands of refugees from a country and an area of the world where enemies of the United States are all around." Vitter emphasized, "this is not from just any part of the world or any country. This is from a hotbed of anti-American terrorist elements."[17] Syrian refugees were defined as threatening on the basis of their origins in places colored by violence and *enemies*. The Middle East emerged as not just an ordinary geography, *not just any part of the world*, but as a uniquely menacing space fixed into a posture of imminent attack. Lawmakers reproduced similarly Orientalist caricatures of Syria in terms of "instability" and "radical Islam,"[18] reducing the country to "a fertile recruiting ground for Islamic extremists and terrorists."[19]

Such portraits allowed the underlying causes of "anti-American" sentiment to remain unaddressed and irrelevant. Casting the region as innately and enduringly hostile closed off avenues of potential US foreign policy culpability in shaping negative perceptions of the United States. Much like the "why do they hate us?" query normalized in domestic identity narratives after the September 11 attacks, crude juxtapositions of an innocent American *us* and an *anti-American* Middle Eastern/Muslim *them* during debates over refugee resettlement diverted attention from US contributions to conditions of violence and instability. These Us/Them maneuvers reproduced co-dependent frameworks of meaning wherein representing the Other as inferior bolstered understandings of the Self as dominant,[20] enabling policymakers to sidestep culpability-based logics of refugee responsibility-sharing.[21]

Orientalist lenses facilitating collective forgetting regarding US involvement in the root causes of displacement were widespread in justifications for curtailing refugee admissions. In October 2015—several weeks prior to the Paris attacks—Rep. Brian Babin (R-TX) proposed H.R. 3314 (Resettlement Accountability National Security Act of 2015) to halt Syrian and Iraqi refugee resettlement. He argued against admitting refugees "who are streaming out of these war-torn areas of the Middle East" and who pose "numerous security risks . . . as entire regions of the Middle East dissolve into chaos."[22] In supporting the passage of the SAFE Act in the House and Senate, Rep. Trey Gowdy (R-SC) and Sen. John Thune (R-SD) conjured up imagery of Middle Eastern conflagration: "There are refugees from the Middle East and northern Africa because those regions are on fire and riddled with chaos," Gowdy stated.[23] Thune similarly described a turbulent Middle East in which "Syria is wracked by civil war, Iraq is in turmoil . . . Saudi Arabia and Iran are immersed in a cold war, and ISIS continues its campaign of terror."[24]

These frameworks elide the role of decades of US foreign policy actions—including the US-led invasion and occupation of Iraq—that helped forge the war-torn conditions of "chaos" and "turmoil" referenced by the legislators.[25] The neglect of that foreign policy context was facilitated in part by systems of meaning rendering the Middle East structurally "irrational, unproductive, uncivilized and backward."[26] Within Orientalist ontologies, characteristics of *chaos, war, terror,* and *turmoil*—which tarnish all inhabitants as potential security risks—are natural and intrinsic features of the region. Terrorism, extremism, and radicalism are thus constructed as cultural forces in which all Muslims are complicit.[27]

Configurations of refugees as terrorist threats built upon WOT frameworks constructing the world in Manichean terms of good and evil and positioning a freedom-defending United States against a Middle East animated by terrorism and the absence of freedom.[28] Rep. Gowdy made sense of halts to Syrian and Iraqi refugee admissions on the basis that "terrorists took the lives of over 100 innocent people in France" because "their objective is evil for the sake of evil."[29] Rep. Hal Rogers (R-KY) similarly supported the SAFE Act in the context of the United States needing to "stamp out this evil . . . to eradicate the threats posed here and abroad . . . to ensure that Americans can tuck in their children at night with a feeling of security that they will be waking up tomorrow morning for school free from fear."[30] These emphases on *evil* recall WOT logics positioning 9/11 as "a simple act of evil whose perpetrators need to be destroyed," preempting any questioning or scrutiny of US foreign policy actions and affirming the WOT as a "natural and just response."[31] By emphasizing the defense of *innocent* Westerners and *American children* from encroaching forces of *evil*, legislators—particularly Republicans—used Orientalist representations of a malevolent Middle East to make sense of retreats from refugee protection.

Gendered Threat

Democrats also drew on Orientalist ontologies in ways that reproduced gendered dimensions of refugee threat. Democratic members of Congress cast support for increased refugee admissions in language emphasizing the vulnerability and helplessness of Syrian women and children. This logic made sense not only in terms of Democratic partisan identity narratives focused on care and compassion—discussed further in chapter 5—but also via Orientalist infantilizing of the Middle East wherein the "vulnerable, helpless and backward children" of the region depend upon a "rational, enlightened, civilized, and strong" United States/West to save them from their local cultures and religions.[32] In this framework, even arguments ostensibly supporting Syrian refugee resettlement masculinized refugee threat such that Syrian men were construed as outside the parameters of deserving protection.

WOT logics bolstered configurations of Syrian refugee men as security threats, reviving post-9/11 discourses wherein women in the Middle East and Central Asia could be understood as "ignorant" and in need of saving while men in those regions were "devious and disposed to violence."[33] Ontologies of counterinsurgency rely on gender to quickly categorize populations into combatants/high-risk and non-combatants/low-risk, resulting in logics of "all-encompassing suspicion against all men . . . while women are afforded the status of being 'naïve' objects of 'protection,' pacification, and humanitarian salvage."[34] Gendering is a microcosm of Orientalist systems of knowledge,[35] and the WOT is bound up with Orientalist notions of saving Muslim women.[36] Images of "oppressed Muslim women" were used to rationalize US interventions and occupations, enabling violent policy actions to be construed as rescue missions to save Muslim women from their cultures.[37] The depiction of Muslim men as primitive and potential terrorists also served as a "foil" for portraying Western soldiers as "modern and peaceful."[38] These Orientalist logics intersected with the broader equating of women and children with non-combatant status in war-making mythologies and gendered social hierarchies.[39]

The essentializing paradigm of "womenandchildren" harmonizes constructions of women as childlike, innocent, and dependent with narratives that states exist to protect feminized victims.[40] The conflation of *women and children* into a singular entity predicated on victimhood was prevalent among Democrats advocating for US refugee responsibility-sharing. Rep. John Conyers (D-MI) argued that Congress should "do its part by properly funding refugee resettlement" on the basis that the United States remain a leader in "providing refuge for the world's most vulnerable . . . especially women and children."[41] Democrats arguing against the SAFE Act opposed the bill for "scapegoating Syrian orphans, widows, and senior citizens,"[42] defending the resettlement program for its focus on "only those who are most vulnerable, who have been tortured, who have been victimized, who are helpless women and children."[43] These configurations reproduced themes within the wider discourse on refugeehood affixing the refugee label to vulnerability in order to justify protection.[44] By relying on passive and feminized representations of refugees to convey their non-threatening status, humanitarian and refugee advocacy actors contributed to these gendered power structures.[45]

While a growing body of work challenges portraits of refugees as gendered objects of humanitarian care,[46] Democrats perpetuated such caricatures in attempting to counter Republican frames of terrorist infiltration. The helplessness and victimhood of Syrian refugees was repeatedly emphasized: "Many of them have been tortured. The women have been raped. The children, for lack of a better term, are destitute."[47] Syrian women were cast as ideal refugee victims—embodying femininity, vulnerability, and helplessness[48]—described as having "nothing but their children in their arms and the clothes on their bodies."[49] Rep. Suzanne Bonamici (D-OR) spoke of the need to protect "women and children" refugees in the context of her own identity "as an American and a mother."[50] Through such language, archetypes of refugee victimhood were woven together with stereotypes about women as the "weaker sex," bound up with child-rearing roles while simultaneously distancing men and fathers from responsibility for the protection of children.[51]

Syrian women doubled as symbols of a "violated" and "suffering" nation, reduced to objects of humanitarian care rather than "genuine participants (with their own ideas, goals, and skills)."[52] These frameworks casting refugee resettlement as unthreatening bolstered Orientalist mythologies of "Islam-Land," where the problems of Islam are "condensed in the figure of the victimized Muslim woman."[53] Portraits of Muslim refugee women as the ultimate vulnerable and voiceless victims[54] rely on and reinforce binaries in which Muslim men are oppressors and attackers. Orientalist depictions of Middle Eastern men as enemies often use the language of "military-aged males" to convey categories of unworthy life.[55] Whereas Muslim refugee women are presumed to need saving and empowering[56] in the form of "outside protection from internal threats,"[57] Muslim refugee men are represented as dangerous.[58] Notions of "violent, oppressive masculinities of the barbarian other" render Syrian refugee men figures of an "uncivilized masculinity."[59] Relying on gendered threat logics, Democratic rhetoric in support of resettling Syrian women and children undermined the broader case for US refugee responsibility-sharing and reproduced gendered binaries.

Republican configurations of refugee threat wielded these gendered binaries to argue against resettlement. Two months prior to the Paris attacks, Trump spoke at a town hall event about the dangers of Syrian refugees: "They could be ISIS, I don't know. Did you ever see a migration like that? They're all men. And they're all strong-looking guys . . . There aren't that many women. And I'm saying to myself, why aren't they fighting to save Syria? Why are they migrating all over Europe?"[60] Syrian refugees were constituted as dangerous on the basis of being *all men* and *strong looking guys*. The notion that "there aren't that many women" reified deservingness of humanitarian protection as feminine. The very act of migrating was feminized, as Trump implied the ideal (civilized) performance of masculinity would require staying in Syria and "fighting to save it." This framing vilified Syrian refugee men as terrorist threats while appealing to traditional gender hierarchies in Republican identity narratives, wherein manhood is bound up with toughness, self-sufficiency, and *fighting*. Syrian men were sufficiently feminized to permit their dehumanization, but not enough to render them non-threatening.

Bifurcated imaginaries casting Syrian refugee men as potential combatants were combined with Orientalist imageries of Middle Eastern/Muslim men as distinctly dangerous. Rep. Francis Rooney's (R-FL) congressional campaign featured ads showing images of armed men in black masks with accompanying narration that "ISIS attacked Paris with Syrian refugees. Now they're trying to use them to infiltrate America." In addition to mug shots of the men who perpetrated the Paris attacks, unidentified news footage showed a large crowd of mostly men walking with bundles and suitcases amid military tanks. These ominous invocations of the threatening *Muslim-migrant-male* triad provided anxiety-inducing visual framing for the ad's caption: "Obama still plans to accept 10,000 Syrian refugees."[61]

This conflation of Syrian refugees with militarized and masculinized imagery among Republicans relied on broader paradigms of gendered threat that were co-constituted by Democrats. In attempting to counter Republican arguments, Democrats ultimately configured Syrian refugee men as outside frameworks of deserving resettlement, normalizing "inattention to adult male civilians" as victims worthy of protection, despite their detention, torture, and targeting for mass execution in conflict situations.[62] Rep. Zoe Lofgren (D-CA) countered logics that Syrian refugees might be terrorist infiltrators by pointing out that "of the 2,000 or so Syrian refugees who have been admitted to the United States, the overwhelming majority are children and widows, who have been victims of torture, who have seen their husbands beheaded."[63] Democrats repeated statistics about Syrian refugees who had been admitted since 2011 to emphasize "half are children," while "young, single males unattached to families constitute only 2% of the Syrian refugee admissions to date."[64] Democratic lawmakers cited a *New York Times* editorial arguing against the SAFE Act during legislative debates to reiterate that Syrian and Iraqi refugees consisted of mostly women and children:

> Half of the Syrian refugees accepted into the United States, officials say, have been children ... Roughly half are female, and many of those applying from abroad are multigenerational families, often with the primary breadwinner missing. About 2 percent are single males of combat age.[65]

Syrian women and children were constructed as deserving of resettlement in the context of having lost their most inimical element—the Arab/Muslim man. The *primary breadwinner* was missing, the fathers and *husbands beheaded*. Syrian refugees were de-weaponized through an emphasis on the absence of men.

This insistence on passive and feminized portraits of Syrian refugeehood among Democratic policymakers further obscured the experiences of refugee men.[66] Discussions of Syrian men as photojournalists, psychiatrists, or caretakers of stray cats,[67] for example, might have disrupted gendered logics of vulnerability and Orientalist caricatures of Middle Eastern male threat. Instead, Syrian refugee men were collapsed into the menacing nomenclature of *males of combat age*. Such framing exacerbated shortfalls within the international refugee regime wherein single Syrian men were repeatedly excluded from resettlement, despite the conditions of vulnerability and insecurity they faced.[68] While adult civilian men often comprise the category most at risk of lethal harm during internal conflicts,[69] Democratic lawmakers persisted in underscoring that only a tiny proportion of admitted refugees were Syrian men.

Some Republicans responded by turning scrutiny onto the small proportion—"2 percent"—of "military aged males," raising concerns that "if even a fraction of those folks are lone wolves, [it] could pose an immense threat to our society."[70] During a campaign rally in Las Vegas, Trump echoed his earlier statements that "the Syrians cannot be allowed to come in" with gendered logics: "Do you ever look at that migration? You say look at all the young men. Where are the women, where are the children, right?"[71] This framing seemingly accepted the premise that women and children are more entitled to protection within humanitarian hierarchies of the relative value of life,[72] focusing on depicting Syrian migrants as predominantly young men to justify blocking their resettlement.

It is important to note that in seeking to delegitimize frames of support for refugee admissions, some Republican lawmakers challenged the supposition that refugee women and children are non-threatening. Rep. Gohmert (R-TX) cited an article claiming, "many of the jihad attempts in the United States are launched by the children of Muslim refugees and migrants."[73] Gohmert pointed to the Tsarnaev brothers responsible for the 2013 Boston Marathon bombings: "You talk to his mother, she said: No, he [the older Tsarnaev brother] is a good boy. And then he went and killed people at the Boston Marathon with his brother."[74] In positioning Muslim refugee women as the mothers of future terrorists, Gohmert's representation aligned with vilifications of *all* Muslims, including "men, women, even children," as "Islamic terrorists intent on killing Americans."[75]

In this vein, New Jersey governor and Republican presidential candidate Chris Christie argued that no Syrian refugees of any age should be resettled in the United States, not even "orphans under five." He defended this comment by pointing to the security risks of "widows and orphans," stating, "we now know from watching the San Bernardino attacks that women can commit heinous, heinous acts against humanity just the same as men can."[76] Syrian widows emerge as undeserving of protection on the basis that they might be "bad victims"—Muslim women who do not want to be "saved" in accordance with WOT logics but who instead turn against their savior (the United States/Western civilization) by participating in terrorism.[77]

The West Under Attack

Dualist matrices juxtaposing the "civilized" West with the non-Western "savage" have long been instrumentalized to justify violence and exploitation in international relations.[78] During the 2015–16 US election cycle, those matrices were used to help justify retreats from refugee responsibility-sharing. Carrying forward the logics at work in President Bush's declaration after 9/11 that "either you are with us, or you are with the terrorists," arguments against refugee resettlement used Us/Them binaries situating Muslims as a non-Western *them*.[79] Rooted in colonial dichotomies of backwardness versus progress and barbarism versus civilization,[80] simplistic dichotomies of a US-led "West" versus an amorphous and inferior non-West reinforced configurations of refugees as terrorist threats. This West/non-West dualism was frequently intertwined with nativist cues to make sense of refugee policy shifts. In line with discursive constructions of "civilization" as "implicitly white,"[81] political elites spoke of *civilization*, *terrorist infiltration*, and *keeping Americans safe* in ways that reinforced the ethnocultural logics of white Christian preservation described in chapter 3.

Arguing against Syrian refugee resettlement, Sen. John McCain (R-AZ) seamlessly wove together threats from ISIS as "the world's largest terrorist army" with "destabilizing refugee flows that have shaken the stability of Syria's neighbors and are now potentially changing the character of European society." McCain warned that "ISIL is determined to attack the heart of the civilized world—Europe and the United States."[82] Europe and the United States were constituted as the vanguard of civilization, while Syrian refugees were configured as threatening along two, overlapping fronts: spreading terrorism and culturally transforming Western society. Representing terrorist aims in terms of civilizational destruction fused the cultural and national security threats posed by Syrian refugees as inseparable dangers. This framing reproduced Orientalist systems of meaning wherein the coding of Middle Eastern actors as terrorists simultaneously codes them as enemies of civilization.[83]

In addition to reifying "the Western world" as a culturally monolithic space endangered by Islamic/terrorist infiltration, policymakers linked its precarity with threats to Christians—creating space for nativist visions of white Christian victimhood. Rep. Keith Rothfus (R-PA) called for "a moratorium on the entry of refugees . . . from Syria and all other countries that have been infiltrated by ISIS," cautioning that, "Islamic State terrorists have the worst intentions not only for Christians and other religious minorities in their own region, but for the entire Western world . . . it is not impossible that ISIS terrorists could enter the country by posing as Syrian refugees."[84] Concerns that non-Western and anti-Christian forces were masquerading as Syrian refugees entangled anxiety-inducing terrorist mystique with the unknowability of the foreigner, portraying refugees as dual threats to safety and culture.[85]

Rep. Hal Rogers (R-KY) similarly argued for halting Syrian and Iraqi refugee admissions in the context of "the senseless and unspeakable violence, the blind fanaticism, the utter and irrational hatred for human life by ISIS" that "present a threat not just to national and global security, but also to the fundamental values that constitute the very fiber of civilization."[86] Such justifications of the SAFE Act collectively tarnished Muslims through repetitions of *violence, fanaticism,* and *irrational hatred* in connection with ISIS along similar lines that WOT discourses tarnished Islam by repeated associations with al-Qaeda—devoid of religious, cultural, or historical context in ways that perpetuated "misreading and misunderstanding."[87] Civilizational orientations of refugee threat opened up space for nativist desires to defend a white Christian European heritage from a fanatical violent infiltrating Islam.

Previous work suggests that multiple categories of threat representation intensify negative perceptions of refugees.[88] Overlapping threat configurations also impact the everyday experiences of refugees awaiting resettlement as they are "battling to be believed."[89] In debates over the SAFE Act, the language of *infiltration* was central to the discursive layering of refugee threat. Rep. Michael McCaul (R-TX) asserted that "Islamic terrorists are seeking to harm our people, destroy our way of life, and undermine the foundational principles of the free world."[90] McCaul went on to emphasize that "at least one of these terrorists [in Paris] may have infiltrated Europe posing as a Syrian refugee . . . to bring terror back to the West." While refugees were embedded in vocabularies of *Islamic terrorists* endangering and infiltrating the West, the United States and Europe were reproduced as civilizationally superior, as the locus of *the free world*. These maneuvers made sense of halts to resettlement by carrying forward WOT visions of defending the West as a vulnerable white vanguard of freedom and civilization.[91]

Such constructions of "the West" rely upon juxtapositions with the non-Western Other not only to maintain narratives of civilizational supremacy but also to deny the validity of non-Western thought.[92] The discrediting of that which is non-Western helps obscure colonial and foreign policy accountability while sustaining desires to preserve a "Western" cultural heritage that is purportedly under attack. Syrian and other Muslim refugees were rendered symbols of a broader civilizational vulnerability wherein Europe and the United States must be defended not only from terrorist attacks but also from an attendant cultural invasion that threatens to destroy "our way of life."

Rep. Gohmert (R-TX) mobilized layered refugee threat configurations by combining concerns about "importing national security problems" with concerns about protecting the US Constitution "against all enemies, foreign and domestic." Terrorist and cultural infiltration frames were interwoven:

> It would be important to ask not simply is this person a terrorist right now, but it would also be important to ask: Are you one of the two-thirds or so that have been reported to be in the United States or wanting to come into the United States as a Muslim who believes that Shari'ah law should replace the Constitution? Because, if those reports are accurate, that two-thirds of the Muslims here believe Shari'ah should replace the Constitution, and they are immigrants and they become citizens, then it means that they absolutely perjured themselves in their oath.[93]

Questioning whether refugees might be terrorists quickly morphed into a focus on their Muslim identity as menacing. Gohmert drew on nativist conspiratorial frameworks of "creeping Sharia"—supposed plots among Muslim Americans to replace the US Constitution and legal system with Sharia law[94]—to elevate the Muslim religious identities of refugees as equally dangerous to potential terrorist connections. These logics amplified conspiracies of "civilization jihad" wherein Muslim organizations "infiltrate and co-opt" branches of the US government to overtake "the West."[95]

The infiltration frame explicitly and implicitly grafted debates over refugee policy onto anxieties about the preservation of the white Christian West. In line with the notion that "whiteness allows bodies to move with comfort through space, and to inhabit the world as if it were home,"⁹⁶ layered refugee threat configurations emphasized the dangers of refugee resettlement to iterations of *our communities* and *our neighborhoods*⁹⁷—extending unspoken claims of whiteness on those spaces. Rep. Francis Rooney (R-FL) combined warnings that refugees could be used by ISIS to "infiltrate America" with the campaign slogan, "let's take our country back."⁹⁸

The infiltration paradigm became so prevalent among Republican lawmakers in their justifications of the SAFE Act that it was deemed "common sense."⁹⁹ Republican governors, too, utilized infiltration logics in arguing against Syrian refugee resettlement within their state jurisdictions. Opposing Syrian refugees was construed as ensuring "terrorists do not enter the nation or our state under the guise of refugee resettlement" and preventing ISIS attempts to "infiltrate the refugee process."¹⁰⁰ Refugees were repeatedly "connected to terrorism"¹⁰¹ and configured as dual threats to safety and culture that could "harm our communities, our institutions, and our people."¹⁰²

Rep. Michael McCaul (R-TX) circulated framing of the "Syrian refugee crisis" in terms of terrorists seeking to "infiltrate the West" through media interviews¹⁰³ and the publication of his book, *Failures of Imagination*. The book described a series of dangers to "the free world," including: "the same sort of radical Islamists who once allied themselves with Hitler. These enemies of civilization seek the death and destruction of the American way of life."¹⁰⁴ Echoing Bush's 2001 declaration depicting "Islamic extremists" as "the heirs of all murderous ideologies of the twentieth century,"¹⁰⁵ McCaul described "Islamist extremism" as the successor to Nazism and communism—propagating WOT logics bound up with defending that which is *Western, civilized,* and *free*. Invoking "the scene of white crosses" in Normandy surrounding the monument to American soldiers who died fighting for their "sacred cause," McCaul's book envisioned a Christian America/West engaged in divine battle against ominous forces connected to Islam.¹⁰⁶ Similar visions were propagated in the discourse of other Republican legislators who spoke of "refugees-turned-jihadis"¹⁰⁷ and questioned whether Syrian refugees were "inserted terrorists" seeking "jihad against Americans and against Western civilization."¹⁰⁸

Republicans attached their partisan identities to the defense of the civilized Christian West amid Orientalist binaries positioning Islam as "the uncivilized and savage 'Other.'"[109] Within these identity narratives, restricting Syrian and other Muslim/Middle Eastern refugee admissions made sense via worldviews of a broader war between r*adical Islam* and the *civilized/Western* world. Republican legislators and governors argued against refugee responsibility-sharing in the context of being "at war" with "radical Muslim extremism"[110] and "radical Islamic terrorists."[111] Such vocabularies contributed to caricatures of Muslims as collectively threatening. The repetition of these associations recycled modes of meaning in which radicalism and extremism are understood as characteristic of Islam,[112] collapsing varieties of Salafi interpretations and myriad complexities in religious and ideological schools of thought[113] into reductionist labels. Portraying Muslims as engaged in a "war against civilization"[114] made sense of refugee policy shifts by commingling terrorist and cultural threats.

Trump's campaign rhetoric also circulated logics of layered threat. Trump often used language amplifying interconnected notions of terrorist conspiracy and unknowability. Syrian refugees were configured as terrorist threats amid refrains that "we don't know who the hell they are"[115] and "we don't want them in our country."[116] During the second presidential debate, Trump opposed "hundreds of thousands of people coming in from Syria when we know nothing about them." This alleged unknowability was augmented with cultural concerns: "We know nothing about their values and we know nothing about their love for our country."[117] Focuses on the unknowability of *their values* cued cultural difference logics less explicitly "tainted with supremacist hierarchy"[118] while implicitly enabling post-biological modalities of racism.[119] Questioning Syrian refugees' affection for the United States conjured neo-Orientalist images of the Middle East as an inherently anti-American space—presumably rooted in cultural/civilizational difference and opposition to American values rather than to US foreign policy actions in the region.

During his speech accepting the Republican presidential nomination at the Republican National Convention in Cleveland, Trump argued against what he described as Hillary Clinton's "radical 550% increase in Syrian refugees" in the context of "massive refugee flows coming into our country already." In addition to warning that "there's no way to screen these refugees in order to find out who they are or where they come from," Trump noted, "I only want to admit individuals into our country who will support our values and love our people. Anyone who endorses violence, hatred, or oppression is not welcome in our country and never ever will be."[120] Syrian refugees were linked with already problematic *massive refugee flows* admitted into the country—pointing to a need for broader US retreats from refugee resettlement beyond restrictions on Syrian admissions. Refugee identities were not only positioned as unknowable, but were also affixed to *violence, hatred,* and *oppression* in mirror image identity contrasts with "our values" and "our people." These frameworks carried forward juxtapositions of the United States as a Western "savior, beacon of light and teacher of democracy and equality" with Orientalist lenses of the Middle East as a "hotbed of terrorism, ignorance, poverty, [and] oppression."[121]

The Specter of 9/11

Interwoven across Orientalist ontologies, gendered threat logics, and constructions of an attack against "the West," the specter of 9/11 loomed large as an implied or overt reference point. The 2015 Paris attacks were represented as a kind of 9/11, experienced by a close ally positioned as similarly "Western" and under assault from Muslim cultural and terrorist infiltration. Extensive references to 9/11 fortified Us/Them binaries, drawing attention away from refugee victimhood to portray "the West" and "the civilized world" as the ultimate victims. Political elites kindled a remembering and reliving of the trauma and horror of September 11 via the surrogate of November 13, effectively "fixing the meaning" of the Paris attacks in terms of 9/11.[122] Retreats from refugee resettlement made sense through distorted West/Other frames, "portraying all acts of terrorism that target the West as connected, regardless of existing similarities between incidents that occur in the East."[123]

In US political discourse, references to 9/11 often reproduce ominous imagery of the Middle East and Islam. On the day of the September 11 attacks, television networks such as CNN, MSNBC, and Fox News circulated "footage of Palestinians dancing in the streets in celebration" alongside "shots of people falling to their deaths from the World Trade towers."[124] Such frames contributed to a "Celebrating Arabs" rumor/legend complex that exaggerated and fabricated instances of Muslims and Arabs rejoicing at the 9/11 attacks and American suffering.[125] This rumor/legend complex was invoked by Trump during his 2015–16 campaign. Trump called for the surveillance of American mosques and the creation of a database of Syrian refugees entering the United States in the context of "thousands and thousands of people cheering" when "the World Trade Center came tumbling down."[126] When questioned about the veracity of the claim, Trump defended the notion that "thousands of Muslims were cheering" on the basis that he had seen it on television at the time of 9/11.[127]

Rep. Louie Gohmert (R-TX) similarly harnessed 9/11 to reproduce snapshots of Arabs and Muslims celebrating anti-Americanism and terrorism. In discussing the threats posed by "so-called Syrian refugees," Gohmert referenced a *Daily Caller* article criticizing Laila Alawa, an "immigrant of Syrian heritage who said 9/11 'changed the world for good' and has consistently disparaged America, free speech, and white people."[128] Gohmert also countered the notion that 9/11 resulted in anti-Arab or anti-Muslim hate crimes: "Well, actually, I don't see a lot of attacks on Muslims in America, especially by true Christians because that is not a Christian thing to do. It is a radical Islamist thing to do."[129] The congressman linked critiques that Syrian refugees could too easily obtain work permits with concerns that American-born children of Muslim immigrants were being recruited for "jihad" because "they have children, and then the children are taught to hate America."[130]

While *radical Islam, jihad, hating America*, and 9/11 became closely linked during the WOT, these associations continued to hover over debates about refugee policy to reinforce constructions of being under attack from a savage Islamic Other. Such WOT vocabularies "narrowed the space for the debate" and constrained "avenues of reply" among policymakers.[131] The 9/11 attacks were used as a "marker of temporal rupture"[132] to justify elevating the terrorist threat of refugees above human rights and refugee protection principles. In emphasizing that the Paris attackers "took advantage of the influx of Syrian refugees into France," Sen. David Vitter (R-LA) warned, "it would be a mistake to retreat to some sort of pre-9/11 posture or mindset."[133]

Bonds between French victims of the Paris attacks and American victims of 9/11 were reproduced extensively by political elites. Tributes and condolences for France became instruments for reliving the trauma of September 11 and reinvigorating WOT logics. Republican lawmakers posited that "the streets of Paris could just have easily been the streets of New York or Chicago or Houston or Los Angeles,"[134] and "based on the number of casualties and population of France, this attack was the equivalent of 9/11."[135] These rhetorical maneuvers bolstered WOT systems of meanings in which an omnipresent terrorist threat "draws a line between the Western, peace-loving world" and "radical Islamic societies."[136] While many Americans increasingly identified issues like climate change, economic instability, and nuclear weapons as major concerns,[137] awakening the specter of 9/11 in debates over refugee resettlement revived fears of terrorism as the preeminent danger of the twenty-first century and the primary lens for evaluating US refugee responsibility-sharing.

Democratic Rep. John Conyers (D-MI) drew on the 9/11-Paris attacks nexus to echo language used by many Republicans arguing against Syrian refugee admissions: "In the wake of the September 11 attacks on our shores and the tragic November 13 terrorist attacks in Paris, we must be vigilant, particularly in the midst of a global refugee crisis."[138] While ultimately arguing against H.R. 4038 and in favor of expanding refugee resettlement, Conyers nonetheless amplified frameworks in which the terminology of "refugee crisis" conveyed "a perceived threat *from* rather than *to* refugees."[139] Democratic policymakers contributed to a narrative wherein "November 13 was France's September 11" and a "reminder" of 9/11,[140] but were more likely to explain how the implications for refugee resettlement were distinct based on procedural differences between European and US admissions processes. Republican legislators typically obscured those differences, drawing parallels in which "at least one of those terrorists in Paris got into France under the Syrian refugee resettlement program there, and that is the same danger that is posed to us."[141] In arguing that "refugees are a huge problem," Sen. John McCain (R-AZ) emphasized "what happened in Paris can happen here."[142] It is worth clarifying that most of the perpetrators of the Paris attacks were residents of Europe already on terrorist watch lists or known to local police. None of the Paris attackers were subject to the extensive vetting measures in place within the US resettlement program, which resulted in refugees being among the most intensively scrutinized populations entering the United States.[143]

Whereas Democrats tended to highlight these details, Republican policymakers repeated a congressional testimony quote by FBI Director James Comey that "if someone has never made a ripple in the pond in Syria in a way that would get their identity or their interests reflected in our database, we can query our database until the cows come home . . . there will be nothing show up."[144] Comey also testified during the same Homeland Security hearing that he believed the United States was "much better" at vetting refugees than it had been in the past, underscoring that "there is no risk-free process." The consensus among US government officials involved in overseas refugee screening was that extensive security vetting was already solidly in place.[145] Such nuances were sidestepped in justifications of retreats from refugee resettlement. Instead, 9/11 was invoked to conflate European and American parallels, summoning recollections of a "Western" identity under attack and enabling terrorist threats to be seamlessly interwoven with nativist visions of cultural crisis.

The Republican governor of Maine, Paul LePage, propagated parallels between the Paris attacks and 9/11 to mobilize such logics:

> To bring Syrian refugees into our country without knowing who they are is to invite an attack on American soil just like the one we saw in Paris last week and in New York City on 9/11 . . . The safety of Maine citizens comes first, and it is about time the United States and Europe wake up to the nature of the threat against us in the form of radical terrorism.[146]

The unknowability of Syrian refugees fueled representations of unassimilable foreign Others culturally disrupting the in-group ("our country," "Maine citizens"). The United States and Europe were projected as kindred spaces of shared Western vulnerability. Implicit in the governor's coded reference to "radical terrorism" was the rhetorical commonplace of *radical Islam*. The Paris attacks were used to revive 9/11 as a staging of the West's encounter with the radical Islamic Other, renegotiating and sustaining the Us/Them imaginaries at the core of WOT spatial maps.[147]

Conclusion

This chapter has shown how political elites positioned Syrian and other Muslim refugees as terrorist threats during the 2015–16 election cycle as part of a multicausal process legitimizing US retreats from the international refugee regime. Legacies of the WOT discursive landscape were prominent in harnessing Orientalist ontologies of the Middle East, gendered threat logics, and visions of a "radical Islamic" attack against "Western civilization." Notions of terrorist infiltration via refugees moved from peripheral to commonsensical after the Paris attacks, which were interpreted as a kind of 9/11. Allusions to 9/11 haunted debates about Syrian and Iraqi refugee admissions to reproduce symbols of a traumatized and vulnerable West/America, elevating terrorist paradigms above humanitarian concerns and enabling configurations of a dual threat wherein refugees were portrayed as both terrorist and cultural/civilizational infiltrators. Beyond making policy shifts away from refugee protection and resettlement possible among Republicans and conservatives, these rhetorical moves construed such shifts as "unavoidable and absolutely legitimate."[148] In addition to showing how refugee policy becomes intimately bound up with discursive practices, the chapter reminds us that gendered and racialized narratives of the past can powerfully reemerge in new contexts and be harnessed by political actors to manipulate Self/Other identities.

Democrats, too, contributed to associations of refugees with terrorist threats, despite often arguing in favor of refugee protection. Democrats were central to perpetuating gendered logics that excluded Syrian refugee men from deserving resettlement, focusing on women and children as acceptable admissions in ways that reinforced feminized and passive accounts of refugeehood[149] and Orientalist assumptions that "it is the men in IslamLand who most need to undergo a moral revolution."[150] The propagation of gendered binaries inscribing all Muslim/Middle Eastern adult men as potential combatants among both Republicans and Democrats enabled the continued stigmatization of Syrian refugee men, calling attention more broadly to the perpetuation of protection gaps within the international refugee regime wherein men are equated with security threats and deemed more easily excludable from access to resettlement and humanitarian services.[151]

Arguments against Syrian and other Muslim refugee admissions in the context of a radical Islamic attack against the West featured most prominently in Republican narratives, enabling harmonization of the terrorist infiltration frame with nativist configurations of refugees as endangering white Christian preservation. Some Democrats also used the language of civilizational threat and reproduced "the West" as a self-evident cultural space. For Democratic members of Congress who spoke of terrorists endangering "Western countries"[152] and "refugees from the Middle East pouring into Europe,"[153] their arguments against restricting refugee resettlement augmented a broader discursive landscape positioning Syrian and Middle Eastern/Central Asian refugees as threatening Islamic Others. Despite the disparate policy positions of Republicans and Democrats regarding refugee admissions, it is important to acknowledge the extent to which Democrats contributed to a collective consciousness wherein refugees were equated with security threats. Indeed, forty-seven Democrats ultimately voted with Republicans to pass the SAFE Act in the House of Representatives.[154]

The partisan divergences discussed in this chapter reiterate the entanglement of refugee threat configurations with domestic identity narratives. Republicans were particularly vocal in positioning themselves as defenders of "Western/Christian civilization" in the wake of attacks from "radical Islamic terrorists" to justify halts on refugee admissions. Republicans also relied heavily on Orientalist ontologies of the Middle East and Islam, reproducing threats of Muslim infiltration and essentializing Muslim men as inherently ominous to construct their party as better equipped to battle civilizational destruction and more willing than Democrats to stand strongly against "refugees-turned-jihadis." This linkage of Republican identity with masculine stereotypes and anti-terrorism supported partisan identity narratives in which the Republican Party "owns" national security while Democrats are linked with feminine stereotypes and feminized policy issues.[155]

5

Refugees as Partisan Symbols

As the number of Syrian refugees registered with the UNHCR exceeded 4 million during the summer of 2015, several Democratic members of Congress criticized resettlement efforts as "unacceptably low" and called for increases in US refugee responsibility-sharing.[1] Democratic presidential candidate Hillary Clinton soon thereafter proposed increasing Syrian refugee admissions to 65,000—a proposal that substantially exceeded the Obama administration's plan to admit 10,000 Syrian refugees for FY2016 and that echoed the resettlement target recommended by the International Rescue Committee.[2] Clinton asserted, "we're facing the worst refugee crisis since the end of World War II and I think the United States has to do more."[3]

In the months ahead of the 2016 elections, Trump's presidential campaign ran a television ad cautioning: "In Hillary Clinton's America, the system stays rigged against Americans. Syrian refugees flood in." Stripped of place, time, or context, large crowds of presumably Middle Eastern migrants stretched ubiquitously into the horizon of the camera angle. The crowd appeared mostly male, with two women wearing hijabs also visible in the shot. Overlaying the image of numerous nameless strangers were the words, "Hillary Clinton: US should take 65,000 Syrian refugees." In shifting away from this and other ominous footage, the narrator stated: "Donald Trump's America is secure. Terrorists and dangerous criminals kept out, the border secured, our families safe."[4]

Trump's campaign ad reflected not only the ascent of logics conflating refugees with terrorists, but also the tethering of those threat configurations to Democrats. Opposition to refugees became central within the meanings surrounding Trump's campaign slogan—"Make America Great Again"—and Republican partisan identity, while support for refugee resettlement became fused with Democratic partisan imagery and Hillary Clinton's "Stronger Together" mantra. Within the domestic scaffolding of partisan and ideological polarization, US political elites made refugee policy constitutive of the shifting group boundaries and symbols separating Republicans and conservatives from Democrats and liberals. These domestic identity processes impaired possibilities of bipartisan support for refugee responsibility-sharing, reconfiguring refugees as accessories of partisan and ideological archetypes.

Political party platforms, congressional rhetoric, gubernatorial statements, and other sources of elite discourse shed light on how refugees were instrumentalized to curate partisan and ideological consciousness during the 2015–16 US election cycle. In addition to constructing diverging maps of reality and boundaries of belonging, conservative and liberal storytelling about refugee resettlement offered disparate accounts of what America means. In Republican narratives, Syrian refugees emerged within gendered and racialized mirror image logics wherein Republicans were masculinized cultural warriors, strong defenders of the in-group—implicitly coded as white and explicitly demarcated as Christian—while Democrats were feminized as weak, submissive, and cast in terms of pro-Muslim/anti-Christian binaries. Democratic support for Syrian refugee resettlement was represented as emblematic of the broader peril posed by liberals regarding their "political correctness" and prioritization of helping distant Others (foreigners, Muslims). In Democratic narratives, retreats from refugee protection were constituted as antithetical to liberal visions of America's Safe Haven status and Statue of Liberty ethos. Embracing refugee resettlement bolstered Democratic claims on compassion and inclusion, simultaneously enabling the juxtaposition of these policy values with Republican intolerance and xenophobia.

It is critical to understand the importance of partisanship and polarization in conditioning (sub)national identity dynamics within the two-party system in the United States. While rarely incorporated into scholarship on international norms or refugee "burden-sharing," work on these concepts is crucial for understanding US retreats from refugee resettlement. Refugees became discursively bound up with partisan identity in ways that constrained possibilities of bipartisan support. Delving into these narratives reveals political elites maneuvering to establish and deepen certain paradigms for understanding reality, to compose and manage the rhetorical commonplaces that become constitutive of policy debates.[5] Republicans sought to center refugee policy discussions around *political correctness* and *radical Islamic terrorism*, attaching these concepts to a broader sense of conservative Christian precarity. Democrats directed these discussions toward liberal prisms of compassion and inclusion, reproducing the Safe Haven mythologies described in chapter 2—wherein the United States has always served as a welcoming caretaker of the world's oppressed—and evoking visions of America oriented around Statue of Liberty imagery.

Republican and Democratic identity narratives were co-constitutive, continuously responding to the constructions of Self and Other articulated by partisan opponents. The chapter offers a window into how debates over refugee resettlement were fashioned into competing and co-dependent accounts of the meaning of America, its greatest existentialist threats, and its most plausible saviors.

Disaggregating National Identity and Refugees as Partisan Symbols

In 2014, amid the intensification of conflict and displacement in Syria, conservative senator Ted Cruz (R-TX) told Fox News interviewers, "We have welcomed refugees—the tired, huddled masses—for centuries. That's been the history of the United States. We should continue to do so."[6] Within two years, such a statement would become associated almost exclusively with Democrats and "the left." Several prominent Republicans initially supported or appeared open to the Obama administration's 2015 announcement accepting at least 10,000 Syrian refugees for the following fiscal year—a sixfold increase from the number previously admitted into the country.[7] As an early frontrunner among Republican presidential candidates, former governor Jeb Bush (R-FL) justified increased refugee responsibility-sharing in the context of allies like Germany promising much higher admissions (over 300,000). Bush elaborated his support for admitting more Syrian refugees on the basis that the United States possessed an "ample process" for security vetting as well as historical roots anchored in welcoming refugees: "We have been a country that has allowed refugees to come in and over the long haul it's been to our benefit."[8] Early in their presidential candidacies in 2015, Governor John Kasich (R-OH) and Sen. Marco Rubio (R-FL) similarly expressed openness to increasing Syrian refugee resettlement. Rubio indicated being "potentially open" to greater acceptances of displaced Syrians into the United States,[9] while Kasich noted, "I think we do have a responsibility in terms of taking some more folks in."[10] Other Republican presidential candidates initially vocalizing support included Sen. Lindsey Graham (R-SC), who contended: "We should take our fair share ... I don't see how we can lead the free world and turn our back on people that are seeking it."[11]

In the following months, the November 2015 Paris attacks accelerated debates over refugee policy and a large field of candidates intensified their competition in advance of the Republican presidential primaries. Traces of conservative rhetoric supportive of Syrian refugee responsibility-sharing diminished. Ted Cruz became a leading figure in introducing legislation to restrict Syrian refugees from entering the United States, and Lindsey Graham, Marco Rubio, and John Kasich all called for variations of a "timeout" or "pause" on resettlement. Jeb Bush shifted his original position from supporting increased refugee admissions to concentrating on the protection of "Christians from Syria" and creating internal safe zones where displaced civilians would remain in Syria.[12] These shifts were manifestations of identity processes that embedded opposition to refugee resettlement within Republican narratives in ways that constrained the parameters of conservative policy options. Positions on refugees became linked with "signals about where one's group belonged,"[13] shaping interpretations of appropriate US responses to displacement along the contours of partisan and ideological identity.

In the US two-party system, ideology (liberal and conservative) and partisanship (Democrat and Republican) have become increasingly entangled amid processes of partisan "sorting"[14] and political polarization.[15] Political parties operate not merely as vehicles of articulating policy positions, but more powerfully as social groups.[16] The power of these group attachments transcends the particularities of ideological orientations.[17] By some accounts partisan identity has become a stronger basis of social identity in US politics than race and religion, increasingly associated with "Us versus Them" interpretations of the political world.[18] Work on political polarization in the United States points to a growing intensity of conflict among partisan elites[19] and an "affective" (emotionally reactive) component wherein Republicans and Democrats increasingly view members of their own party more positively and members of the opposing party more negatively.[20] Accompanying growing partisan antipathy and animosity is an increased "dehumanizing" of partisan opponents.[21] Even for Americans who do not explicitly identify with a political party, those actively engaged in politics typically "lean" toward the Republican or Democratic Party and show similar trends toward moral disengagement with and dehumanization of partisan opponents.[22]

Like partisanship, ideology has social identity aspects—"the sense of belonging to the groups called liberal and conservative."[23] In-group/out-group boundary delineations determine insiders and outsiders, who is worthy of trust and protection and who can be morally excluded and denied help.[24] International Relations scholars and others studying human rights and refugee protection can benefit from considering the extent to which competing partisan narratives fashion disparate normative environments wherein logics of inclusion/protection and exclusion/denial make sense. Because norms depend on intersubjectivity, they are powerful only insofar as they are accepted within a group.[25] This chapter underscores the extent to which standards of appropriateness vary across conservative and liberal frameworks, highlighting diverging group norms among Republicans and Democrats.

The reconfiguration of refugees into partisan and ideological identity symbols during the 2015–16 election cycle was an important component in the multicausal process characterizing US retreats from refugee resettlement. Those retreats were rooted in fractured, polarized, and competing domestic identities. The chapter contributes to work on how interests and identities are contested and become discursively dominant.[26] Beyond problematizing notions of unitary state interests or identities driving refugee "burden-sharing," it explains how policy logics evolve and become hegemonic within partisan and ideological systems of meaning. Republican and Democratic constructions of refugees were not just articulations of policy positions but became symbols of partisan group attachment mired in emotionally reactive "pernicious polarization" cycles.[27] Representations of refugees were often linked to concerns about ethnocultural preservation and Christian precarity in Republican narratives and were fused with the championing of multicultural diversity and inclusion among Democrats—reproducing partisan identity as a "mega-identity" bound up with religion and race.[28]

During the 2015–16 election cycle, political elites embedded refugee protection within cultural and partisan conflict, configuring refugees along coordinates of ideological and partisan social imagery in ways that rendered refugee policy stances "non-negotiable."[29] They used the Syrian "refugee crisis" to widen the perceived moral gap between in-party and out-party identities.[30] Democrats constructed refugee responsibility-sharing in ways that bolstered liberal visions of safeguarding the Safe Haven status and Statue of Liberty ethos of America and anchored refugees within Democratic commitments to diversity and inclusion. Democrats often directed debates over refugee resettlement toward dimensions of non-discrimination and equal treatment of groups (fairness), and toward the importance of caring for the vulnerable (compassion)—fortifying these values as liberal group norms and "moral foundations."[31]

Partisan elites often draw on gendered group norms in their representations of refugees. Conservatives and Republicans tend to construct masculine notions of power and authority, to build and be perceived through masculinized prisms of toughness, and to use "masculine language" evoking dominant and negative valence in political speech.[32] In discussions of refugee resettlement during the election cycle, Republicans assembled masculinized portraits of cultural warriors, fighting to defend Christianity from liberal collusion with "radical Islam." Republican toughness, strength, and loyalty to insiders was contrasted with Democratic weakness vis-à-vis political correctness and the prioritization of helping distant Others.

Fractures between liberal and conservative interpretations of Christianity bifurcated religious justifications for supporting and restricting refugee resettlement. Republicans reconfigured refugees in ways that delegitimized and reframed previous paradigms of bipartisan support to cast Syrian and other Muslim refugee admissions as incongruent with conservative Christian group norms and preservation. Through Christian victimhood frames and anti-universalist conceptualizations of hospitality, Republican policymakers "made sense" of retreats from refugee protection in ways that reinforced conservative Christian belonging.

Safeguarding the Statue of Liberty

Decades of bipartisan justifications for refugee resettlement prior to the 2016 elections were bound up with providential exceptionalist themes and imagery of the United States as a global Safe Haven and "leader" of international refugee and human rights regimes. Understanding how these logics broke down unwinds an important thread in US retreats from refugee responsibility-sharing. Legitimations of refugee admissions did not break down in a blanketed manner but fractured along partisan identity boundaries. Democrats tethered exceptionalist vocabularies to emphases on multicultural diversity and the inclusion of Others, embedding Safe Haven mythologies in distinctly partisan frameworks. Democrats also configured refugees in alignment with partisan group imagery cultivated around compassion and care for the vulnerable, reinforcing party "ownership" of care-adjacent traits and policy issues.[33] Support for resettlement was tied to desires to preserve the Statue of Liberty ethos of America as a welcoming and diverse "nation of immigrants"[34] and caretaker of the oppressed.

Under a section entitled "Protect Our Values," the 2016 Democratic Party platform promoted *inclusion, tolerance, human rights*, and *safeguarding vulnerable minorities*.[35] The platform included "refugees" within its list of vulnerable groups in need of protection—alongside, for example, "LGBT people," women and girls, and religious minorities. "Muslim refugees" were further distinguished as a disadvantaged group in need of defense given that Trump's campaign proposed "banning" them from entry. Another section of the platform argued that the United States should "lead the international community in providing greater humanitarian assistance to the civilian victims of war in Syria and Iraq, especially displaced refugees."[36]

In linking refugee protection with *our values*, categorizing *Muslim refugees* as one of the *vulnerable* groups the party should protect, and conceiving of care for displaced Syrians and Iraqis in terms of *leading the international community*, the Democratic Party platform situated refugee responsibility-sharing within particular understandings of what is morally right in the world and what America's role in that world ought to be. These visions affirmed liberal group norms regarding empathy for the disadvantaged, affirmation of human rights, and inclinations toward "internationalist" approaches elevating multilateralism, foreign aid, and humanitarianism.[37]

In response to the effort among mostly Republican governors to discontinue Syrian refugee resettlement in state jurisdictions, Democratic governors coupled support for refugees with calls for "compassion."[38] During debates over H.R. 4038 (the SAFE Act) restricting Syrian and Iraqi refugees, Democratic members of Congress defended refugee resettlement in the context of "a fight of values"[39] and standing up for "our values."[40] Refugee responsibility-sharing was legitimized on the basis that "we are facing a global refugee crisis that requires a global response," and "the United States must do its part to help" and "show compassion."[41] Democrats linked refugee admissions with "openness and inclusiveness" and protection of "the most vulnerable,"[42] reproducing these values as constitutive of Democratic partisan identity.

At stake in these debates were not only US refugee policies, but also the moral core of America and—according to Democrats—its lineage as a Safe Haven for the marginalized and oppressed. Rep. Betty McCollum (DFL-MN) condemned the SAFE Act as "a political weapon to attack Democrats who still believe our nation should be a safe haven for vulnerable people seeking freedom from persecution and the threat of death."[43] House minority leader Nancy Pelosi (D-CA) additionally criticized the legislation on the basis that it "fails to meet our values," contrasting imagery of the bill "slamming the door to mothers and children" with "the proud American tradition" of welcoming desperate people.[44] Rep. Jerry Nadler (D-NY) condemned efforts to restrict Syrian refugees from entry as morally wrong and antithetical to the essence of America: "To stop thousands of desperate people who are fleeing unspeakable violence is unconscionable. We might as well take down the Statue of Liberty."[45]

Through quotations of the words inscribed on the Statue of Liberty, Democratic lawmakers positioned refugee responsibility-sharing as intrinsic to America's roots—to "our history of a nation of what America is."[46] Democratic configurations of refugees as emblematic of *what America is* reproduced visions of a diverse, multicultural polity founded on immigrant origins. Sen. Elizabeth Warren (D-MA) reinforced this image in defending refugee resettlement: "We are a country of immigrants and refugees, a country made strong by our diversity, a country founded by those crossing the sea."[47] Democratic policymakers used refugee resettlement to deepen origin stories wherein "our Nation was founded by immigrants and has historically welcomed refugees"[48] and "America was built on the values of acceptance and compassion."[49]

Democrats situated themselves as safeguarding America's Statue of Liberty iconography and its attendant portraits of American exceptionalism.[50] As discussed in chapter 2, exceptionalist fantasies of America as an "exemplar nation" and Americans as "a divine and righteous people above all others" have long pervaded US cultural and political discourse, spanning Republican and Democratic narratives.⁵¹ The appropriation of providential exceptionalist imagery by Democrats in debates about refugee resettlement, however, entangled tropes of America as a "shining city on a hill" and "leader of the free world"⁵² with explicitly liberal ideological cues and partisan antipathy toward Republicans. Deliberately refuting ethnocultural lenses of American heritage as derived from white Anglo-Saxon Protestantism, Democrats emphasized a diverse provenance: "We are a nation of Native Americans, descendants of slaves, and immigrants."⁵³

Democratic political elites leveraged these iterations of multicultural origins and inclusive historical foundations to attach refugees to signals of partisan identity. Configurations of refugees within vocabularies of diversity and inclusion aligned with Hillary Clinton's campaign slogan, "Stronger Together."⁵⁴ During the second presidential debate, Clinton defended refugee responsibility-sharing on the basis that: "There are a lot of refugees—women and children ... suffering in this catastrophic war ... we need to do our part. We by no means are carrying anywhere near the load that Europe and others are."⁵⁵ In addition to wielding gendered logics to reinforce partisan imagery, the refrain of "doing our part" cued Democratic group norms championing multilateralism and the benefits of working collectively with allies. These frameworks helped entrench refugee admissions as a "liberal cause," contributing to elite polarization over refugee resettlement.

As Democrats transformed refugees into symbols of partisan values, they simultaneously instrumentalized them to differentiate Republicans as morally opposite—as exclusionary, discriminatory, and threatening to America's Statue of Liberty ethos. Arguing against restrictions on Syrian and Iraqi refugees meant simultaneously arguing against Republican beliefs that "only White Christians can come into this country."⁵⁶ Partisan antipathy cues painted Republican efforts to restrict refugees as unAmerican, as "slamming our doors to the world's most vulnerable" and "betraying our values."⁵⁷ Hillary Clinton distinguished her supportive stance toward Syrian refugees from Trump's desire to "ban people based on a religion," countering his discriminatory approach with the assertion that "we are a country founded on religious freedom and liberty."⁵⁸

Democratic presidential contender Bernie Sanders similarly condemned Republican "fear-mongering" while underscoring the need to safeguard America's welcoming and inclusive moral core: "We will not succumb to Islamophobia . . . We will not turn our backs on the refugees who are fleeing Syria and Afghanistan. We will do what we do best and that is be Americans—fighting racism, fighting xenophobia, fighting fear."[59] Governor Jay Inslee (D-WA) compared Republican efforts to restrict Syrian refugees in state jurisdictions with the internment of Japanese Americans during World War II: "It was a bad decision, and it wasn't consistent with who we are as a country."[60] Within these Democratic interpretations, refugee protection was fused with *who we are as a country* and what it means to be American. Partisan opponents (Republicans) were simultaneously disowned from genuine national belonging via their opposition to refugees, which was equated with racial and religious intolerance.

The Democratic Party platform also wielded refugees as instruments of partisan differentiation: "While Donald Trump proposes banning Muslim refugees, we will look for ways to help innocent people who are fleeing persecution while ensuring rigorous screening and vetting." Another section of the platform reiterated, "We reject attempts to impose a religious test to bar immigrants or refugees from entering the United States" since it is "un-American and runs counter to the founding principles of this country."[61] Republicans, via their desires to block refugees, were interpreted as unpatriotic while Democrats were positioned as protectors of virtuous victims and defenders of America's true moral core.

Referring to the SAFE Act as "the Republican bill" and "Republican-led refugee bill,"[62] Democratic lawmakers reinforced refugee resettlement as a conduit for partisan antipathy. Democrats rejected the bill as a manifestation of Republicans' "cruel, callous . . . blatant display of xenophobia" and "hatred of immigrants."[63] Republican efforts to restrict refugees were likened to the "racist, xenophobic, and anti-Semitic" national origin quotas established in the Immigration Act of 1924, without which "perhaps 2 million of the 6 million Jews who were murdered in the Holocaust would have been living safely in the United States instead."[64] Amid a polarized environment in which Republicans and Democrats were "enemies,"[65] arguments for refugee resettlement situated Republicans in mirror image frameworks wherein Democrats were tolerant, inclusive protectors of America's Safe Haven status while Republicans were intolerant, exclusionary, and un-American.

In sustaining providential exceptionalist justifications of refugee resettlement, Democrats circulated sanitized accounts of US hegemony as a benign and welcomed force, promulgating fantasies of the United States as a superpower savior that "the world always looks to" in times of distress.[66] Eclipsed within this paradigm were the harmful effects of US foreign policy and its myriad violations of human rights regarding refugee and asylum standards. Speaking against the SAFE Act, Sen. Ben Cardin (D-MD) corralled exceptionalist motifs toward a portrait of refugee "rescue" in which Republican-led restrictions on refugees were an anomaly in US history:

> I will start by saying that the world looks to the United States, and when there are tough problems, they look to our leadership . . . This Republican bill we considered today dishonors our proud history of providing a safe haven . . . We should not let knee-jerk reactions keep us from being the beacon of hope for Syrians and other refugees in the Middle East, Africa, and around the world.[67]

Sen. Cardin recounted the US resettlement of displaced persons from Nazi-controlled areas, refugees from Vietnam, Jews from the Soviet Union, and Cuban refugees to support this exceptionalist retelling of America's past, neglecting the degree to which deviations from refugee protection principles also animated that history (as discussed in chapter 2).

Democrats defended the refugee resettlement program as a testament to America's status as a "beacon of light, of democracy, of freedom in the world."[68] Sen. Elizabeth Warren (D-MA) championed "our commitment to a world of open minds and open hearts" as "the reason the people of Syria and people all around this world look to us for hope."[69] Refugees were used to promulgate visions of America as a benevolent rescuer, such that "people who are abused, people who are oppressed, can still look to this country"[70] as a polity "born of persecution, forged in liberty's name with equality for all . . . that shining city upon the hill."[71] Within Democratic identity narratives, refugee resettlement spotlighted the best features of America's silhouette, sidestepping the deep roots of US discriminatory and exclusionary policies.

Republican and Democratic partisan identity narratives were mutually constitutive. Appeals to providential exceptionalism in support of refugee responsibility-sharing among Democrats pressed Republicans to reconcile restrictions on refugees with beliefs about the special and divine duties of America. Rep. Trey Gowdy (R-SC) affirmed that, "America always stands as a beacon of hope for everyone fleeing oppression and terror. Nothing will stop us from protecting the innocent while continuing our fight against evil." The congressman reoriented these exceptionalist appeals along a distinction between *the innocent* (which deserve *protecting*) and *evil* (which America must fight). Gowdy further countered Democratic logics tethering refugee admissions to American values by positing that, "it is against the values of our Nation and the values of a free society to give terrorists the opening they are looking for to come into our country and harm the American people."[72] This framing left exceptionalist visions of American rescue ostensibly uncorrupted by desires to block threatening outsiders.

Justifying the SAFE Act through logics of terrorist infiltration, Rep. Richard Hudson (R-NC) offered arguments harmonizing exceptionalist mythology with America First ideology: "America is a compassionate country. We are a good country. We have a long history of accepting refugees, people fleeing oppression and violence. But we have an obligation to the American people."[73] Similarly, before becoming the Republican nominee for vice president, Indiana governor Mike Pence opposed Syrian refugee resettlement within his state jurisdiction on the basis that: "Indiana has a long tradition of opening our arms and homes to refugees from around the world but, as governor, my first responsibility is to ensure the safety and security of all Hoosiers."[74] The term "Hoosier"—a colloquial way of referring to native inhabitants of Indiana—is often used as part of a local cultural lexicon constructing state identity as "rustic, rural, and White."[75] The Republican Party platform, too, framed retreats from refugee responsibility-sharing in ways that were sensitive to the exceptionalist paradigm while creating space for nativist and Orientalist interpretations. The platform acknowledged that, "from its beginning, our country has been a haven of refuge and asylum," adding, "that should continue—but with major changes." Policy shifts were legitimized through the need to prevent the entry of refugees "whose homelands have been the breeding grounds for terrorism."[76]

Republican narratives redirected providential exceptionalism toward visions of defending Western values—"the values of a free society"—from

Islamic attack and toward the defense of the local ("Hoosiers," "the American people") over the global ("refugees from around the world"). That these arguments were made from the premise of reaffirming America's history of refuge points to the endurance and malleability of providential exceptionalism. Constructions of America as a protector of the oppressed were not explicitly contested by Republicans but were channeled toward a more urgent priority of defending the in-group—"protecting the American people."[77] Such interpretations complemented the "America First" mantra of Trump and other Republicans without wholly rejecting or retelling the "American legacy of being a welcoming nation."[78]

Republican Warriors and Democratic Doormats

As partisan elites continuously respond and react to the constellations of meaning circulated by their opponents, they construct conceptual frameworks that help group members "make sense of the political world" and demarcate allies and enemies.[79] In the decades following the Civil Rights Movement, Republicans became more conservative on issues of race, more resistant to racial pluralism, and more suspicious of racial and cultural outsiders in part as a "reaction" to the Democratic Party's embrace of progressivism and increasingly liberal views on race.[80] During the 2015–16 election cycle, Republicans utilized debates over refugee resettlement to reproduce one-dimensional caricatures of Muslim enemies in ways that positioned Republicans and conservatives as cultural warriors. Responding to Democratic narratives emphasizing diversity and inclusion, Republicans infused the need to defend against Islamic attack with imagery of masculinized, militarized strength drawing on deeper genealogies of conservative identity construction oriented around "toughness" and the use of force.[81]

Such narratives persist through time, repurposed and refined in response to shifting contexts. Past and present are discursively connected and interwoven.[82] Ten years prior to the 2016 election, for example, conservative television host Bill O'Reilly authored a book entitled *Culture Warrior*, which became a *New York Times* bestseller. O'Reilly outlined the need to fight against "secular-progressives" destroying America: "Traditionalists are fighting for their neighborhoods, their country, and their world. Since there's a huge amount at stake, the traditional cause must become a way of life. There are no 'weekend warriors' in this culture war. We are in it to win it, which will require courage, commitment, and discipline."[83] This call to arms portrayed liberals as "not capable of understanding true evil" and unable to recognize the threat posed by "Islamic fascist terror cells."[84] Similar themes reemerged in Republican justifications for restricting refugee resettlement.

In legitimizing retreats from refugee responsibility-sharing, Republican lawmakers traced the carved-out paths of masculinized warrior discourses pitting conservative fighters against liberal weakness. Rep. Steven Palazzo (R-MS) invoked wartime lexicon of being "under attack," specifying "this enemy is radical Muslim extremism . . . we must fight back, and we must do more." Palazzo challenged Obama, "I dare the President to veto this bill because he is angrier at Republicans than he is at terrorists."[85] Palazzo combined partisan antipathy cues with warrior vocabulary—*fight, attack, enemy*. Republicans emerged as "fighters" ready to take action against the Islamic threat surreptitiously lurking within Syrian refugees, while Democrats were depicted as weak and irrationally emotional, misdirecting their anger toward partisan opponents instead of terrorists. Portraits of liberal emotionality and irrationality similarly manifested in Republican claims that "Hillary is pathologically committed to bringing more refugees here, knowing full well that there will be Islamists and jihadists among them."[86]

Republicans reproduced mirror image dyads contrasting Democratic weakness and passivity with Republican strength and assertiveness. Sen. John Thune (R-SD) attributed "the Syrian refugee crisis" to Obama's "failure to back up his tough talk with action," emphasizing, "if you don't take action to solve the problem, the people who are suffering will end up on your doorstep."[87] Refugee resettlement was feminized and softened as part of the juxtaposition between Democratic *talk* and Republican *action*, between liberal sentimentality and conservative toughness. As desires to protect Syrian refugees were linked with Democratic feebleness, debates over refugee responsibility-sharing became bound up with co-dependent partisan identity narratives dichotomizing Republican warriors and Democratic doormats.

Republican representations blamed "the flood of Syrians" on Democratic "inaction in Syria, and failure to take seriously the ISIS threat."[88] Logics in which "we cannot allow America's welcome mat to become a doormat for radicalized Islamic extremists who are hardwired to kill innocent people and destroy our way of life"[89] replicated notions of liberal passivity in the face of Islamic threat and reinforced Republican cultural warrior self-concepts. Such references to defending the American "way of life" also created space for nativist visions of Republicans and conservatives as the sentinels of ethnocultural preservation, enmeshing partisan and nativist prisms.

In the battle to preserve the American way of life, Republicans wielded political correctness as a sword against Democrats. Conservative reinventions of political correctness in the 1990s created rhetorical structures pitting cultural diversity and liberal resistance to discrimination against "individuality and value neutrality."[90] Political correctness often accompanies logics of white victimhood, wherein "line cutters" have disrupted white privilege and pushed native-born white Americans "to the back of the line" behind "blacks, women, immigrants, [and] refugees."[91] In debates over the SAFE Act, Republicans contrasted their unapologetic confrontation with the enemy, "radical Islam," against the "political correctness" of Democrats who "refuse even to say the words 'radical Islamic terrorist.'"[92]

Rejections of refugees became fused with refutations of political correctness. Rep. Brian Babin (R-TX) condemned the Obama administration's "plans to increase from 70,000 to 85,000 the number of refugees allowed into the United States," linking concerns that "most of the increase is from Syria and western Iraq" with "Islamic jihadists" and "ISIS infiltrators." The congressman continued:

> I am compelled by the oath of office that I took when I was sworn in as a Member of the United States Congress to put the safety and security of the American people above political correctness. I didn't come to Congress to be politically correct. I came to uphold the US Constitution and to protect our national security. Protecting our American way of life, the greatest experiment in liberty and freedom in all human history, is our highest calling as elected leaders of this great Nation.[93]

Defenses of the in-group—*our American way of life, the American people, this great Nation*—were situated against the political correctness of Democratic support for refugee admissions.

These associations were reproduced explicitly and implicitly in Republican identity narratives. Sen. John McCain argued for refugee restrictions in the context that "this is radical Islamic terrorism, whether the President [Obama] ever wants to say it or not."[94] Denying the presence of "radical Islamic terrorism" within refugee admissions became a surrogate for being politically correct. This framing enabled Republicans to deliberately preempt Democratic arguments that Syrian and other Muslim refugees were not terrorists, for insistence that refugees were *not* ISIS infiltrators only reinforced liberal subservience to political correctness via a refusal to recognize Islamic threats.

Political correctness frames were amplified across Republican voices. On the campaign trail, Trump criticized Obama for allowing "Syrian refugees to pour into our country at unbelievable rates," which "could be the all-time great Trojan horse." This threat was heightened amid a battle against "radical Islamic terrorism—words that our president won't use and words that Hillary Clinton won't use."[95] Refugee resettlement as "one of the great Trojan horses" became a prominent frame among Republicans following the Paris attacks,[96] fueling nativist and Orientalist prisms of Muslim infiltration discussed in chapter 3. Through repeated associations with *radical Islamic terrorism* and Democrats' unwillingness to name the enemy as such, refugees were configured as symbols of liberal submissiveness to political correctness, bound up with feminized connotations of fragility and weakness. Republicans dichotomized this Democratic feebleness with vocabularies of masculinized toughness wherein restrictions on refugees made sense to "defend the homeland" and "take the fight to the enemy."[97] The SAFE Act was part of a broader arsenal of defense from "monsters in the world that seek to destroy us."[98] On the campaign trail, Trump paired assertions that "Syrians cannot be allowed to come in" with promises of strength: "that border is going to be so strong."[99] Amid imagery of *fighting monsters, strong borders,* and *defending the homeland,* US retreats from refugee responsibility-sharing deepened Republican group norms surrounding muscular patriotism and foreign policy toughness.

These narratives relied on the Orientalist ontologies described in chapters 3 and 4, making use of tropes representing Islam and the Middle East as innately dangerous. The Republican Party platform described the Middle East as "more dangerous now than at any time since the Second World War," recycling ominous caricatures through language of *Islamic terror-*

ists, Mullahs, ballistic missiles, Death to Israel, murderous fanaticism, and *nations imploding*.[100] Such discourses facilitated warrior image-building within Republican and conservative identity formations and the conflation of restrictions on refugees with masculinized toughness.

Christianity Divided

Partisan and ideological identities have "loose edges and indeterminate centers,"[101] and discursive practices connected to religion help contour and shift those boundaries. When potentially competing group attachments manifest among American Christians, and religious teachings are not necessarily congruent with overriding partisan imagery, rhetorical frameworks can enable certain interpretations to transcend contradictory cues. Divisions between liberal and conservative renderings of Christianity regarding refugee resettlement during the 2015–16 election cycle exemplified how the language and meanings associated with religious doctrines adapt to accommodate partisan identities.

While Republicans are more likely to espouse and emphasize Christian convictions, majorities of Democrats endorse Christian beliefs and symbols.[102] The Social Gospel emphasizing "structural inequality, social justice, and the status of refugees"[103] has played an important role in shaping liberal Christian identity narratives in US politics. Democratic partisan norms have been harmonized with elements of scripture foregrounding equality, compassion, hospitality, and neighborly love.[104] These theological underpinnings were used by Democrats to legitimize refugee responsibility-sharing within liberal Christian logics.

During congressional debates over refugee admissions, Democratic lawmakers leveraged faith-based opposition to the SAFE Act. A letter from the Christian Reformed Church emphasized that "as Christians, we must speak clearly and loudly: we are called to welcome the stranger, protect the vulnerable, and love fearlessly."[105] Democrats also cited a letter by the US Conference of Catholic Bishops describing Republican attempts to limit the resettlement of Syrians and Iraqis as a threat to "our moral leadership in the world."[106] House Minority Leader Nancy Pelosi (D-CA) located liberal Christian support for refugees within a "coalition of more than 80 faith, humanitarian, and human rights groups." Pelosi's elevation of *faith* and *family* in refugee protection logics aligned with her complex political image foregrounding motherhood and Catholicism.[107] She highlighted "families in Syria and Iraq" and "desperate mothers and children" in need of resettlement.

Pelosi also justified refugee admissions within interreligious intertwinements of human rights and American values:

> With regard to those mothers and children, I join with labor, civil, human rights, and faith groups from the U.S. Conference of Catholic Bishops, from the Episcopalians, the Lutherans, the Methodists, the Presbyterians, the evangelicals, and Jewish groups. I join them in saying that the Republican bill before the House today fails to meet our values and fails to strengthen the security of the American people.[108]

Invoking partisan antipathy cues by describing the SAFE Act as a *Republican bill*, Pelosi positioned Republican-led restrictions as antithetical to *our values*. Partisan group norms championing multicultural and interreligious diversity were bolstered through the bridging of Jewish organizations with a varied list of Christian denominations supportive of refugee resettlement.

Liberal Christian arguments were amplified by advocacy groups like Catholic Relief Services, which linked calls to support Syrian refugees with Pope Francis."[109] Catholic Relief Services also encouraged solidarity with Syrian refugees in its monthly prayers during the spring 2016 holidays of Lent and Easter: "In our longing for the paradise you have made for us, are we not all refugees? . . . Lord, let my Lenten sacrifice remind me of my desire for my heavenly home. And may my exile help me grow in solidarity with refugees everywhere: Sharing food for the journey, rest for the weary, protection for the vulnerable."[110] Logics in which *we are all refugees* before God, longing for refuge in an afterlife, encouraged a sense of cosmopolitan spiritual unity with refugees around the world. In line with liberal moral frameworks of caretaking, the prayer elevated *protection for the vulnerable* as a religious lens for thinking about refugees. Catholic Charities similarly drew parallels in which "Jesus, Mary and Joseph" were "the archetype of every refugee family."[111]

Justifications of refugee resettlement in terms of religious obligations to protect the vulnerable and biblically charged notions of "mercy"[112] challenged Republican ownership of faith-based identity appeals, pressing Republicans to clarify conservative Christian and religious values vis-à-vis their efforts to suspend and restrict refugee admissions. Decades of discourse interweaving conservative white evangelical identities with Republican partisan group norms provided crucial foundations. Increasingly sorting into the Republican Party during the 1980s, conservative Christians forged biblical justifications for opposition to immigration and hawkish foreign policies.[113] The continuity of these justifications in the context of retreats from refugee responsibility-sharing manifested in scriptural notions of *loving thy neighbor* framed in "anti-universalist" terms, wherein not everyone is considered a neighbor and principles of hospitality are conditioned by group membership.[114] These themes animated arguments against refugee resettlement among groups like Evangelicals for Biblical Immigration, as discussed in chapter 3. They also emerged in Republican congressional discourse surrounding the SAFE Act.

Countering liberal Christian logics emphasizing "compassion" for refugees in the context of faith, Rep. Jeff Duncan (R-SC) framed theological notions of compassion as dependent on national belonging:

> As a Christian, I have compassion and sympathy for the refugees in Syria . . . We are criticized for not having compassion on this issue. Let me tell you, compassion cuts two ways. We should also be cognizant of the compassion we should show our fellow citizens here in America. That compassion is exemplified by using the good sense that God gave us in addressing this national security concern that our Nation faces.[115]

In protest that "we are criticized," the congressman defended Republican identity from arguments that opposing refugee resettlement was inherently un-Christian. His conservative Christian interpretation of compassion narrowed the boundaries of applicability to "fellow citizens." The debate over refugee resettlement was transformed into a vehicle for articulating Republican identity narratives contrasting conservative Christian loyalty to "our Nation," insiders, with liberal Christian prioritization of distant Others, outsiders—Muslims and Syrian refugees.

Rep. Duncan went on to legitimize halting Syrian and Iraqi refugee admissions so that "no harm comes to our fellow countrymen," reiterating anti-universalist conceptualizations of hospitality. Duncan positioned the SAFE Act as necessary "to make sure that the elements of evil are not introduced, due to our compassionate hearts, into the neighborhoods, the towns, the cities, and the States that we represent in this great Nation."[116] Diverging from more cosmopolitan liberal Christian constructions of neighborly love as encompassing distant Others, this framing accentuated localized boundaries focused on protecting American *neighborhoods, towns,* and *cities.* There is a danger of excessively "compassionate hearts" that are too inclusive of outsiders and thus might endanger local communities. Sharpening the edges of what it means to be a conservative Christian, such language encircled group belonging within logics of defending local brethren—*countrymen, this great Nation*—against foreign "evil" and Muslim infiltration (symbolized by Syrian and Iraqi refugees).

In Republican legitimizations of refugee restrictions, cultural warrior self-concepts drew heavily on appeals to Christian victimhood. Speaking at the Values Voter Summit of the Family Research Council—a conservative Christian organization designated by the Southern Poverty Law Center as an anti-LGBTQ hate group[117]—Trump affirmed, "there are no more decent, devoted, or selfless people than our Christian brothers and sisters here in the United States." Trump simultaneously idealized the moral status of *Christian brothers and sisters* while positioning them as an attacked and marginalized minority, lamenting that "our media culture often mocks and demeans people of faith . . . our politicians have really abandoned you." Casting his candidacy as a vanguard of Christendom, he promised that under "a Trump administration, our Christian heritage will be cherished, protected, defended, like you've never seen before." It was in this context of protecting and defending Christian identity that Trump criticized President Obama for allowing Syrian refugees to "pour into our country at unbelievable rates" and warned that Hillary Clinton intended to "allow 550 percent more." Amid allusions to Muslim infiltration, Democratic support for refugee resettlement was equivocated with anti-Christian discrimination: "It's almost impossible to get a Christian in from Syria. They take others, but they don't take Christians."[118]

Christian victimhood was also tethered to Syrian refugee resettlement during Trump's visit with the American Renewal Project—a gathering of conservative evangelical pastors in Orlando, Florida:

> You know that Christianity and everything we're talking about today has had a very tough time. You know in Syria when—this is before the

migration—if you were a Christian in Syria it was virtually impossible to come into the United States. If you were a Muslim from Syria, it was one of the easier countries to be able to find your way into . . . just think of what that means.[119]

In addition to rendering Christianity as a religious underdog having "a very tough time," US immigration policies were depicted as pro-Muslim and anti-Christian. It is worth noting that more Christian refugees were admitted in total numbers during the Obama administration than during the Republican administration of George W. Bush, and non-Muslim refugees were admitted in excess to their proportion of the population in areas where they were a religious minority.[120] But Republican claims of Christian discrimination in refugee resettlement enabled a powerful fusion of Christian victimhood with nativist anxieties. Trump's call to "just think of what that means" invited catastrophizing thoughts of Christian precarity exacerbated by Syrian Muslim refugee admissions.

Republican political elites configured Syrian refugees as symbols of discrimination toward Christians,[121] neglecting the nuances of Syria's demographic and political context and the Assad regime's targeting of predominantly Sunni Muslim areas of the country—factors that help explain why most Syrian refugees in need of resettlement were Muslim. In addition to generating a sense of Christian victimhood, Republican identity narratives reproduced representations of Democrats and liberals as agents of existential demise, with their advocacy for Syrian refugee protection providing further evidence of their role as co-conspirators in the destruction of America's Christian heritage. Republican and conservative identities were constituted in terms of preserving and protecting Christianity from internal and external attack.

In a meeting with evangelical leaders in New York City, Trump merged imagery of Syrian refugees as "the greatest Trojan horse" with the decline of Christianity in America—"you used to go to church . . . the young people aren't going much"—and the need to *bring back* Christian ways of life: "We have to bring those values back. We have to bring that spirit back . . . it's been taken away from you." Trump championed his "temporary ban on Muslims" amid claims that his policies would be "incredible for evangelicals."[122] Retreats from refugee responsibility-sharing were legitimized as protecting conservative Christians. Republican identity, tethered to defense against the *Trojan Horse* of Muslim infiltration, was inscribed with the preservation of threatened evangelical values and nostalgic longing for Christian hegemony.

The Republican Party platform positioned Syrian and Iraqi Muslim refugees as less persecuted and less deserving of protection than Christians, discussing them in terms of "foreign nationals seeking to enter the United States from terror-sponsoring countries or from regions associated with Islamic terrorism." In contrast, "Christian communities" in Iraq were described as "displaced persons and urban refugees" threatened by "genocide." The platform linked the Obama administration and the UN as complicit in discrimination toward Iraqi Christians through withholding assistance despite their status as the ones "who have suffered the most."[123] Republican lawmakers similarly contended that "Christians in the Middle East are targeted for genocide," countering Democratic efforts to draw parallels between Syrian Muslim refugees in the contemporary era and Jewish refugees during World War II. Rep. Dana Rohrabacher (R-CA) implied that Christians, not Muslims, were the genuine victims: "Christians should get the priority in the same way those Jews should have been given the priority in 1938."[124] Republican reframing of the Jewish refugee analogy undermined recollections of the rejected *St. Louis* and its attendant Holocaust parallels drawn on by Democrats and liberal Jewish voices advocating for resettlement.[125]

Within domestic identity tapestries, Republican lawmakers stitched together Christian victimhood, opposition to refugees, and political correctness. In a speech criticizing the Obama administration for its "accelerated pace" of resettling "so-called Syrian refugees,"[126] Rep. Louie Gohmert (R-TX) blamed liberal submissiveness to political correctness for discrimination and violence against Christians. He recounted examples of *radical Islamists killing* Christians: "Political correctness has now gotten so far afield, it is killing people. Let's talk about banning political correctness that keeps our FBI and intelligence from being able to talk about radical Islam." Gohmert offered a sympathetic understanding of why "right-wing extremists are mad" on the basis that "we are not doing enough to stop radical Islamists from destroying our country . . . we can't practice our Christian beliefs as the Bible teaches, because it may offend someone." The congressman conceptualized Democrats within a pro-Muslim/anti-Christian binary:

I know the President [Obama] loves to castigate Christians and say, hey, you know, Christians had the Crusades. Anybody that was out there saying, I kill you in the name of Christ, is not killing people legitimately in the name of Christ, because Jesus said, "Greater love hath no one than this, that a man lay down his life for his friends" ... There is a pretty clear, distinct difference between what radical Islamists believe as well as what Christians who truly believe the teachings of Christ, what they believe.[127]

Christians with authentic faith in scripture were depicted as incapable of killing based on religious motives, but a similar delegitimization of violence was not extended to "true" followers of Islam. Muslims were homogenized as "radical Islamists" and permanent outsiders who could be sharply distinguished from Christian insiders.

Political correctness and advocacy for Muslim refugees were bound together to castigate Democrats as allies to anti-Christian outsiders. Sen. Ted Cruz entangled these elements to categorize Democrats as "apologists for radical Islamic terrorism," opening the door to "tens of thousands of Syrian Muslim refugees" with the potential to "wage jihad." Cruz invoked Christian victimhood, adding that Democrats neglected "persecuted Christians" who were "facing genocide."[128] This embedding of Democrats within pro-Muslim/anti-Christian binaries bolstered partisan antipathy. Refugee resettlement was affixed to Democratic alliances with dangerous outsiders and the destruction of traditional Christian ways of life. "Political correctness" cued animosity toward Democrats as both proponents of Muslim infiltration and facilitators of Christian discrimination. These webs of meaning made sense of blocking Syrian and other Muslim refugees as a matter of preserving Christian identities and norms.

Trump instrumentalized these logics in his appeals to Christian conservatives, who were initially divided regarding his candidacy. Observers of the intragroup schism pondered: "Does Trump's irreverence toward political correctness override his rakish indecency in the eyes of many cultural conservatives?"[129] At conservative Christian events, Trump highlighted the nexus between political correctness and Christian victimhood. He assured evangelical leaders, "I'm so on your side," and condemned being "politically correct" in the context of Democratic leaders "selling Christianity down the tubes, selling the evangelicals down the tubes."[130] Democratic support for Syrian refugees was framed as a dual manifestation of political correctness and anti-Christian agendas. Beyond operating as a surrogate for overtly racist language, political correctness was used as a tool in foregrounding concerns about the preservation of conservative Christian identity.

Republicans implicated both Democrats and the UN in depicting refugee admissions through prisms of anti-Christian discrimination. These depictions were co-dependent with Democratic references to the centrality of the UNHCR in registering and referring refugees as part of an internationally structured vetting process. The multilateral aspects of refugee resettlement were legitimizing within Democratic narratives, aligning with partisan group norms championing international institutions and responsiveness to transnational advocacy.[131] In contrast, Republican and conservative Christian suspicions of the UN and international institutions interpreted them as threatening American sovereignty and religious traditionalism.[132] Representations of the UNHCR as complicit in the abandonment of Christian refugees were palatable within conservative Christian narratives constituting the UN as "a secular affront to God's rule on earth."[133] Decades of meaning-making among conservative Christians established threatening interpretations of international organizations and international human rights norms as harbingers of US foreign policy secularization and moves away from white Christian supremacy.[134] Within conservative Christian maps of reality primed to perceive the UN and international legal frameworks as anti-Christian, the Christian victimhood logics circulated by Republican political elites made sense of retreats from refugee responsibility-sharing and reinforced the urgency of defensive postures focused on Christian preservation.

Conclusion

Refugees were configured as partisan and ideological identity symbols during the 2015–16 election cycle. Political elites embedded refugees within juxtapositions of contrasting policy values, constructing support or opposition for refugee admissions in ways that innovated and reproduced meanings surrounding what constitutes *liberal* versus *conservative* and *Democrat* versus *Republican*. Policymakers from both parties affixed Syrian refugee resettlement to signals of liberal and Democratic identity, construing refugee admissions as "a cause of the left"[135] in ways that constrained bipartisan possibilities of support. Democrats and Republicans also largely ignored decades of US foreign policy actions in the Middle East and Central Asia that contributed to the dynamics of the Syrian conflict and displacement, arranging the parameters of the debate in ways that sidestepped US culpability logics for refugee responsibility-sharing.

Refugee policy was positioned within "a fight of values" not only at the global level, between the United States and "monsters like ISIS,"[136] but also at the local level, between competing partisan and ideological interpretations of America's moral core. Republicans constructed narratives around refugee resettlement portraying their group members as cultural warriors—masculinized, tough, and unapologetic in their defense of Christianity and the American "way of life" from Islamic enemies and Democrats incapable of confronting those enemies. Syrian and other Muslim refugees were configured within conservative critiques of political correctness and logics of Christian victimhood, which depicted Democrats as simultaneously weak, submissive, and nefariously operating within pro-Muslim/anti-Christian binaries in their efforts to increase refugee admissions.

Democrats built alternative systems of meaning in which refugee responsibility-sharing symbolized the safeguarding of America's Safe Haven status and Statue of Liberty ethos oriented around compassion, diversity, and inclusion. Providential exceptionalist motifs of America as a "beacon of light" were used to insist upon international obligations to engage in refugee responsibility-sharing and domestic imperatives to rebuff Republicans' exclusionary and xenophobic policies. The exceptionalist architecture previously utilized by both parties to legitimize refugee resettlement sustained a distinctly partisan transformation, with Democrats curating parallels between Safe Haven imagery and liberal group norms emphasizing inclusion and caretaking of the vulnerable. Democrats drew on exceptionalist vocabularies to cast Republicans as discriminatory and un-American partisan opponents. Republican efforts to restrict resettlement were condemned as forsaking the genesis of the United States. These discursive processes detached refugees from bipartisan referents and destabilized previous bipartisan logics of justification for US "leadership" in refugee resettlement. Foundations for intersubjective cross-partisan interpretations of refugee protection diminished.

The ramifications of these (sub)national dynamics and their attendant language wars paved the way for US moves away from global refugee responsibility-sharing upon Trump's 2016 election. With conservative maps of reality conditioned to understand refugee resettlement in terms of political correctness, "radical Islam," and anti-Christian discrimination, the Trump administration's travel bans, cuts to refugee admissions ceilings, and other refugee policy shifts could easily be accommodated in Republican identity matrices. Democratic refutations of those policies could subsequently be interpreted as reinforcing liberal collusion with enemies of cultural preservation, tracing the trails of meaning carved out during the 2015–16 election cycle.

Domestic identity narratives establish logics wherein certain policies make sense in accordance with discrete ideological norms and boundaries while others are understood as incongruent or iconoclastic. That Republican and Democratic articulations of refugee resettlement drew upon vastly different webs of meaning underscores the importance of recognizing how refugee groups become enmeshed in partisan imagery at local levels. Attention to these evolving rhetorical structures deepens our understanding regarding the role of language and identity in fashioning "the national politics of international institutions"[137] and in facilitating shifts in refugee policies across time. What might be considered an inordinate conceptual leap or hypocritically shifting goalpost can be reanimated within identity narratives to represent an unbroken progression of the protagonist's storytelling tied to a sense of what is right in the world. This reinforces but also moves beyond the instrumentalization of refugees for domestic political gain.[138] Syrian refugees were not only "unwilling props in the political theater of borders,"[139] but also became constitutive of partisan and ideological identities, intertwined with discrete representations of America's ethos and moral core. These fragmented discourses destabilize notions of *America* or *American* as "unified, unproblematic, and settled,"[140] underscoring the dilemmas of approaching refugee responsibility-sharing via premises of cohesive national identities or interests.

6

Enduring and Evolving Identity Narratives

In exploring how domestic meaning-making shapes refugee protection, this book presses work on international norms, migration, and refugee responsibility-sharing to contend with the complexities of (sub)national identities. It foregrounds how discursive processes affect interpretations of appropriate and acceptable policymaking—what "makes sense" and why. Refugeehood emerges as contestable and open to reinterpretations through representational practices that describe as well as constitute group belonging.[1] Mapping out the complexities of arguments around refugee resettlement in the US context, the book shows how local articulations of meaning can legitimate and de-legitimate international frameworks of protection. In doing so, it addresses calls for greater attention to the wide array of factors shaping government responses toward displacement.[2]

As a result of shifts associated with the 2015–16 US elections, representations of refugees as cultural threats, terrorist infiltrators, and symbols of partisan identity worked in tandem to shape a pivotal period of US retreats from refugee protection and responsibility-sharing. From the particular moments and sites of interaction examined in the preceding chapters, we can better understand how partisan, gendered, and racialized identity narratives propagate support for and resistance to refugee resettlement. The discriminatory policies and severe curtailments in refugee admissions that unfolded under Trump were not exclusively wedded to the particularities of his administration. Rather, these moves both innovated and built upon the foundations laid by previous discourses and policy trajectories. Justifications for future humanitarian migration policies, too, will likely draw upon traces of past discourses, even as refugeehood is continuously reconfigured. We might expect forthcoming portrayals of displacement and considerations of appropriate policy responses to both invoke and alter the parameters of refugee protection debates outlined in these chapters—perhaps layering similar partisan, gendered, and racialized logics with renovated representations of refugeehood adapted to new contexts.

The case study at the center of the book underscores the complexity of continuities and transformations in refugee policymaking. Domestic institutional and electoral factors converged with the 2015 Paris attacks to produce a particular milieu in which the identity narratives studied in the preceding chapters gained traction. These narratives made sense of humanitarian migration policies in ways that contributed to a breakdown in decades-long bipartisan acceptance and even vocal support for US "leadership" in global refugee resettlement. While that leadership role was exaggerated and idealized (as discussed in chapter 2), its deterioration had drastic effects on the international refugee regime, the ability of people around the world to access safety amid life-threatening situations, and the daily circumstances of insecurity refugees experienced. In addition to pushing back against tendencies to singularize or oversimplify national interests and identities,[3] tracing the unraveling of bipartisan support for refugee resettlement among US policymakers underscores the value of comprehending how local identity processes and domestic interpretations mediate contributions to international protection.

In exploring how lawmakers and civil society actors co-create, amplify, and alter refugee configurations, the previous chapters show how nativist and racialized prisms are adapted to shifting circumstances and modes of classification. Deeply rooted genealogies evolve to reproduce familiar yet innovated imageries of the Other. As logics of terrorist infiltration became paradigmatic in structuring debates over refugee resettlement, "Syrian" operated as a proxy for entangled etymologies of Muslim, Arab, Middle Eastern, and non-Western.[4] These conflations were reinforced by Trump's campaign calls for "a total and complete shutdown of Muslims entering the United States"[5] and "strengthening and promoting Western civilization."[6] As described in chapters 3 and 4, nativist and Orientalist frameworks intermingled to position refugees as culturally foreboding in ways that bolstered logics wherein whiteness and Christianity were in need of defense and preservation. As discussed in chapter 1, such imageries reemerged and adapted to new "refugee crises" during the first portion of the Biden presidency as a cohort of conservative policymakers resisted Afghan resettlement efforts and prevented Afghan parolees from gaining permanent residency rights.

Refugeehood is continuously in flux. While recognizing the plasticity of refugee meanings, it is also important to grapple with their resilience. The remainder of this final chapter considers some of the shifting and persisting refugee configurations in the post-2016 and post-2020 electoral contexts. Following Trump's election, refugees continued to be embedded in polarization dynamics through the repetition and innovation of identity narratives via tropes of Muslim infiltration, Christian victimhood, and political correctness. There were, however, moments in which bipartisan justifications for refugee protection reemerged as some Republican lawmakers pushed back against Trump's policy changes and joined with Democratic colleagues to voice support for resettlement.

Domestic identity narratives around refugees endured and evolved during the 2019–20 election cycle. While the COVID-19 pandemic siphoned attention away from refugee policy, it also added a new layer to refugee threat configurations. Augmenting purported dangers of cultural change, terrorist infiltration, and the agendas of "globalists" and "the left," the pandemic enabled domestic opponents of resettlement to link refugees with the spread of the novel coronavirus. Additionally, there were continuities and reconfigurations in refugee representations following the 2021 transition to the Biden administration. Discriminatory approaches were not vanquished with the conclusion of the Trump presidency or the end of the Travel Ban but endured in more subtle manifestations of racial hierarchy. Ukrainians were more widely welcomed and offered greater measures of protection than displaced people of other nationalities as the racialized symbols and identities associated with refugees shifted. These examples have important implications for the future of US refugee policy.

Enduring Logics Under Trump

Many of the logics established during the 2015–16 US election cycle persisted throughout the Trump presidency. Specters of Syrian and other predominantly Muslim refugees plotting to infiltrate, invade, and victimize vulnerable American communities helped make sense of the 2017 Travel Ban—Executive Order 13769—which halted Syrian refugee admissions indefinitely, restricted travel from several Muslim-majority countries, and temporarily suspended the US refugee resettlement program. The order was justified on the basis of "protecting the nation from foreign terrorist entry," with refugees cast as "would-be terrorists." Drawing on Orientalist and anti-Muslim ontologies equivocating Islam with narrow understandings of Sharia law, the order claimed to prevent the entry of "those who do not support the Constitution" and "place violent ideologies over American law."[7] These logics also justified the designation of refugee arrivals from eleven mostly Muslim-majority countries as "high risk" and therefore subject to "extra vetting" measures.[8]

Key segments of the public, including majorities of self-identified Republicans, continued to perceive Syrian refugees as a "major threat to the well-being of the United States."[9] Enduring representations of refugees as terrorist infiltrators were instrumentalized for political purposes. In a 2017 special election in Georgia's sixth congressional district, for example, the National Republican Congressional Committee launched a television ad linking Democratic candidate Jon Ossoff with Syrian refugee resettlement. Alongside footage of masked militants with Islamic State flags, ominous narration asserted: "ISIS is infiltrating America and using Syrians to do it. The FBI warned we can't simply screen every Syrian. Yet Jon Ossoff's liberal party bosses brought 10,000 Syrian refugees to America."[10] Ossoff narrowly lost the race to his Republican opponent, Karen Handel, whose campaign drew attention for fundraising messages promising voters she would "end Muslim immigration."[11] Nativism, Orientalism, and partisanship operated concomitantly to reproduce familiar rhythms in representations of refugeehood.

Despite the fact that Syrian refugees continued to represent the largest forcibly displaced population worldwide with the highest level of resettlement needs,[12] by 2019, Syrian refugee admissions into the United States fell by 96 percent.[13] This closure had global consequences, severing responsibility-sharing with smaller countries confronting diminished resources and infrastructure such as Jordan and Lebanon, which hosted over one million UNHCR-registered Syrian refugees.[14] The Fiscal Year (FY) 2020 US refugee admissions ceiling (18,000)—established *prior* to the onset of the pandemic—represented roughly an 80 percent decline from FY2016 (85,000).[15] The anti-Muslim and conservative Christian prisms described in the preceding chapters continued to help make sense of these cuts and the subsequent downsizing of the domestic refugee resettlement infrastructure, contributing to growing grassroots pressures on local and state officials to further curtail resettlement programs and restrict refugee accommodations.[16] At the end of 2016, there were approximately 325 local offices across the United States that resettled refugees in their areas. By the end of 2019, more than one hundred had shut down or suspended their services.[17] This erosion of the refugee admissions infrastructure at the local level reverberated across worldwide resettlement chains.[18] These effects also lingered into the first years of the Biden presidency, constraining the ability of the new administration to follow through on increased pledges of resettlement slots.[19]

Muslim identity was marginalized by US political elites and evaluated negatively by members of the public throughout the Trump presidency,[20] and spikes in anti-Muslim[21] and anti-immigrant[22] hate crimes underscored the consequences of discursive threat configurations beyond refugee policymaking. Violence toward such groups often emerges when local actors perceive their cultural power to be waning.[23] The perpetuation of racialized refugee representations within nativist narratives contributed to that climate. Iranian American author Porochista Khakpour, whose family fled the Iran-Iraq War and Islamic Revolution as refugees, reminds us how the political rhetoric around the Travel Ban was experienced as an acute mainstreaming of racism and discrimination: "You are suddenly a Muslim. No one doubts your brownness anymore. You realize that every day is a lesson in America, the real America, the violent one."[24]

Public opinion surveys during the first years of the Biden presidency pointed to enduring divisions over refugee protection based on partisan identity, and white evangelical Protestants remained more resistant to refugee responsibility-sharing than other domestic communities.[25] The persistence of conservative Christian skepticism toward refugees can be understood in the context of repeated articulations of scriptural justifications for restricting migration along the logics described in chapter 3. In a letter to then-President Trump and Republican leaders—promoted by the nativist group, NumbersUSA—Evangelicals for Biblical Immigration argued:

> In Scripture, we learn that God placed us each in a family, a land, an epic story of creation, the fall and redemption. The Bible envisions a world of beautiful and unique nations, not a stateless "open society" run by global oligarchs. Each of us is called to be a blessing where God has placed us in the world.[26]

Recalling white evangelical justifications for racial segregation,[27] biblical visions of *unique nations* enabled immigration and refugee restriction to be understood as fulfilling a divine plan to keep culturally different peoples separated on distinct territories—a religious version of the "Desert Island Model" of international borders.[28] Condemnation of *a stateless open society* as discordant with biblical teachings discredited cosmopolitan conceptualizations of belonging and perceived calls for "open borders" among some liberals. The language of *global oligarchs* alluded to the conspiratorial caricature of "globalists" as power-hungry corporate elites (often depicted as Jewish) who espouse cosmopolitan identities as "citizens of the world" to weaken national sovereignty for financial gain.[29]

Focus on the Family, a conservative Christian group, similarly linked refugees to "a new globalist consensus among leaders and influential groups in Europe and the United States" working toward "eliminating national borders."[30] These logics bolstered resistance to refugee responsibility-sharing and global governance in tandem. Cooperative multilateral frameworks of refugee protection could be interpreted as menacing projects among global oligarchs/globalists colluding to abolish sovereign territorial borders. These themes were reiterated in Trump's 2020 reelection campaign highlighting "promises kept" in fulfilling the America First vision: "President Trump pulled the United States out of negotiations for a 'Global Compact on Migration,' a plan for global governance of immigration and a refugee policy that may have compromised US sovereignty."[31] The implicit and explicit linkage of refugee protection with globalist conspiracy reinforced the centrality of identity narratives in making sense of migration governance.[32]

Conservative Christian logics of refugee restriction were reproduced by figures like Sam Rohrer, a former Pennsylvania state representative and president of the American Pastors Network: "All through the beginning of Scripture, through to the end, God emphasizes the establishment of nations . . . [Acts 7] talks about the Lord establishing the nations and, even before the beginning of time, having determined their geographical boundaries." In addition to the divine separation of nations logic, Rohrer countered the notion that the Bible mandates the welcoming of strangers and foreigners. In his alternative interpretation of Leviticus 19:34, the "stranger" whom God instructs should be loved and welcomed refers exclusively to foreigners "who want to assimilate," adding: "if they're not here to assimilate, they're enemies."[33] As discussed in chapter 3, such invocations of assimilation are often premised on notions of racial hierarchy and Anglo-conformity in ways that render Muslim migrants perpetual outsiders. Assimilation was once again reinscribed as a one-directional process reaffirming the superiority of America's white Christian Self and the potentially disruptive status of the stranger as a non-white/non-Christian Other.[34]

In support of the Travel Ban, a Christian Coalition post described the policy as "a crucial and determining factor for keeping America and other Western democracies safe." Warning of a "radical Islamic immigration strategy," the post pointed to a Muslim Brotherhood plot to subjugate the United States and "destroy Western civilization from within" through four stages, beginning with Muslim immigration and ending with "transformation of the host state to an Islamic theocracy under sharia law." Muslims were excluded from the "melting pot" vision of American democracy on the grounds that "Islam and freedom cannot coexist."[35] The Muslim Brotherhood infiltration plot was also circulated by the Center for Security Policy, one of the anti-Muslim groups discussed in chapter 3. The plot exemplifies the racialized theme of reverse colonization, positioning white/Christian/Western polities as vulnerable in ways that elide intensifications of imperial violence and military interventionism in the Middle East and Central Asia.[36]

As anti-Muslim and conservative Christian narratives persisted in making sense of US retreats from refugee resettlement, nativist groups such as FAIR and CIS (discussed in chapter 3) amplified their influence through connections to Trump administration advisers and officials.[37] Logics of terrorist infiltration were combined with invocations of "left-wing" and "globalist" agendas to help justify continued moves away from international norms and responsibility-sharing.[38] These frameworks reemerged in Republican opposition to Afghan resettlement during the first year of the Biden administration. Former Trump adviser Steve Cortes, for example, tweeted a photo of hundreds of Afghan civilians aboard a US Air Force cargo plane and linked the image to "uniparty globalists,"[39] while State Rep. Anthony Sabatini (R-FL-32) warned that more than 100,000 Afghans might be granted permanent residency status due to "#AmericaLast Globalists."[40]

Bipartisan Legacies

During the Trump presidency there were notable moments in which Republican policymakers pushed back against the administration's retreats from responsibility-sharing. One such moment unfolded around an effort to devolve the authority to block refugee resettlement to the state and local levels. During the 2015–16 election cycle, some Republican members of Congress endorsed this decentralization of authority on the basis that "many Governors expressed a desire, shared by their constituents, that Syrian refugees not be resettled in their States."[41] In 2019, Trump signed Executive Order (EO) 13888 enabling states and municipalities to block refugee arrivals by requiring their "written consent,"[42] offering an opportunity to reignite anti-refugee fervor among conservative officials at local levels.

In what was described as "a spectacular blowback" for the administration,[43] the executive order sparked a reemergence of bipartisan support for refugee resettlement. The extent to which local state and municipal officials are more insulated from partisan polarization in responding to immigration and refugee issues remains unclear.[44] In the response to EO 13888, subnational identities often intervened. Policymakers in Utah, for instance, advocated for continuing the resettlement program and creating a welcoming environment for refugee arrivals, despite the majority of the state voting for Trump in the 2016 and 2020 elections. Gov. Gary Herbert (R-UT) was one of the first governors to send a letter to the Trump administration expressing support for resettling refugees within his jurisdiction. Referencing the experiences of the Church of Jesus Christ of Latter-day Saints members, Gov. Herbert justified his position in terms of both religious (Mormon) and state (Utahn) identities: "Our state was founded by religious refugees fleeing persecution in the eastern United States. Those experiences and hardships of our pioneer ancestors 170 years ago are still fresh in the minds of many Utahns."[45] The governor's reference to *our pioneer ancestors* reproduced white settler narratives of refugeehood discussed in previous chapters and perpetuated colonial fantasies of uncharted American lands,[46] while also using refugees to curate a distinct story about the purpose and place of his local constituents.

Governors in forty-two states along with more than a hundred mayors announced support for hosting refugees. These included nineteen

Republican-led states. Gov. Mike DeWine (R-OH) joined notions of state identity and tradition with religious support for refugees: "The State of Ohio has a long and successful history of welcoming and assimilating refugees from all corners of the globe... primarily lead by our faith-based communities."[47] Gov. Doug Ducey (R-AZ) similarly pointed to his state's heritage of *welcoming* and positioned support for refugee resettlement within the Safe Haven mythologies described in chapter 2: "Throughout our nation's history, the United States has been a refuge for individuals fleeing religious and political persecution in their homeland, and Arizona has historically been one of the most welcoming states in terms of the number of refugees resettled here."[48] Such frameworks show how local interpretations of national identity can reinforce narratives of hospitality.

Gov. Mike Parson (R-MO) echoed these approaches of intermingling state and religious identity appeals: "Missouri has a long and rich history of immigration, dating back to America's earliest explorers, fur traders, and missionaries." He also praised the "thousands of refugees who have become vital members of our communities."[49] Gov. Eric Holcomb (R-IN) invoked state heritage—"our long tradition of welcoming and helping to resettle refugees"—while also alluding to the bifurcation between overseas refugees and southern border crossers,[50] emphasizing that refugees were "deserving, qualified individuals" distinct from undocumented migrants: "These are NOT illegal or unlawful immigrants but individuals who have gone through all the proper channels."[51] Such language revived earlier decades of bipartisan interpretations wherein the refugee admissions process reaffirms rather than undermines migration management and authority over borders. The resettlement of *qualified* refugees through *proper channels* emerges as part of a broader border control ontology used to achieve a sense of civilizational sovereignty.[52]

Standing apart from these Republican voices was Governor Greg Abbott (R-TX), who declined consent for hosting refugees within his jurisdiction on the grounds that Texas was already overburdened by a "broken" immigration system and "carried more than its share in assisting the refugee resettlement process." Abbott employed a localized interpretation of the America First ideology that prioritized Texans first and *those who are already here*: "the state and non-profit organizations have a responsibility to dedicate available resources to those who are already here, including refugees, migrants, and the homeless—indeed, all Texans."⁵³ The inclusion of *refugees*, *migrants*, and *the homeless* within Texas suggested a preemption of logics labeling the governor's rejection of refugee resettlement as xenophobic or lacking compassion. This framing resembles the conservative Christian counter-logics to refugee responsibility-sharing described in chapter 3, whereby prioritizing support for the "neighbor next door" over distant strangers in faraway lands was construed as aligning with Christian ethics of charity. The governor's emphasis on preserving resources echoes the "resource-guarding rationales" circulated in arguments for decentralizing federal immigration policies to state and municipal authorities, rationales that often operate as surrogates for cultural and racial exclusion.⁵⁴ Shortly after Gov. Abbott refused consent, a federal judge blocked the implementation of EO 13888 on the basis that it violated the 1980 Refugee Act.

This opposition to refugee arrivals in Texas prompted repetitions of the partisan narratives described in chapter 5. In criticizing Gov. Abbott's announcement, Rep. Ilhan Omar (D-MN) tweeted a quote from "The New Colossus" poem mounted at the base of the Statue of Liberty: "Give me your tired, your poor, your huddled masses yearning to breathe free."⁵⁵ To this framing Abbott replied, "The values America needs you to believe in are the: US Constitution & the Declaration of Independence."⁵⁶ The exchange points to enduring instrumentalizations of refugees as partisan symbols, with Democrats elevating Statue of Liberty visions of an inclusive and multicultural America and Republicans countering with America First interpretations of national identity. Debates over refugees were once again linked to debates over what America means as well as contested constructs of American values. Additionally, Gov. Abbott's questioning of Rep. Omar's loyalty to the Constitution reproduced the racialized logics described in chapter 3. Suggesting Rep. Omar—a Black Muslim legislator of Somali refugee origins—might not believe in the US Constitution and Declaration of Independence left unchallenged Orientalist portrayals of Muslim Americans prioritizing Sharia law over constitutional principles and created space for race-based assumptions regarding which groups are "fit" for political equality and democratic self-governance.⁵⁷

As Canada overtook the United States as the world's leading country of refugee resettlement,⁵⁸ Trump proposed further lowering the FY2019 admissions ceiling to 30,000. Bipartisan support for refugee responsibility-sharing resurfaced. The Bipartisan Refugee Caucus sent a letter to the White House emphasizing "the importance of maintaining the life-saving United States Refugee Admissions Program" and an admissions level that would "signal to the international community the US will continue to be a global leader in refugee protection." The leadership paradigm described in chapter 2 was reiterated: "American global leadership in refugee resettlement is more critical now than ever." The lawmakers also reproduced notions of refugee policy as an important pillar of *foreign policy* and support for *human rights*:

> The refugee resettlement program has always been part of the US foreign policy strategy . . . when we resettle refugees and support our allies in refugee hosting countries, we are helping to keep ourselves safe. Moreover, the United States' historic commitment to refugee resettlement is a clear manifestation of America's longtime pledge to defend human rights . . . this retreat in our commitment to this durable solution could signify the United States is turning its back on these ideals, as well as the international community.[59]

Refugee resettlement could be interpreted as distinct from domestic immigration and asylum policy insofar as it was connected to foreign policy, alliances, and international obligations.

The letter went on to distinguish refugees as "legal" immigrants and foregrounded exceptionalist motifs wherein the United States has a special "duty to protect refugees." The linkage of Safe Haven mythologies with providential exceptionalism animated calls for restoring higher levels of refugee admissions so that "the United States will remain a beacon of hope for individuals and families seeking safety from war, violence, and persecution." The letter also recycled images of refugees as emblematic of the industrious core of *what it means to be American* and to achieve *the American Dream*: "Refugees resettled in the United States exemplify what it means to be American . . . refugees invest in and start businesses at a rate twice that of the general population . . . refugees in the United States contribute billions to our economy . . . purchase homes, invest in educating their children, and become civically engaged all in pursuit of the American dream."[60] These themes point to the legacy of the bipartisan frameworks described in chapter 2, reopening possibilities for mutually intelligible constructions of refugee responsibility-sharing across partisan identities when those constructions bolster refugee/migrant binaries and neoliberal idealizations of economic productivity and entrepreneurship. Refugees might be intersubjectively understood as deserving welcome so long as they are associated with legality and foreign policy and so long as they generate economic benefits.

The letter was signed by six Democratic and four Republican members of the House of Representatives. All four Republicans represented "moderate" wings of the party. Rep. John Katko (R-NY) was a member of the Tuesday Group—a congressional caucus of more ideologically moderate and liberal Republican members of the House—and was one of just ten Republicans who voted to impeach Trump during his second impeachment.[61] Rep. Ileana Ros-Lehtinen (R-FL), co-chair of the Bipartisan Refugee Caucus, was part of a group of Republican legislators who stated that they would not endorse or vote for Trump.[62] She did not seek reelection in 2018. The other two Republican signatories—Representatives Randy Hultgren (R-IL) and David Young (R-IA)—were both defeated by their Democratic challengers several weeks after signing the letter. In sum, three of these four Republicans pushing back against the Trump administration's retreats from refugee responsibility-sharing were no longer in Congress by the end of 2018.

One year later, another small group of Republican legislators joined Democratic colleagues to speak out against further cuts to refugee admissions. These efforts included a letter from the Bipartisan Congressional Refugee Caucus led by Rep. Joe Neguse (D-CO) and signed by more than thirty House caucus members, including Republican Representatives Mario Díaz-Balart (R-FL), Steve Stivers (R-OH), and John Katko (R-NY).[63] The group called on the Trump administration to "allow for a refugee resettlement number that reflects America's historic leadership in openness and protection."[64] A separate letter was sent from a bipartisan group of senators, led by James Lankford (R-OK) and Chris Coons (D-DE), and including Republican senators John Thune (R-SD), Lisa Murkowski (R-AK), Mike Rounds (R-SD), Rob Portman (R-OH), Susan Collins (R-ME), Roy Blunt (R-MO), Marco Rubio (R-FL), and Cory Gardner (R-CO). While a few of these senators were ideologically moderate, most were considered consistently conservative in their legislative records,[65] suggesting a more significant rift was afoot. By the time these senators spoke out in 2019, the domestic refugee resettlement infrastructure was already greatly diminished and there were reports that the administration was considering entirely eliminating admissions for FY2020.

In pushing back against further retreats from refugee responsibility-sharing, the senators redeployed many of the bipartisan logics of appropriateness outlined in chapter 2. They urged the administration to increase resettlement because "America has a responsibility to promote compassion and democracy around the world." Exceptionalist vocabularies of a special responsibility to promote democracy—logics that have long been profoundly racialized[66]—were combined with appeals to America's "legacy as a protector of human rights" and "global leadership" in refugee protection, suspending realities of undemocratic behavior abroad and repeated violations and evasions of human rights and refugee protection principles in the treatment of asylum-seekers. Reproducing associations of refugee resettlement with migration management and border control, the senators emphasized "the legal refugee process." Tracing the threads of decades-old discourses, the senators inscribed refugees as deserving protection on the basis that they "seek freedom" and symbolize industriousness and productivity, praising the "talent, drive, and ambition" of refugees and their contributions to "local and national economies."[67] These triumphant storylines become commonsensical as they are repeatedly employed, but they are also damaging insofar as they equate refugeehood with a kind of flawlessness that filters out the blemishes of the Self and Other.

Rep. Ken Buck (R-OH) soon thereafter led an effort among seventeen Republican members of the House to advocate for higher levels of refugee admissions, foregrounding his Christian faith: "As a Christian, I believe we should assist those who are forced to flee their homes."[68] The letter from the House members echoed familiar bipartisan systems of meaning around US leadership, Safe Haven mythologies, and exceptionalist claims of serving as a "beacon of hope," additionally aligning refugee resettlement with Republican policy values regarding religiosity and industry through references to "faith groups" joining businesses in welcoming and integrating refugees.[69] Schisms within Christian identity narratives endured as evangelical leaders brought together under the banner of the Evangelical Immigration Table (EIT) disavowed continued cuts to resettlement slots through combinations of exceptionalist "beacon of liberty" imagery and appropriations of biblical constructs whereby "God calls us to love the foreigner and the stranger . . . that means loving the refugee in our country who has fled violence and persecution in their own country." Configuring refugees as proximate to in-group identity, the EIT lamented that "persecuted Christians" would be among those harmed by the Trump administration's "closed door" approach.[70]

The potential for Christian civil society actors and religious appeals in support of refugee responsibility-sharing to undermine America First unity among Republicans and conservatives was recognized as problematic, and such moves were actively delegitimized. Lutheran Social Services, World Relief, and the EIT were discredited as "refugee contractors" and "pro-mass immigration organizations" with links to "globalists" like "billionaire George Soros."[71] Representations of religious refugee advocacy and other voluntary resettlement organizations as predatory, anti-American, and connected with a Jewish/George Soros conspiracy reignited "white genocide" logics and inspired anti-Jewish violence.[72] Conservative and right-leaning media outlets amplified such claims through citations of the nativist civil society groups discussed in chapter 3.[73] As the embers of bipartisan support for refugee resettlement flickered across the examples outlined above, these arguments enabled conservative Christian narratives to disown more liberal and cosmopolitan Christian interpretations of refugee protection and paved the way for refugeehood to remain embedded within fractured domestic identity narratives.

The 2019–20 Election Cycle

While the 2020 US elections were dominated by focuses on economic and health recovery amid the COVID-19 pandemic, debates about refugees continued. Rep. Glenn Grothman (R-WI), for example, mailed out a "constituent survey" linking Democratic presidential candidate Joe Biden with refugee resettlement: "Currently, 15,000 refugees per year are relocated to the US. Joe Biden has pledged that his administration will raise this number to 125,000. This is in addition to the more than 1 million legal immigrants accepted into the country. Do you agree with his pledge?"[74] The question contrasted the Trump administration's low refugee admissions ceiling (15,000) with much higher figures linked to Biden—"125,000 refugees and 1 million legal immigrants"—without providing context for understanding how those numbers compared with historical levels of immigration and refugee responsibility-sharing or how those figures related to the causes and scale of global displacement. Both the framing and inclusion of this question in the congressman's campaign mailer reflected a persistent positioning of refugees within partisan identity narratives and continued instrumentalization of refugee "counting" for political purposes.[75]

Biden's 2020 presidential campaign also positioned refugees within partisan identity frameworks. The campaign website made sense of a series of immigration-focused policy changes as a means to "restore our moral leadership," including promises to "terminate the travel ban against people from Muslim-majority countries" and "raise our target for refugee admissions to a level commensurate with our responsibility and unprecedented global need." Refugee resettlement was also constructed in vocabularies of "who we are" as a "nation of immigrants," "our deepest-held values," and commitments to "advancing human rights and democracy around the world."[76] On World Refugee Day—several months before the 2020 general elections—Biden vowed to work toward an annual refugee admissions target of 125,000, "commensurate with our responsibility, our values," and commitments to "building a more inclusive and welcoming America." Imageries of America as a "safe haven" were contrasted with "the heartless policies of the Trump administration."[77] Refugees were used as vehicles to articulate Democratic partisan identity as oriented around an inclusiveness and multicultural diversity that was at odds with the xenophobia of Republican opponents.

Much like the previous election cycle, Trump's campaign recited gendered and nativist storylines in which "our way of life has been threatened" and there is a need to "defend, protect, and preserve American way of life," to "safeguard our values, traditions, customs, and beliefs." Republican identity was intertwined with warrior imagery: "We are Americans, and we never back down, we never give in, and we never give up, and we will never yield [in] defense of our nation . . . we will only fight to win."[78] In a worldview wherein the 2020 elections determined "whether we will defend the American way of life, or whether we allow a radical movement to completely dismantle and destroy it,"[79] refugees were once again configured in ways that linked Democrats with cultural threat and the infiltration of *radical Islam*. At a rally in Duluth, Minnesota, Trump prompted crowds to boo refugees by claiming Biden would "inundate your state with a historic flood of refugees . . . from the most dangerous places in the world including Yemen, Syria, and your favorite country [referencing the birthplace of Minnesota's Democratic Rep. Ilhan Omar] Somalia, right?" Trump continued with warnings that "Biden will turn Minnesota into a refugee camp . . . opening the floodgates to radical Islamic terrorism." The crowd of supporters transitioned from boos to cheers as Trump praised his own administration for "keeping them the hell out of Minnesota" and for having "ended the refugee influx into your state."[80]

Days before the general elections, Trump corralled these meanings into a tweet commending his administration for having "suspended the entry of refugees from terror-compromised nations such as Syria, Somalia and Yemen." He cautioned that "Biden's plan surges refugees 700% into Minnesota, Michigan & Pennsylvania—burdening schools & hospitals while opening the floodgates to Radical Islamic Terror."[81] A Trump campaign ad echoed warnings that Biden would be "increasing refugees by 700% from the most unstable, vulnerable, dangerous parts of the world," linking refugee resettlement to Democratic weakness: "America can't afford weak Joe Biden." Presumably Middle Eastern and African men and women were depicted in grainy, monochromatic footage. A long line of women in hijabs and bearded men amid fires and rubble reinforced visual framing of Islamic threat. Alongside narration describing *unstable, vulnerable, dangerous parts of the world*, the words "Syria, Somalia, Yemen" appeared over images of explosions and burning debris.[82] Extending the anti-Muslim and Orientalist prisms described in previous chapters, the ad paralleled Trump's FY2021 refugee admissions policy banning most refugees from Syria, Somalia, and Yemen[83]—all countries where populations were at risk of mass atrocity crimes.

Configurations of refugees as terrorist infiltrators also persisted ahead of the 2020 elections, drawing on the arrest of Mustafa Mousab Alowemer—who arrived in the United States in 2016 as a teenager in a Syrian refugee family—for planning to bomb a Pittsburgh church as part of an ISIS-inspired plot.[84] Rep. Mo Brooks (R-AL) used the story to defend the Travel Ban and continued cuts to refugee resettlement:

> As of 2016, so-called refugee admissions from the Middle East, Near East, South Asia, and Africa accounted for 80 percent of so-called refugee admissions into America. I say "so-called refugees" because the United Nations states no country is obligated by international law to take refugees

from a country in which they are already protected. The result of America's flawed policy? America is the world's top refugee resettlement country on the planet. In a 2015 Breitbart interview, I opposed these dangerous refugee policies . . . Fortunately, the FBI stopped Alowemer from blowing up a church and slaughtering innocent American Christians. Unfortunately, American lives are still at risk from terrorists masquerading as refugees.[85]

In referring to *so-called refugees, terrorists masquerading as refugees*, and suggesting refugees were *already protected* in their current locations, Brooks discredited legal and humanitarian arguments for resettlement. Countering refugee advocacy frameworks emphasizing international law, the congressman pointed to the lack of explicit responsibility-sharing obligations. This sidestepping of the spirit and intent of refugee protection principles to claim technical compliance with legal requirements exemplifies how norm evasion[86] becomes thinkable and justifiable in domestic discourse.

Rep. Brooks coded refugees as non-Western and non-white through references to their origins in *the Middle East, Near East, South Asia*, and *Africa*. In this framing, the US status as a major refugee resettlement destination was not interpreted as emblematic of US leadership or as upholding providential exceptionalism but was reinscribed as flawed and dangerous. The congressman used the story of Alowemer to bolster both anti-Muslim and Christian victimhood logics, casting Muslim refugees as potentially violent aggressors intent on *slaughtering* while narrating American Christians as vulnerable and *innocent*. Brooks subsequently reinforced partisan identity narratives, linking refugee protection and opposition to the Travel Ban with "socialist Democrats" and "radical leftists." Democrats and refugees were entangled in a lexicon of peril, with the former portrayed as "open border advocates" prioritizing refugees over the safety of the in-group: "Socialist Democrats have shown there is no amount of American blood on their hands that will cause them to protect American lives by securing America's borders."[87]

With the onset of the COVID-19 pandemic in 2020, refugee meanings were innovated to elevate the dangers of spreading disease alongside the dangers of terrorist infiltration and cultural threat. Refugee Resettlement Watch (RRW) warned about refugees fleeing "COVID-saturated" countries and "spreading the coronavirus." Concerns about COVID-

19—often termed "the Chinese virus" in RRW posts—were positioned as mutually exclusive with support for refugee admissions. To "bring in refugees" was to "import new cases of the virus."[88] RRW also cast refugees already living in the United States as "spreading the virus" due to deficiencies in assimilation and English language skills. A chart listing "the top ten languages spoken by refugees" showed Arabic at the top of the list. Alongside RRW's banner slogan that "they are changing America by changing the people," these logics adapted nativist vocabularies to pandemic-specific contexts.[89] Such examples remind us that refugee threat constructions are malleable and can be reconfigured according to the latest moments of "crisis" and most salient modes of classification.

Conservative voices in civil society similarly promulgated representations of refugees as coronavirus carriers. The Heritage Foundation's James Jay Carafano argued in a Fox News editorial that "refugees from the Middle East . . . clamoring to get into Europe" were no longer welcome, combining logics of cultural menace ("assimilation") and encroachment on sovereignty ("refugee policies dictated from Brussels") with "a new concern" specific to the pandemic:

> The coronavirus outbreak in Iran has been particularly acute and is already working its way through the region. It is bound to get into refugee camps, where the state of hygiene and health care is already subpar. Europeans know that an uncontrolled wave of migration is likely to carry the virus with it . . . a migrant flood could be overwhelming across the continent.[90]

These portrayals of refugees as transmitters of coronavirus elevated familiar anti-immigrant tropes. In addition to depictions of migration through marine metaphors of *uncontrolled waves* and *overwhelming floods*, focuses on the deficient cultural assimilation and hygiene of refugees from the Middle East resembled decades of image-building surrounding Mexican and Central American asylum-seekers along the US southern border with Mexico. The COVID-19 pandemic offered another pathway for merging malevolent images of overseas refugees and southern border crossers through conflations of *all* categories of migrants as spreaders of disease. These logics speak to how refugees become interpreted as "at worst, an infestation, at best, a particle in transit."[91]

The Illusions of Endings

When Trump refused to concede to Biden following the November 2020 presidential election, prominent Republicans such as senators Ted Cruz (R-TX) and Lindsey Graham (R-SC) initially stood by his rejection of the results. Sen. Mitt Romney (R-UT)—one of the Republican Party's most vocal critics of Trump—spoke to NBC's *Meet the Press* about Trump's post-election persistence:

> He is without question the most powerful voice in our party. He will have an enormous impact on our party going forward . . . I believe the great majority of people who voted for Donald Trump want to make sure that his principles and his policies are pursued. So, yes, he's not disappearing by any means. He's the 900-pound gorilla when it comes to the Republican Party.[92]

Retiring Republican Rep. Francis Rooney (R-FL), whose 2016 campaign circulated threatening depictions of Syrian refugees, spoke to the dearth of Republican lawmakers coming forward to recognize the legitimacy of Biden's victory: "There will be books written about this hold that President Trump has over a lot of the Republican leadership and base, and I don't understand it . . . it was never that way with previous Republican leaders."[93]

In some ways, this book is one of those books. It contextualizes Trump's ascent and subsequent retreats from refugee responsibility-sharing within trajectories that had been in place long before the 2016 elections. These include the identity dynamics of partisan polarization, discourses chastising multiculturalism and political correctness, narratives of Christian victimhood, Islamophobic conspiracies warning against Muslim infiltration, Orientalist ontologies of the Middle East and Central Asia, and violations and evasions of refugee protection principles for asylum-seekers deemed racially threatening. To the extent that "Trumpism" is entangled with novel iterations of nativism, the end of the Trump era is as illusory as its beginning. Such movements do not begin or end; they evolve and continue as manifestations of ever-present anxieties about identity. In the US context, these anxieties are often oriented around shifting conceptualizations of white Christian supremacy and perceptions of declining power in a multicultural and multiracial society.

The zeitgeist of Trumpism fixates on those anxieties as an organizing principle of politics. Other political figures and voices in civil society are likely to carry forward visions of "America First" and "Make America Great Again," elevating racialized rhetoric within Republican identity narratives and employing unabashedly exclusionary and anti-Muslim modes of making sense of the world. Following Trump's 2020 electoral loss, for example, RRW condemned the Hebrew Immigrant Aid Society for "working tirelessly from before Trump won the White House to defeat him" in order to hasten "the immediate arrival of the promised 125,000 refugees to America." Refugees were bound up with conspiratorial visions of Democrats claiming electoral gains through importing "immigrant voters"[94] and concerns that Biden would lift the "Muslim ban" to resettle people "from countries that hate us." RRW used racialized representations of refugees to heighten anxieties around Trump's departure, cautioning that "12,924 Somalis and 14,084 Syrians" would enter the United States if Biden were inaugurated and there would be "more Ilhan Omars coming our way!"[95]

Relatedly, racialized representations of refugees have become part of a more recent "anti-woke" narrative that draws on earlier critiques of multiculturalism and political correctness. Following the dramatic storming of the US Capitol Building by Trump supporters on January 6, 2021, outgoing Secretary of State Mike Pompeo tweeted about the dangers of "wokeism" and "multiculturalism" on the basis that "they're not who America is. They distort our glorious founding and what this country is all about." The tweet contained an image of Pompeo with a quote condemning "censorship, wokeness, political correctness" as "authoritarianism, cloaked as moral righteousness." Anticipating that Democrats would continue to describe refugees in terms of diversity, tolerance, and inclusion, Republican narratives were poised to interpret those arguments through prisms of multiculturalism and political correctness, delegitimizing their logics as disingenuous and antithetical to what America means. These frameworks preempt accusations of nativist, racist, and discriminatory policies by suggesting such accusations are merely mirages of liberal wokeness and censorship. This discourse carries forward logics circulated during the 2015–16 election cycle that suggested Democrats were self-censoring in submission to political correctness by refusing to say the words "Islamic extremism" when discussing Syrian refugees.

After the inauguration of President Biden in 2021, Republican leaders denounced the new administration's plans to increase the annual refugee resettlement cap from 15,000 up to 62,500 and pushed back against Biden's executive actions related to ending the Travel Ban and "rebuilding and expanding" the US refugee admissions program.[96] More than two dozen House Republicans authored a letter claiming the policy changes would "disregard terrorist risk" and encourage "polygamists seeking to bring multiple wives to the United States," invoking Orientalist specters of Muslim threat through cues around terrorism and polygamy.[97] The legislators also delegitimized "resettling more refugees from abroad" in light of the "refugee crisis" of people seeking asylum from Central America "who are already inside the United States."[98] With the bifurcation between overseas refugees and domestic asylum-seekers previously geared toward sustaining bipartisan support for resettlement (as discussed in chapter 2), the blurring of that distinction among Republicans to argue against resettlement underscores the malleability of meanings surrounding refugeehood.

While the new administration moved away from America First frameworks, ended the discriminatory Travel Ban, restored funding to UNRWA, and began to regenerate humanitarian migration pathways, it fell short of its pledges to rebuild the resettlement program and reestablish leadership in refugee protection. Violations and evasions of non-refoulement, non-detention, and non-penalization persisted in the treatment of asylum-seekers. Efforts to lift Title 42—the public health rule used by the Trump administration to rapidly expel migrants without asylum screenings on the basis of the COVID-19 pandemic[99]—stalled in federal courts amid Republican-led lawsuits, and aspects of the policy were ultimately maintained and expanded throughout 2021 and 2022. In migration policy areas perceived as less "controllable," such as the arrivals of asylum claimants, the transition from Trump to Biden appeared to be marked by more continuity than change.[100] Despite raising the annual refugee admissions ceilings to 62,500 and 125,000 for FY2021 and FY2022, formal refugee admissions remained very low (11,411 and 25,465, respectively),[101] with most domestic resettlement resources geared toward humanitarian parolees from Afghanistan and Ukraine. More liberal lawmakers in the Democratic Party pressed the administration on "upholding the xenophobic and racist policies of Trump"[102] and "reneging" on its campaign promises around refugees,[103] as did refugee advocacy and aid groups.[104]

Amid critiques of continuity with Trump-era approaches, Biden officials emphasized the hospitality extended to Afghan and Ukrainian parolees who were widely discussed as "refugees." In the first year of Russia's 2022 invasion, more than 270,000 Ukrainians were admitted into the United States through a combination of migration pathways—including roughly 115,000 who entered via the Uniting for Ukraine humanitarian parole program.[105] US responsibility-sharing for displaced Ukrainians exceeded that of any other refugee group during the first portion of Biden's presidential term. Resettlement priorities were bound up with racialized discourses narrating Ukrainians as proximate to white/Western/European belonging. Political elites made sense of support for Ukrainian refugees in mythologies of the United States as a vanguard of the free world, positioning Ukrainians as "freedom-loving" protagonists within a familiar story of tenacity and democracy and identifying the villains (Putin and his supporters) who stood in the way of redemption.[106]

Discriminatory approaches were not vanquished with the conclusion of the Trump presidency or the end of the Travel Ban but endured in more subtle manifestations of racial hierarchy. While the United States was directly culpable in contributing to conditions of harm that left hundreds of thousands of Afghans at risk of Taliban persecution in the aftermath of the US and NATO troop withdrawal, Ukrainians were more widely welcomed and offered greater measures of protection on the basis of "common civilizational attributes."[107] Policymakers made exceptions for approximately 20,000 Ukrainians admitted at the southern border with Mexico at the same time that Title 42 policies were used to rapidly expel asylum-seekers of other nationalities.[108] Ukrainian nationals already in the United States were granted Temporary Protected Status (TPS)—which provided work authorization and protection from deportation—within weeks of the Russian invasion, whereas Afghan nationals were not offered TPS until nearly seven months after the Taliban takeover of their country. Responses to Afghan refugees revealed a significant intraparty schism among Republican lawmakers who were divided over whether resettled Afghans were loyal American "allies" or unassimilable terrorist infiltrators,[109] but both Democrats and Republicans configured Ukrainian refugees as kindred and easily enfranchised into white Western identities.

In contrast to parallel layered threat configurations that emerged across debates regarding Afghans and Syrians seeking refuge, Ukrainian deservingness of protection in the months following the invasion was largely unquestioned. Policymakers—including conservative Republicans—rendered Ukrainians "kindred spirits" and analogized them to "American Revolutionary War heroes like George Washington and Patrick Henry."[110] Ukrainians were inscribed as "true refugees"[111] and "innocent people"[112] rather than suspicious harbingers of violence. Legislators who just months prior cautioned that Afghan evacuees "might have terrorist affiliations" and "endanger our communities"[113] championed local sponsorship for Ukrainian refugees: "Let's welcome these people into our community . . . we are all Ukrainians."[114] The offices of Republican governors such as Doug Ducey (R-AZ), who previously called for an "immediate halt" to Syrian refugee placement within his state,[115] raised the Ukrainian flag outside the State Capitol building and proclaimed, "we're ready to welcome Ukrainian refugees."[116] While communities became increasingly divided along partisan identity regarding the evacuation and resettlement Afghan refugees,[117] polls conducted in 2022 found most Americans, including most Republicans, supportive of admitting Ukrainian refugees.[118]

As the context and construction of Self/Other positioning changed, the racialized symbols and identities associated with refugees shifted. Some Democratic lawmakers of color pushed back against these inconsistencies. Sen. Bob Menendez (D-NJ) noted the double standard in enthusiasm for admitting Ukrainian parolees while "too many Black and Brown migrants in our hemisphere have been denied the opportunity to seek humanitarian protection."[119] Legislators connected to the Congressional Black Caucus called attention to "the treatment of people of African and Asian descent who are trying to flee Ukraine" and reports that "many Black families, immigrants from the African diaspora and other people of color are subject to discriminatory or inhumane treatment."[120] Rep. Lou Correa (D-CA) asked about the discrepancy in understandings of who counts as a "political refugee," observing, "you also have Central Americans with AK-47s to their head, not by Russian soldiers but by cartel soldiers . . . why is it that one group is credible and the other group is not?"[121] The meanings around refugeehood were once again fluid, rooted in racial hierarchies, and subject to different interpretations.

Looking Ahead

Partisan polarization entails members of opposing parties increasingly perceiving each other as threatening, and the rhetoric of political leaders is central to this trend in US politics.[122] As constructions of refugee "crises" and contexts around displacement evolve, bipartisan logics of support for refugee protection in the United States may at times be rekindled when political elites across both major parties talk about refugees in ways that reaffirm local group identities, decenter partisan antipathy frameworks, and make sense of responsibility-sharing as aligning with intersubjective mythologies of what America means. Associations of refugees with values like patriotism and loyalty and amplifications of such frameworks among religious groups and veterans in civil society will likely be important for bolstering Republican and conservative-leaning interpretations of refugees as deserving protection and resettlement. When more "Trumpian" Republican leaders emphasize America First ideologies and instrumentalize racialized depictions of refugees as cultural threats, and when nativist civil society actors help co-create and circulate logics discrediting religious voices of support for refugees, we might expect bipartisan inclinations toward responsibility-sharing to diminish. Language among Democrats weaponizing refugee protection to attack partisan opponents can also further entrench refugees within dynamics of polarization, embedding refugeehood in symbols of liberal policy values and visions of local and national identities that are not mutually intelligible across partisan attachments.

Drawing on his experiences as a refugee, Vietnamese American author Vu Tran writes that the "space between what is real and imaginary is ultimately where the refugee resides. Like a ghost, her state of being—to others and even to herself—is ambiguous."[123] Future pathways of humanitarian migration are unlikely to be opened or closed by US policymakers based on which representations of refugees are most factual or "true," or which representations are most authentic to refugees themselves. In contrast, this book underscores the extent to which refugees are used as vehicles and symbols for other group identities—e.g., conservative Christians, Utahns, Hoosiers, Republicans, Democrats—as a means of crafting and reproducing narratives about their place and purpose in the world. To study discourse is to grapple with the stories we tell ourselves about reality. The plasticity of refugee configurations points to the importance of pliable perceptual maps of reality in making sense of migration policy. At the heights of bipartisan support for US refugee responsibility-sharing, policymakers did not draw on indisputable renderings of refugeehood but on idealized and exaggerated mythologies of America's providential exceptionalism, Safe Haven origins, and leadership in the international refugee regime.

Support for refugee protection among US policymakers will likely continue to draw upon gendered archetypes of refugees as feminized victims and elevate "women and children" frameworks that downplay the deservingness of protection for refugee men. We can expect debates about refugee policy—particularly in response to displacement linked with the Middle East, Central Asia, and Muslim-majority polities—to propagate Orientalist ontologies and to both innovate and recycle War on Terror vocabularies in considering the potential security threats posed by Muslim refugees, reproducing 9/11 as an irrevocable turning point in domestic meaning-making and reifying battles against "radical Islam" (or some variation of the concept) as indefinite and geographically limitless.[124] Binaries juxtaposing overseas refugees and humanitarian parolees who are resettled through highly selective and tightly controlled admissions procedures with southern border crossers and asylum-seekers arriving directly on US territory will probably endure to some extent among both Republicans and Democrats, though more liberal coalitions within the Democratic Party will at times push back against the double standards inherent in hierarchies deeming the former group more deserving of protection. Conservative opponents to resettlement, too, might collapse those binaries in arguments delegitimizing increased refugee admissions from abroad so long as the backlog of domestic asylum cases remains unresolved.

US lawmakers will likely continue to silence many refugee voices and elide the diverse perspectives of displaced people that do not fit neatly within their narratives, turning more often to fantasies of America as either a vanguard of Western civilization in need of defense or a shining city upon the hill and rescuer of oppressed peoples.[125] These systems of meaning tend to perpetuate accountability evasion regarding US culpability in violating human rights and in contributing to the underlying forces of danger and displacement in refugee origin countries. As such, they remain problematic even if they are used to justify returns to higher levels of refugee resettlement and other forms of responsibility-sharing.

In many ways, the story of the breakdown in intersubjective understandings of refugee responsibility-sharing that unfolded during the 2015–16 election cycle parallels the plotlines of domestic political polarization,[126] reminding those who study international norms, migration, and refugee policy to scrutinize (sub)national schisms and the trajectories of contested meanings. The coding of the United States as a cohesive "liberal democracy" to assess and predict its contributions to human rights and refugee regimes is not viable. With the language of political elites spurring on diverging perceptions of reality, a future of stable and consistent shared domestic interpretations regarding refugees or the US role in the refugee regime is unlikely. The growth of global displacement due to climate and environmental forces portends further fragmentation and polarization in domestic visions of refugeehood. Republican policymakers have already expressed skepticism around "so-called 'climate refugees'"[127] and emphasized that "asylum should be limited to cases of political, ethnic or religious persecution."[128] Polling in 2022 found that Americans were most divided along partisan lines in perceptions of immigration and climate change, with only 5 percent of self-identified Republicans viewing climate change as an issue of major concern.[129] With most of the emerging class of "environmental refugees" originating in parts of the Global South that have been racialized as non-white and non-Western,[130] we can anticipate that many US lawmakers opposing responsibility-sharing will likely employ the kinds of layered threat constructions studied in this book.

ACKNOWLEDGMENTS

The completion of this book unfolded over many years, and its core ideas strengthened and evolved thanks to the encouragement, advice, and contributions of numerous scholars and colleagues. Examples include Lamis Abdelaaty, Claire Adida, Julia Azari, Carl Bon Tempo, Kiran Banerjee, Zoltán Búzás, Elizabeth Cohen, David Coury, Jeff Crisp, Marcelo Cruz, Emily Farris, Elizabeth Ferris, David FitzGerald, Rebecca Hamlin, Colton Heffington, David Helpap, Ray Hutchison, Edwin Daniel Jacob, Debbie Kang, Shauna Labman, Anna Law, Matthew Leep, Jamie Mayerfeld, Elizabeth Oldmixon, David Owen, Jeremy Pressman, Jason Ralph, Andrea Silva, Tahseen Shams, Matthew Shannon, Craig Damian Smith, Chana Soloman-Schwartz, James Souter, Patrick Thaddeus Jackson, Lewis Turner, Michael Wagner, Aaron Weinschenk, and Kelly Zvobgo. I received thoughtful comments and questions during presentations at conferences hosted by the University of Leeds, the Midwest Political Science Association, the Western Political Science Association, and the Canada Excellence Research Chair in Migration & Integration at Toronto Metropolitan University (formerly Ryerson University). I drew valuable insights from participating in events hosted by the Immigration and Ethnic History Society. I also drew inspiration from the creative work of photographers, authors, artists, and poets such as Amina Abou Kerech, Aula Al Ayoubi, Tammam Azzam, Behrouz Boochani, Oussama Diab, Safwan Dahoul, Hosam Katan, Porochista Khakpour, Dina Nayeri, Viet Thanh Nguyen, and Warsan Shire.

I am thankful to the book's anonymous reviewers and to my New York University Press editor, Sonia Tsuruoka, for providing helpful suggestions and support. My writing was also shaped by the feedback I received from community members and civil society groups at presentations through the Manitowoc Public Library, Lester Public Library, Mead Public Library, Weidner Center for the Performing Arts, Manitowoc City Hall, and the Door Community Auditorium. Special thanks to the League of Women Voters of Manitowoc County, Kathie Fishbeck, Linda Hunter, Jackie Joseph-Silverstein, and the organizers of the Great Decisions lecture series in Green Bay, Sheboygan, and Manitowoc for encouraging me to share my research with local audiences. Interviews on developments around US refugee, asylum, and immigration policy on Wisconsin Public Radio's Central Time program pressed me to improve the accessibility and articulation of my ideas. I am appreciative of my University of Wisconsin-Green Bay students, colleagues, staff, and administrators across multiple campuses, and particularly within the Public & Environmental Affairs Unit and the College of Arts, Humanities, and Social Sciences, for engaging and supporting my work on this project. The university librarians were crucial sources of support throughout my research process.

I owe my deepest gratitude to Matt, Moszka, and Razeem. They motivated me to move this book forward through the many sharp turns of life's unforeseen challenges.

NOTES

CHAPTER 1. RECONFIGURING REFUGEES

1. Donald Trump (@realDonaldTrump), "Refugees from Syria are now pouring into our great country. Who knows who they are—some could be ISIS. Is our president insane?" Twitter, November 17, 2015, 7:54am, https://twitter.com/realdonaldtrump/status/666615398574530560.
2. Cheryl Teh, "Trump Claims Biden's Afghanistan Evacuation Could Be Bringing 'Terrorists' to America," *Business Insider*, August 25, 2021, www.businessinsider.com.
3. Tori Richards, "Afghan Refugees at Wisconsin Army Base Lack Complete Vetting But Can Leave Any Time, House Member Says," *Washington Examiner*, September 2, 2021, www.washingtonexaminer.com.
4. Rep. Matt Rosendale (R-MT) (@RepRosendale), "See my statement below on Afghanistan," Twitter, August 16, 2021, 4:08pm, https://twitter.com/RepRosendale/status/1427376741631340544?s=20.
5. Rep. Tom Tiffany (R-WI). See "Statement of Rep. Tom Tiffany on Biden Administration Plans to Send Afghan Nations to Fort McCoy in Wisconsin," *Congressman Tom Tiffany*, August 18, 2021, https://tiffany.house.gov.
6. Rep. Paul Gosar (R-AZ) (@DrPaulGosar), "These are not refugees. These are afghan fighting age men who chose not to fight against the taliban. Not one shot was fired. They do not belong in our country. They belong in their country. We are not the world's dumping ground for every third world country," Twitter, August 16, 2021, 10:57am, https://twitter.com/DrPaulGosar/status/1427298487004286978.
7. A. G. Gancarski, "Rick Scott Questions Vetting of Florida-Bound Afghan Refugees," *Florida Politics*, September 8, 2021, https://floridapolitics.com.
8. Interview with Matthew Continetti on The Ezra Klein Show. See "Donald Trump Didn't Hijack the G.O.P. He Understood It." *New York Times*, May 6, 2022, www.nytimes.com.
9. Interview with Sophia Jordán Wallace. "What Do Americans Think About Immigration Policy?" *Politics in Question*, March 24, 2022, www.politicsinquestion.com.
10. This approach can be situated within growing attention to the power of language among Republican Party strategists since the 1990s. See Frank Luntz, *Words That Work: It's Not What You Say, It's What People Hear* (New York: Hyperion, 2007), and "The Politics of Slash and Burn," *New York Times*, September 20, 1990, www.nytimes.com.
11. These analogies drew on prior discourses among domestic religious and voluntary groups appealing to the memory of the US failure to assist Jews in the 1930s. See

Geoffrey Cameron, *Send Them Here: Religion, Politics, and Refugee Resettlement in North America* (Chicago: McGill-Queen's University Press, 2021), 144.
12 Robbie Shilliam, *Race and the Undeserving Poor* (Newcastle upon Tyne, UK: Agenda Publishing, 2018), 4.
13 See Geoffrey Cameron and Shauna Labman, "The Dynamics and Divergences of Executive Discretion in Refugee Resettlement," ch. 5 in Kiran Banerjee and Craig Damian Smith, eds., *Migration Governance in North America: Policy, Politics, and Community* (Montreal: McGill-Queen's University Press, 2024), 143–170.
14 Damir Utrzan, Elizabeth Wieling, and Timothy Piehler, "A Needs and Readiness Assessment of the United States Refugee Resettlement Program: Focus on Syrian Asylum-Seekers and Refugees," *International Migration* 57:1 (2019): 127–144, 133.
15 "U.S. Annual Refugee Resettlement Ceilings and Number of Refugees Admitted, 1980–Present," *Migration Policy Institute*, n.d., www.migrationpolicy.org.
16 See David S. FitzGerald, *Refuge Beyond Reach: How Rich Democracies Repel Asylum Seekers* (New York: Oxford University Press, 2019), 3.
17 Molly Fee and Rawan Arar, "What Happens When the United States Stops Taking in Refugees?," *Contexts* 18:2 (2019): 19–23, 22.
18 "New IRC Analysis of U.S. Refugee Resettlement," *International Rescue Committee*, June 18, 2019, www.rescue.org.
19 See "Desperate Journeys," *UNHCR*, December 2018, www.unhcr.org, and "Death Rates in the Western, Eastern, and Central Mediterranean Routes, 2015–2019," *Missing Migrants Project*, n.d., https://missingmigrants.iom.int.
20 Muzaffar Chishti and Sarah Pierce, "Despite Trump Invitation to Stop Taking Refugees, Red and Blue States Alike Endorse Resettlement," *Migration Policy Institute*, January 29, 2020, www.migrationpolicy.org.
21 See "Executive Order 13769 of January 27, 2017—Protecting the Nation from Foreign Terrorist Entry into the United States," *The Federal Register*, February 1, 2017.
22 Susan Fratzke, "Top 10 of 2017—Issue #6: In Wake of Cuts to U.S. Refugee Program, Global Resettlement Falls Short," *Migration Policy Institute*, December 13, 2017, www.migrationpolicy.org.
23 See "Proclamation 9645 of September 24, 2017—Enhancing Vetting Capabilities and Processes for Detecting Attempted Entry into the United States by Terrorists or Other Public-Safety Threats," *The Federal Register*, September 27, 2017.
24 The "high-risk" designated countries included Egypt, Iran, Iraq, Libya, Mali, North Korea, Somalia, South Sudan, Sudan, Syria, and Yemen. See Chishti and Pierce, "Despite Trump Invitation to Stop Taking Refugees, Red and Blue States Alike Endorse Resettlement."
25 See Zaha Hassan, "Trump's Funding Cuts to Palestinian Refugees Put Lives at Risk," *Al Jazeera*, July 28, 2018, www.aljazeera.com, and Stephen Farrell and Nidal al-Mughrabi, "U.N. Refugee Agency for Palestinians Appeals for Money to Pay Salaries," *Reuters*, November 9, 2020, www.reuters.com. For additional background on the centrality of UNRWA to Palestinian refugees, see Anne Irfan, *Refuge and Resistance: Palestinians and the International Refugee Regime* (New York: Columbia University Press, 2023).

26 Alise Coen, "Trump, Biden, and the U.S. Role in the International Refugee Regime," ch. 6 in Banerjee and Smith, eds., *Migration Governance in North America*, 171–206.
27 Seyla Benhabib, "The End of the 1951 Refugee Convention? Dilemmas of Sovereignty, Territoriality, and Human Rights," *Jus Cogens* 2:1 (2020): 75–100.
28 See, for example, Kemal Derviş, "The Post-Trump Reconstruction of America and the World," *Brookings*, January 19, 2021, www.brookings.edu, and Julia Spiegel, "Embracing Foreign Affairs Federalism in a Post-Trump Era," *Lawfare*, March 3, 2021, www.lawfareblog.com.
29 Caroline Coudriet, "'Decimated' Refugee Infrastructure Threatens a Key Biden Promise," *Roll Call*, May 26, 2021, https://rollcall.com.
30 "U.S. Annual Refugee Resettlement Ceilings and Number of Refugees Admitted, 1980–Present."
31 "You're Going to Your Death: Violations against Syrian Refugees Returning to Syria," *Amnesty International*, September 7, 2021, www.amnesty.org.
32 See "UNRWA Raises Alarm on the Situation of Palestine Refugees in Lebanon," *UNRWA*, April 1, 2021, www.unrwa.org, and "Palestinian Refugees Face Hitting 'Rock Bottom,' Warns UNRWA in $1.6 Billion Appeal," *UN News*, January 24, 2023, https://news.un.org.
33 The book scrutinizes the use of "refugee crisis" language for political purposes, bearing in mind that phrasing tends to imply refugees are a "problem" and tends to obscure the extent to which refugees often comprise a relatively small proportion of populations. Elizabeth G. Ferris and Katharine M. Donato, *Refugees, Migration and Global Governance* (New York: Routledge, 2020), 79.
34 See Alise Coen, "Localizing Refugeehood: Norms and the U.S. Resettlement of Afghan Allies," *International Affairs* 98:6 (2022): 2021–2038.
35 Mat Nashed, "One Year On, Few Options for Afghans Escaping Hunger and Taliban Persecution," *The New Humanitarian*, August 10, 2022, www.thenewhumanitarian.org.
36 The Afghan Adjustment Act of 2022 attempted to normalize the legal status of Afghan parolees—which was set to expire after two years—and facilitate access to permanent residency. See Katherine Gypson, "U.S. Lawmakers Fail to Pass Afghan Adjustment Act by Year's End," *VOA*, December 20, 2022, www.voanews.com.
37 Michel Agier, *Managing the Undesirables: Refugee Camps and Humanitarian Government* (Malden, MA: Polity Press, 2011), 16–17.
38 Lucy Mayblin and Joe Turner, *Migration Studies and Colonialism* (Medford, MA: Polity Press, 2021), 18.
39 Abdelaaty and Kukathas point out that the use of these terms is often deliberate and politically motivated, though Lipman notes at other times it is an arbitrary convergence of "influence, luck, and chance." See Lamis Elmy Abdelaaty, *Discrimination and Delegation: Explaining State Responses to Refugees* (New York: Oxford University Press, 2021), 192; Chandran Kukathas, *Immigration and Freedom* (Princeton, NJ: Princeton University Press, 2021), 17; and Jana K. Lipman, *In Camps: Vietnamese Refugees, Asylum Seekers, and Repatriates* (Oakland: University of California Press, 2020), 19.

40. Rebecca Hamlin, *Crossing: How We Label and React to People on the Move* (Stanford, CA: Stanford University Press, 2021), 152.
41. See Angela S. García, *Legal Passing: Navigating Undocumented Life and Local Immigration Law* (Oakland: University of California Press, 2019), 3–4; Porochista Khakpour, *Brown Album: Essays on Exile and Identity* (New York: Vintage Books, 2020); and Dina Nayeri, *The Ungrateful Refugee: What Immigrants Never Tell You* (New York: Catapult, 2019).
42. Rawan Arar and David Scott FitzGerald, *The Refugee System: A Sociological Approach* (Hoboken, NJ: Polity Press, 2023), 23.
43. Chris Abani, "The Road," in Viet Thanh Nguyen, ed., *The Displaced: Refugee Writers on Refugee Lives* (New York: Abrams Press, 2018), 23–30, 25.
44. Nayeri, *The Ungrateful Refugee*, 13.
45. See Alexis Okeowo's interview with Shire in "Warsan Shire's Portraits of Somalis in Exile," *The New Yorker*, February 7, 2022, www.newyorker.com.
46. Irfan, *Refuge and Resistance*, 24.
47. See Article I of the 1951 Convention and 1967 Protocol Relating to the Status of Refugees.
48. "Critical Vocabularies," *The Critical Refugee Studies Collective*, n.d., https://criticalrefugeestudies.com.
49. "An Overview of U.S. Refugee Law and Policy," *American Immigration Council*, October 22, 2022, www.americanimmigrationcouncil.org.
50. See Celia Medrano, "Securing Protection for De Facto Refugees: The Case of Central America's Northern Triangle," *Ethics & International Affairs* 31:2 (2017): 129–142.
51. "Global Trends At-a-Glance," *USA for UNHCR*, n.d., www.unrefugees.org.
52. B. S. Chimni, "The Birth of a 'Discipline': From Refugee to Forced Migration Studies," *Journal of Refugee Studies* 22:1 (2009): 11–29, 18.
53. Aleksandar Hemon, "God's Fate," in Nguyen, ed., *The Displaced*, 99–112, 100.
54. Heba Gowayed, *Refuge: How the State Shapes Human Potential* (Princeton, NJ: Princeton University Press, 2022), 19.
55. Behrouz Boochani, *No Friend but the Mountains: Writing from Manus Prison* (Toronto: Anansi International, 2019), 69.
56. Viet Thanh Nguyen, "Introduction," in Nguyen, ed., *The Displaced*, 13.
57. Nayeri, *The Ungrateful Refugee*, 6.
58. See Kristina Shull, *Detention Empire: Reagan's War on Immigrations & the Seeds of Resistance* (Chapel Hill: University of North Carolina Press, 2022), xix.
59. "Refugee Processing and Security Screening," *U.S. Citizenship and Immigration Services*, n.d., www.uscis.gov.
60. See Silvia Pasquetti, Noemi Casati, and Romola Sanyal, "Law and Refugee Crises," *Annual Review of Law and Social Science* 15 (2019): 289–310, and Romola Sanyal, "Managing Through Ad Hoc Measures: Syrian Refugees and the Politics of Waiting in Lebanon," *Political Geography* 66 (2018): 67–75.
61. Leo R. Chavez, *The Latino Threat: Constructing Immigrants, Citizens, and the Nation, Second Edition* (Stanford, CA: Stanford University Press, 2008/2013).

62 Clare Sheridan, "Contested Citizenship: National Identity and the Mexican Immigration Debates of the 1920s," *Immigration & Ethnic History Society* 21:3 (2002): 3–35.
63 Samuel P. Huntington, "The Hispanic Challenge," *Foreign Policy* 141 (2004): 30–45.
64 Labman similarly notes this point with regard to Canadian policy distinguishing between well-controlled and orderly resettlement versus the "unpredictable nature" of asylum-seekers who enter the country irregularly. Shauna Labman, *Crossing Law's Border: Canada's Refugee Resettlement Program* (Toronto: UBC Press, 2019), 27.
65 Kim Monin, Jeanne Batalova, and Tianjian Lai, "Refugees and Asylees in the United States," *Migration Policy Institute*, May 13, 2021, www.migrationpolicy.org.
66 Christina Boswell, Andrew Geddes, and Peter Scholten, "The Role of Narratives in Migration Policy-Making: A Research Framework," *British Journal of Politics and International Relations* 13:1 (2011): 1–11, 4.
67 Gowayed, *Refuge*, 33.
68 Monin et al., "Refugees and Asylees in the United States."
69 See Amanda C. Demmer, *After Saigon's Fall: Refugees and U.S.-Vietnamese Relations, 1975–2000* (New York: Cambridge University Press, 2021).
70 See Didier Fassin, *Humanitarian Reason: A Moral History of the Present* (Berkeley: University of California Press, 2012).
71 Matthew Leep, "Introduction to the Special Issue: Multispecies Security and Personhood," *Review of International Studies* 49:2 (2023): 181–200, 184.
72 Lamis Abdelaaty and Rebecca Hamlin, "Introduction: The Politics of the Migrant/Refugee Binary," *Journal of Immigrant & Refugee Studies* 20:2 (2022): 233–239, 239.
73 Nayeri, *The Ungrateful Refugee*, 8.
74 See, for example, Simon Behrman and Avidan Kent, eds., *"Climate Refugees": Beyond the Legal Impasse?* (New York: Routledge, 2018); Nicole Bates-Eamer, "Border and Migration Controls and Migrant Precarity in the Context of Climate Change," *Social Sciences* 8:7 (2019): 198; Andrew Geddes, "Governing Migration from a Distance: Interactions between Climate, Migration, and Security in the South Mediterranean," *European Security* 24:3 (2015): 473–490; Benoît Mayer and François Crépeau, eds., *Research Handbook on Climate Change, Migration and the Law* (Northampton, MA: Edward Elgar, 2017); Jane McAdam, "Should I Stay or Should I Go? Shaping International Responses to Climate Change, Disasters and Displacement," *Law Society Journal* 32 (2017): 36–39; and Gaia Vince, *Nomad Century: How Climate Migration Will Reshape Our World* (New York: Flatiron Books, 2022).
75 See, for example, how Nguyen and Tran position "immigrant" as at times a more desirable label than "refugee" in Jon Wiener, "'Call Me a Refugee, Not an Immigrant': Viet Thanh Nguyen," *The Nation*, June 11, 2018, www.thenation.com, and Vu Tran, "A Refugee Again," in Nguyen, ed., *The Displaced*, 165–171, 163.
76 Hannah Arendt, "We Refugees," in Jerome Kohn and Ron H. Feldman, eds., *The Jewish Writings: Hannah Arendt* (New York: Schocken Books, 1943/2007), 264–274, 264–265.
77 Nayeri, *The Ungrateful Refugee*, 8.

78 Irfan, *Refuge and Resistance*, 6.
79 See Stephen D. Krasner, "Structural Causes and Regime Consequences: Regimes as Intervening Variables," *International Organization* 36:2 (1982): 185–205.
80 See Alexander Betts, "The Normative Terrain of the Global Refugee Regime," *Ethics & International Affairs* 29:4 (2015): 363–375, 363.
81 See Jeff Crisp, "No Solution in Sight: The Problem of Protracted Refugee Situations in Africa," *The Center for Comparative Immigration Studies*, Working Paper No. 68 (2002): 1–30, 3.
82 Alexander Betts, "The Refugee Regime and Issue-Linkage," in Rey Koslowski, ed., *Global Mobility Regimes* (New York: Palgrave Macmillan, 2011), 73–91, 78.
83 See Alexander Betts and Phil Orchard, "Introduction: The Normative Institutionalization-Implementation Gap," in Alexander Betts and Phil Orchard, eds., *Implementation and World Politics: How International Norms Change Practice* (New York: Oxford University Press, 2014), 1–26, and Thomas Risse, *Domestic Politics and Norm Diffusion in International Relations: Ideas Do Not Float Freely* (New York: Routledge, 2017).
84 Examples include the International Covenant on Civil and Political Rights, the Convention against Torture, the European Convention on Human Rights, the Cartagena Declaration on Refugees, the Organization of African Unity Refugee Convention, UN resolutions, and UNHCR Executive Committee conclusions.
85 Luke Glanville, *Sharing Responsibility: The History and Future of Protection from Atrocities* (Princeton, NJ: Princeton University Press, 2021), 7.
86 See Alise Coen, "Can't Be Held Responsible: Weak Norms and Refugee Protection Evasion," *International Relations* 35:2 (2021): 341–362; Cathryn Costello, Michelle Foster, and Jane McAdam, *The Oxford Handbook of International Refugee Law* (New York: Oxford University Press, 2021); and Rebecca Dowd, "Dissecting Discrimination in Refugee Law: An Analysis of Its Meaning and Its Cumulative Effect," *International Journal of Refugee Law* 23:1 (2010): 28–53.
87 "Advisory Opinion on the Extraterritorial Application of *Non-Refoulement* Obligations under the 1951 Convention Relating to the Status of Refugees and Its 1967 Protocol," *UNHCR*, January 26, 2007, www.unhcr.org.
88 Susan Akram, "UNRWA and Palestinian Refugees," in Elena Fiddian-Qasmiyeh et al., eds., *The Oxford Handbook of Refugee and Forced Migration Studies* (New York: Oxford University Press, 2014), 227–240.
89 See Raja Shehadeh, "Am I a Refugee?" in Nguyen, ed., *The Displaced*, 159–164, 161.
90 Irfan, *Refuge and Resistance*, 5.
91 Yasmeen Abu-Laban, "Re-Defining the International Refugee Regime: UNHCR, UNRWA, and the Challenge of Multigenerational Protracted Refugee Situations," in Catherine Dauvergne, ed., *Research Handbook on the Law and Politics of Migration* (Northampton, MA: Edward Elgar, 2021), 310–322.
92 Alexander Betts, "From Persecution to Deprivation: How Refugee Norms Adapt at Implementation," in Betts and Orchard, eds., *Implementation and World Politics*, 29–49, 29–30.

93 See Ian Goldin, Geoffrey Cameron, and Meera Balarajan, *Exceptional People: How Migration Shaped Our World and Will Define Our Future* (Princeton, NJ: Princeton University Press, 2011), 266–267. For additional discussions of how the figure of the "refugee" reveals tensions between conceptions of belonging in a discrete political community and universal proclamations of human rights, see Hannah Arendt, *The Origins of Totalitarianism* (New York: Harcourt Brace Jovanovich, 1973), and Kiran Banerjee, "Re-Theorizing Human Rights through the Refugee: On the Interrelation between Democracy and Global Justice," *Refuge* 27:1 (2010): 24–35.
94 See B. S. Chimni, "The Geopolitics of Refugee Studies: A View from the South," *Journal of Refugee Studies* 11:4 (1998): 350–374, 353, and Milena Chimienti, "The Failure of Global Migration Governance," *Ethnic and Racial Studies* 41:3 (2018): 424–430, 427.
95 Jeff Crisp, "Forced Displacement in Africa: Dimensions, Difficulties, and Policy Directions," *Refugee Survey Quarterly* 29:3 (2010): 1–27, 7.
96 See Alexander Betts, Gil Loescher, and James Milner, *UNHCR: The Politics and Practice of Refugee Protection, Second Edition* (New York: Routledge, 2012), 5.
97 Antoine Pécoud, "Narrating an Ideal Migration World? An Analysis of the Global Compact for Safe, Orderly and Regular Migration," *Third World Quarterly* 42:1 (2021): 16–33, 20.
98 Abani, "The Road," 30.
99 Glanville, *Sharing Responsibility*, 176.
100 See Alise Coen, "Capable and Culpable? The United States, RtoP, and Refugee Responsibility-Sharing," *Ethics & International Affairs* 31:1 (2017): 71–92; Rebecca Dowd and Jane McAdam, "International Cooperation and Responsibility-Sharing to Protect Refugees: What, Why, and How?," *International & Comparative Law Quarterly* 66:4 (2017): 863–892; Tally Kritzman-Amir, "Not in My Backyard: On the Morality of Responsibility Sharing in Refugee Law," *Brooklyn Journal of International Law* 34:2 (2009): 355–393; David Owen, "Refugees and Responsibilities of Justice," *Global Justice: Theory Practice Rhetoric* 11:1 (2018): 23–44; and Volker Türk, "Prospects for Responsibility Sharing in the Refugee Context," *Journal on Migration and Human Security* 4:3 (2016): 45–59.
101 See David Miller, "Justice in Immigration," *European Journal of Political Theory* 14:4 (2015): 391–408, 395. See also David Owen, "Refugees, Economic Migrants, and Weak Cosmopolitanism," *Critical Review of International Social and Political Philosophy* 20:6 (2017): 745–754.
102 See Lewis Turner, "Explaining the (Non-)Encampment of Syrian Refugees: Security, Class and the Labor Market in Lebanon and Jordan," *Mediterranean Politics* 20:3 (2015): 386–404.
103 See Alexander Betts, "Introduction: Global Migration Governance," in Alexander Betts, ed., *Global Migration Governance* (New York: Oxford University Press, 2011), 1–33, 26; Labman, *Crossing Law's Border*, 5; and Beth Elise Whitaker, "Funding the International Refugee Regime: Implications for Protection," *Global Governance* 14:2 (2008): 241–258, 243.

104 Coen, "Capable and Culpable," 73.
105 See Nils Holtug, "A Fair Distribution of Refugees in the European Union," *Journal of Global Ethics* 12:3 (2016): 279–288. Also note that Pattison elevates capability-based factors as central to determining which countries should be responsible for humanitarian protection. See James Pattison, *Humanitarian Intervention and the Responsibility to Protect: Who Should Intervene?* (New York: Oxford University Press, 2010).
106 See Luara Ferracioli, "The Appeal and Danger of a New Refugee Convention," *Social Theory and Practice* 40:1 (2014):123–144; Matthew J. Gibney, "Refugees and Justice Between States," *European Journal of Political Theory* 14:4 (2015): 448–463; Owen, "Refugees and Responsibilities of Justice"; and Astri Suhrke, "Burden-Sharing during Refugee Emergencies: The Logic of Collective versus National Action," *Journal of Refugee Studies* 11:4 (1998): 396–415.
107 Benedicta Solfa and Katherine Rehberg, "The Resettlement Gap: A Record Number of Global Refugees, But Few Are Resettled," *Migration Policy Institute*, October 22, 2021, www.migrationpolicy.org.
108 See Jeff Crisp and Katy Long, "Safe and Voluntary Refugee Repatriation: From Principle to Practice," *Journal on Migration and Human Security* 4:3 (2016): 141–147, 142, and Peter Gatrell, *The Making of the Modern Refugee* (New York: Oxford University Press, 2015), 200. Note that nearly 90 percent of the agency's funding is often provided by donor states. See Jeff Crisp, "As the World Abandons Refugees, UNHCR's Constraints Are Exposed," *News Deeply*, September 13, 2018, www.newsdeeply.com.
109 See E. Tendayi Achiume, "Syria, Cost-Sharing, and the Responsibility to Protect Refugees," *Minnesota Law Review* 100:2 (2015): 687–761; Hamza S. Aldoghmi, "R2P and Refugee Protection: Framing the Responsibility to Protect Prima Facie Refugees Fleeing Mass Atrocity Crimes," *Global Responsibility to Protect* 11:1 (2019): 104–134; Dan Bulley, "Shame on EU? Europe, RtoP, and the Politics of Refugee Protection," *Ethics & International Affairs* 31:1 (2017): 51–70; Alise Coen, "R2P, Global Governance and the Syrian Refugee Crisis," *International Journal of Human Rights* 19:8 (2015): 1044–1058; Jean-François Durieux, "The Duty to Rescue Refugees," *International Journal of Refugee Law* 28:4 (2016): 637–355; Chloë M. Gilgan, "Exploring the Link between R2P and Refugee Protection: Arriving at Resettlement," *Global Responsibility to Protect* 9:4 (2017): 366–394; Olivia Lwabukuna, "The Responsibility to Protect Internally Displaced Persons in Africa," *Journal of African Law* 65:S1 (2021): 73–100; Jason Ralph and James Souter, "A Special Responsibility to Protect: The UK, Australia and the Rise of Islamic State," *International Affairs* 91:4 (2015): 709–723; and Susan Harris Rimmer, "The Rwanda Paradigm: The Responsibility to Protect Displaced Persons," in Cecilia Jacob and Alistair D. B. Cook, eds., *Civilian Protection in the Twenty-First Century: Governance and Responsibility in a Fragmented World* (New York: Oxford University Press, 2017), 79–104.
110 Glanville, *Sharing Responsibility*, 92.
111 David Owen, *What Do We Owe to Refugees?* (Medford, MA: Polity Press, 2020), 104.
112 Susan Kneebone, "The Bali Process and Global Refugee Policy in the Asia-Pacific Region," *Journal of Refugee Studies* 27:4 (2014): 596–618, 597.

113 Glanville, *Sharing Responsibility*, 91.
114 Arar and FitzGerald note that the international system of refugee management is dependent on refugee-hosting countries in the Global South—countries that are less powerful and tend to have histories of being colonized. *The Refugee System*, 134–135.
115 Richa Shivakoti and James Milner, "Beyond the Partnership Debate: Localizing Knowledge Production in Refugee and Forced Migration Studies," *Journal of Refugee Studies* 35:2 (2022): 805–826, 809.
116 Alexander Betts, *Protection by Persuasion: International Cooperation in the Refugee Regime* (Ithaca, NY: Cornell University Press, 2009), 36.
117 "Which Countries Host the Most Refugees?," *International Rescue Committee*, July 28, 2021, www.rescue.org.
118 See E. Tendayi Achiume, "Migration as Decolonization," *Stanford Law Review* 71:6 (2019): 1509–1574.
119 See James Souter, *Asylum as Reparation: Refuge and Responsibility for the Harms of Displacement* (Cham, CH: Palgrave Macmillan, 2022).
120 Luke Glanville, "Hypocritical Inhospitality: The Global Refugee Crisis in the Light of History," *Ethics & International Affairs* 34:1 (2020): 3–12, 6.
121 Alise Coen, "International Order, the Rule of Law, and U.S. Departures from Refugee Protection," *International Journal of Human Rights* 22:10 (2018): 1269–1284; Constance Duncome and Tim Dunne, "After Liberal World Order," *International Affairs* 94:1 (2018), 25–42; Tim Dunne, "'The Rules of the Game Are Changing': Fundamental Human Rights in Crisis after 9/11," *International Politics* 44:2/3 (2007): 269–286; Stephen Hopgood, *The Endtimes of Human Rights* (Ithaca, NY: Cornell University Press, 2013); G. John Ikenberry, "The Future of Liberal World Order," *Japanese Journal of Political Science* 16:3 (2015): 450–455; and Dirk Messner and Silke Weinlich, eds., *Global Cooperation and the Human Factor in International Relations* (New York: Routledge, 2016), 4. For a critique of the conceptualization of US-led liberal international order, see Amitav Acharya, *The End of American World Order* (Medford, MA: Polity Press, 2014/2018).
122 See Gurminder K. Bhambra, "The Current Crisis of Europe: Refugees, Colonialism, and the Limits of Cosmopolitanism," *European Law Journal* 23:5 (2017): 395–405, 404.
123 See Hamlin, *Crossing*.
124 Paulina Ochoa Espejo, *On Borders: Territories, Legitimacy, & The Rights of Place* (New York: Oxford University Press, 2020), 84.
125 Matthew Leep, *Cosmopolitan Belongingness and War: Animals, Loss, and Spectral-Poetic Moments* (Albany: State University of New York Press, 2021), 8–9.
126 Michael Barnett, "Humanitarianism with a Sovereign Face: UNHCR in the Global Undertow," *International Migration Review* 35:1 (2001): 244–277, 269. See also Arendt's note that problems of refugeehood and statelessness will persist so long as people are organized into "the old system of nation-states." Hannah Arendt, "The Disenfranchised and Disgraced," in Kohn and Feldman, eds., *The Jewish Writings*, 232–235, 235.

127 Coen, "Can't Be Held Responsible"; FitzGerald, *Refuge Beyond Reach*; and Daniel Ghezelbash, "Hyper-Legalism and Obfuscation: How States Evade Their International Obligations towards Refugees," *American Journal of Comparative Law* 68:3 (2020): 479–516.
128 Glanville, *Sharing Responsibility*, 97.
129 Chishti and Pierce, "Despite Trump Invitation to Stop Taking Refugees, Red and Blue States Alike Endorse Resettlement."
130 María Cristina García, *The Refugee Challenge in Post-Cold War America* (New York: Oxford University Press, 2017), 3.
131 Sen. Ted Kennedy (D-MA), *The Congressional Record*, May 2, 2002, S3845.
132 "Republican Party Platform of 1956," *The American Presidency Project*, August 20, 1956, www.presidency.ucsb.edu.
133 "Republican Party Platform of 1988," *The American Presidency Project*, August 16, 1988, www.presidency.ucsb.edu.
134 See, for example, Obama's 2016 statement that "all nations ought to share in our collective responsibilities" regarding refugees, quoted in Andrew Geddes, *Governing Migration Beyond the State: Europe, North America, South America, and Southeast Asia in a Global Context* (New York: Oxford University Press, 2021), 189. See also the findings of Pew surveys from 2017 and 2018 regarding Democratic support for the notion that "the U.S. has a responsibility to accept refugees into the country." Hannah Hartig, "Republicans Turn More Negative toward Refugees as Number Admitted to U.S. Plummets," *Pew Research Center*, May 24, 2018, www.pewresearch.org.
135 Mallory Newall and Jocelyn Duran, "Over Two-Thirds of Americans Support Resettling Afghan Allies in the United States," *IPSOS*, September 9, 2021, www.ipsos.com.
136 "Executive Order 13769 of January 27, 2017," *The Federal Register*, February 1, 2017.
137 See Antoine Pécoud, *Depoliticising Migration: Global Governance and International Migration Narratives* (London: Palgrave Macmillan, 2015), 53, and Roxanna Sjöstedt, "The Discursive Origins of a Doctrine: Norms, Identity, and Securitization under Harry S. Truman and George W. Bush," *Foreign Policy Analysis* 3:3 (2007): 233–254, 237.
138 Roxanne Lynn Doty, *Imperial Encounters: The Politics of Representation in North-South Relations* (Minneapolis: University of Minnesota Press, 1996), 72.
139 For overviews of these contributions, including their roots in the work of scholars such as Edward Said, Michel Foucault, Jacques Derrida, Ernesto Laclau, and Chantal Mouffe, see Homi K. Bhabha, ed., *Nation and Narration* (New York: Routledge, 1990); Doty, *Imperial Encounters*; Philippe Fournier, "Michel Foucault's Considerable Sway on International Relations Theory," *Bridges: Conversations in Global Politics and Public Policy* 1:1 (2012): 18–43; Matthew Coen Leep, "The Affective Production of Others: United States Policy towards the Israeli-Palestinian Conflict," *Cooperation and Conflict* 45:3 (2010): 331–352; and Dirk Nabers, "Filling the Void of Meaning: Identity Construction in U.S. Foreign Policy After Septem-

ber 11, 2001," *Foreign Policy Analysis* 5:2 (2009): 191–214. For a critique of Foucault's Eurocentricity and "silence" on the violence of imperialism and enslavement, see also Gurminder K. Bhambra, "Postcolonial and Decolonial Dialogues," *Postcolonial Studies* 17:2 (2014): 115–121.

140 See Jamie Gaskarth, "Discourses and Ethics: The Social Construction of British Foreign Policy," *Foreign Policy Analysis* 2:4 (2006): 325–341, 327; Jarrod Hayes, "Identity, Authority, and the British War in Iraq," *Foreign Policy Analysis* 12:3 (2016): 334–353; Jennifer Milliken, "The Study of Discourse in International Relations: A Critique of Research and Methods," *European Journal of International Relations* 5:2 (1999): 225–254; and Carina Van de Wetering, "Policy Discourses and Security Issues: U.S. Foreign Policy toward India During the Clinton Administration," *Foreign Policy Analysis* 13:2 (2017): 460–479.

141 See Bhambra, "The Current Crisis of Europe"; Roxanne Lynn Doty, *Anti-Immigrantism in Western Democracies: Statecraft, Desire, and the Politics of Exclusion* (New York: Taylor & Francis, 2003); and Cecilia Lynch, "The Moral Aporia of Race in International Relations," *International Relations* 33:2 (2019): 267–285.

142 Randolph B. Persaud, "Situating Race in International Relations: The Dialectics of Civilizational Security in American Immigration," in Geeta Chowdhry and Sheila Nair, eds., *Power, Postcolonialism and International Relations: Reading Race, Gender and Class* (New York: Routledge, 2022), 56–81, 66–67.

143 See Darlene Xiomara Rodriguez, Paul N. McDaniel, and Matthew Tikhonovsky, "Human Service Providers' Perspectives on Refugee Resettlement in the United States Before and After the 2016 Presidential Election," *Journal of Immigrant & Refugee Studies* 18:4 (2020): 448–466, and Shoba Sivaprasad Wadhia, *Banned: Immigration Enforcement in the Time of Trump* (New York: New York University Press, 2019).

144 Lipman, *In Camps*, 15. See also the implications of Turkey labeling Syrians "guests" rather than "refugees," and the effects of nomenclature regarding refugee "camps," "settlements," and "individual accommodations" in Uganda. Lamis Abdelaaty, "Refugees and Guesthood in Turkey," *Journal of Refugee Studies* 34:3 (2019): 2827–2848, and Ulrike Krause, *Difficult Life in a Refugee Camp: Gender, Violence, and Coping in Uganda* (New York: Cambridge University Press, 2021).

145 Jenny Phillimore, "Refugee-Integration-Opportunity Structures: Shifting the Focus from Refugees to Context," *Journal of Refugee Studies* 34:2 (2021): 1946–1966, 1954.

146 See Ronald R. Krebs and Jennifer K. Lobasz, "Fixing the Meaning of 9/11: Hegemony, Coercion, and the Road to War in Iraq," *Security Studies* 16:3 (2007): 409–451, 449, and "The Sound of Silence: Rhetorical Coercion, Democratic Acquiescence, and the Iraq War," ch. 7 in A. Trevor Thrall and Jane K. Cramer, eds., *American Foreign Policy and the Politics of Fear: Threat Inflation Since 9/11* (New York: Routledge, 2009), 117–134, 118.

147 See Heba Gowayed, "Resettled and Unsettled: Syrian Refugees and the Intersection of Race and Legal Status in the United States," *Ethnic and Racial Studies* 43:2 (2020): 275–293.

148 These samples of discourse were collected by the author over the course of several years, beginning in 2015 and extending through 2022, predominantly through searches of government documents, online news stories, campaign websites, C-SPAN videos and transcripts, televised events, public blogs and social media accounts, the websites of non-governmental and advocacy organizations, and databases such as *The Congressional Record* and *The American Presidency Project*.
149 Geddes, *Governing Migration*, 6.
150 Matthew Leep, "Specters of Minks: Postcapitalist Elegies and Multispecies Solidarities," *Millennium* 51:1 (2022): 237–260 1–24, 241.
151 Jeremy Pressman, "History in Conflict: Israeli-Palestinian Speeches at the United Nations, 1998–2016," *Mediterranean Politics* 25:4 (2020): 476–498, 482.
152 Dan P. McAdams et al., "Family Metaphors and Moral Intuitions: How Conservatives and Liberals Narrate Their Lives," *Journal of Personality and Social Psychology* 95:4 (2008): 978–990, 979.
153 Tahseen Shams, *Here, There, and Elsewhere: The Making of Immigrant Identities in a Globalized World* (Stanford, CA: Stanford University Press, 2020), 24.
154 Ronald R. Krebs, *Narrative and the Making of U.S. National Security* (New York: Cambridge University Press, 2015), 9.
155 Chavez, *The Latino Threat*, 45.
156 Pressman, "History in Conflict," 481–482.
157 For more on the value of studying party platforms, see Rasmus Sinding Søndergaard, *Reagan, Congress, and Human Rights: Contesting Morality in U.S. Foreign Policy* (New York: Cambridge University Press, 2020), 23.
158 See Julia Azari, "The Platforms Are Windows into the Future of the Parties," *FiveThirtyEight*, July 19, 2016, https://fivethirtyeight.com.
159 See Matthew S. Weinert, *Making Human: World Order and the Global Governance of Human Dignity* (Ann Arbor: University of Michigan Press, 2015), 45.
160 William J. Brady et al., "Emotion Shapes the Diffusion of Moralized Content in Social Networks," *PNAS* 114:28 (2017): 7313–7318, 7317.
161 Interview with Felix Salmon on *The Ezra Klein Show*. See "Elon Musk Might Break Twitter. Maybe That's a Good Thing," *New York Times*, April 29, 2022, www.nytimes.com.
162 See, for example, Paul Goren, Christopher M. Frederico, and Miki Caul Kittilson, "Source Cues, Partisan Identities, and Political Value Expression," *American Journal of Political Science* 53:4 (2009): 805–820; Mark R. Joslyn and Donald P. Haider-Markel, "Should We Really 'Kill' the Messenger? Framing Physician-Assisted Suicide and the Role of Messengers," *Political Communication* 23:1 (2006): 85–103; and Michael W. Wagner and Mike Gruszczynski, "When Framing Matters: How Partisan and Journalistic Frames Affect Individual Opinions and Party Identification," *Journalism & Communication Monographs* 18:1 (2016): 5–48.
163 See Homi K. Bhabha, "Introduction: Narrating the Nation," in Bhabha, ed., *Nation and Narration*, 1–7, 3, and Roxanne Lynn Doty, "Immigration and National Identity: Constructing the Nation," *Review of International Studies* 22:3 (1996): 235–255, 240.

164 Geeta Chowdhry and Sheila Nair, "Introduction," in Chowdhry and Nair, eds., *Power, Postcolonialism and International Relations: Reading Race, Gender and Class* (New York: Routledge, 2002), 1–32, 18–19.

165 See Bhabha, *Nation and Narration*, and Doty, *Imperial Encounters*. See also Arendt's point that the meaning of "refugee" changed in the context of the Jewish diaspora in the 1940s, and Fassin's discussion of how refugees and asylum policies were redefined in France between the 1970s and 1990s. Arendt, "We Refugees," and Didier Fassin, "Truth Ordeal: Attesting Violence for Asylum Seekers," in *Humanitarian Reason*, 109–130.

166 Matthew Leep, "Toxic Entanglements: Multispecies Politics, White Phosphorous, and the Iraq War in Alaska," *Review of International Studies* 49:2 (2023): 258–277, 264.

167 Doty, *Anti-Immigrantism in Western Democracies*, 7.

168 As Krebs and Jackson note, the language elites use can influence political outcomes regardless of individual-level motivations. Ronald R. Krebs and Patrick Thaddeus Jackson, "Twisting Tongues and Twisting Arms: The Power of Political Rhetoric," *European Journal of International Relations* 13:1 (2007): 35–66, 42.

169 Yến Lê Espiritu, *Home Bound: Filipino American Lives across Cultures, Communities, and Countries* (Berkeley: University of California Press, 2003), 207.

170 Krebs, *Narrative and the Making of U.S. National Security*, 3.

171 See Betts, "Introduction: Global Migration Governance," 3, and Cameron, *Send Them Here*, 8.

172 Most studies on refugee and asylum policy do not concentrate on discourse. It is notable that Demmer emphasizes the central role played by members of Congress in crafting US policy toward Vietnamese refugees and highlights the power of particular frames around "moral obligations" and "human rights." Previous studies by Pécoud and Geddes have more broadly elevated the importance of narratives and interpretations, focusing on the role of international organizations and regional repertoires, respectively. Cameron sheds light on the role of religious and voluntary NGOs, while Farris, Halabi, and Mohamed underscore the importance of media coverage in shaping understandings of refugees and immigrants. See Cameron, *Send Them Here*; Demmer, *After Saigon's Fall*; Heather Silber Mohamed and Emily M. Farris, "'Bad Hombres'? An Examination of Identities in U.S. Media Coverage of Immigration," *Journal of Ethnic and Migration Studies* 46:1 (2020): 158–176; Geddes, *Governing Migration*; Nour Halabi, *Radical Hospitality: American Policy, Media, and Immigration* (New Brunswick, NJ: Rutgers University Press, 2023); and Pécoud, *Depoliticising Migration*.

173 Utrzan et al., "A Needs and Readiness Assessment," 7.

174 See Jennifer McCoy and Murat Somer, "Toward a Theory of Pernicious Polarization and How It Harms Democracies: Comparative Evidence and Possible Remedies," *ANNALS of the American Academy of Political and Social Science* 681:1 (2019): 234–271, and Aaron C. Weinschenk, Costas Panagopoulos, and Sander van der Linden, "Democratic Norms, Social Projection, and False Consensus in the

2020 U.S. Presidential Election," *Journal of Political Marketing* 20:3–4 (2021): 255–268.
175 See, for example, Drew DeSilver, "U.S. Public Seldom Has Welcomed Refugees Into Country," *Pew Research Center*, November 19, 2015, www.pewresearch.org.
176 Mariano Sana, "Public Opinion on Refugee Policy in the United States, 1938–2019," *International Migration Review* 55:2 (2021): 574–604.
177 Interview with Dara Lind on *The Weeds*. See "Immigration, Democracy, and the Rise of the Western Far Right," *Vox*, May 24, 2022, www.vox.com.
178 See, for example, Boochani, *No Friend but the Mountains*; Cameron, *Send Them Here*; Sara de Jong, "Resettling Afghan and Iraqi Interpreters Employed by Western Armies: The Contradictions of the Migration-Security Nexus," *Security Dialogue* 53:3 (2022): 220–237; Demmer, *After Saigon's Fall*; Gatrell, *The Making of the Modern Refugee*; Georgios Giannakopoulos, "Depicting the Pain of Others: Photographic Representations of Refugees in the Aegean Shores," *Journal of Greek Media & Culture* 2:1 (2016): 103–113; Halabi, *Radical Hospitality*; Richard Hugman, Eileen Pittaway, and Linda Bartolomei, "When 'Do No Harm' Is Not Enough: The Ethics of Research with Refugees and Other Vulnerable Groups," *British Journal of Social Work* 41:7 (2011), 1271–1287; Irfan, *Refuge and Resistance*; Pécoud, *Depoliticising Migration*; Ellen Reichel, "Navigating between Refugee Protection and State Sovereignty," in Klaus Dingwerth et al., eds., *International Organizations Under Pressure: Legitimating Global Governance in Challenging Times* (New York: Oxford University Press, 2019), 195–231; Warsan Shire, *Bless the Daughter Raised by a Voice in Her Head: Poems* (New York: Random House, 2022); and Shull, *Detention Empire*.
179 See Alexi Peristianis, "Syrian Refugee Artist," *BBC*, October 30, 2017, www.bbc.com; Camila Domonoske, "After Surviving Aegean Sea, Syrian Swimmer Hopes for Spot in Olympics," *NPR*, March 20, 2016, www.npr.org; "Treating the Trauma of Young Syrian Refugees," *New York Times*, October 12, 2015, www.nytimes.com; and Killian Fox, "The 13-Year-Old Syrian Refugee Who Became a Prizewinning Poet," *The Guardian*, October 1, 2017, www.theguardian.com.
180 Madeline O. Campbell, *Interpreters of Occupation: Gender and the Politics of Belonging in an Iraqi Refugee Network* (Syracuse, NY: Syracuse University Press, 2016), 64.
181 See, for instance, the work of Somali refugee women resettled in Wisconsin in Bisharo Abdullahi et al., *The First Winter* (Green Bay, WI: Two Shrews Press, 2019) and a series of public events hosted by the United ReSisters of Green Bay, www.unitedresisters.com. Other examples include media interviews, events, and editorials by Vietnamese refugee Anh "Joseph" Cao and Liberian refugee Wilmot Collins—both of whom were resettled in the United States and elected to political office.
182 See David Coury, "Giving Immigrants a Voice: Exploring Migration and Identity in the Video Series Germania," *Papeles del CEIC* 2 (2022): 1–17; Heather L. Johnson, "Narrating Entanglements: Rethinking the Local/Global Divide in Ethnographic Migration Research," *International Political Sociology* 10:4 (2016): 383–397; and Nguyen, ed., *The Displaced*.

183 Banerjee, "Re-Theorizing Human Rights through the Refugee," 33.
184 Halabi, *Radical Hospitality*, 23. See also Sadeghi's discussion of the myths associated with "immigrant America" as a "colorblind" society and "nation of many nations." Sahar Sadeghi, *Conditional Belonging: The Racialization of Iranians in the Wake of Anti-Muslim Politics* (New York: New York University Press, 2023).
185 Abani, "The Road," 27.
186 Evyn Lê Espiritu Gandhi, *Archipelago of Resettlement: Vietnamese Refugee Settlers and Decolonization across Guam and Israel-Palestine* (Oakland: University of California Press, 2022), 4.
187 Phil Zuckerman, ed., *The Social Theory of W.E.B. Du Bois* (Thousand Oaks, CA: Sage, 2004), 26.
188 Kevin Kenny, *The Problem of Immigration in a Slaveholding Republic: Policing Mobility in the 19th-Century United States* (New York: Oxford University Press, 2023), 14.
189 See, for example, Carl J. Bon Tempo and Hasia R. Diner, *Immigration: An American History* (New Haven, CT: Yale University Press, 2022); Noelle Brigden, *The Migrant Passage: Clandestine Journeys from Central America* (Ithaca, NY: Cornell University Press, 2018); Jason De León, *The Land of Open Graves: Living and Dying on the Migrant Trail* (Oakland: University of California Press, 2015); García, *Legal Passing*; Pratheepan Gulasekaram and S. Karthick Ramakrishnan, *The New Immigration Federalism* (New York: Cambridge University Press, 2015); S. Deborah Kang, *The INS on the Line: Making Immigration Law on the US-Mexico Border, 1917–1954* (New York: Oxford University Press, 2017); Anna O. Law, *The Immigration Battle in American Courts* (New York: Cambridge University Press, 2010); Andrea Silva, "Direct-Democracy Rules: The Effect of Direct Democracy on State Immigration Legislation," *PS: Political Science & Politics* 51:2 (2018): 298–303; Abigail Fisher Williamson, *Welcoming New Americans? Local Government and Immigrant Incorporation* (Chicago: University of Chicago Press, 2018); and Jia Lynn Yang, *One Mighty and Irresistible Tide* (Durham, NC: Carolina Academic Press, 2020).
190 See, for example, Abdelaaty, *Discrimination and Delegation*; Fiona B. Adamson and Gerasimos Tsourapas, "The Migration State in the Global South: Nationalizing, Developmental, and Neoliberal Models of Migration Management," *International Migration Review* 54:3 (2020): 853–882; Haya Al-Dajani, Maysa Baroud, and Nasser Yassin, *Refugee Resilience and Adaptation in the Middle East: Reclaiming Agency in the Informal Economies of Lebanon and Jordan* (New York: Routledge, 2023); Betts, "From Persecution to Deprivation"; Clayton Boeyink, "Deconstructing the Migrant/Refugee/Host Ternary in Kigoma, Tanzania: Toward a Borderland Politics of Solidarity and Reparation," *Journal of Immigrant & Refugee Studies* 20:2 (2022): 240–252; Katarzyna Grabska, "Marginalization in Urban Spaces of the Global South: Urban Refugees in Cairo," *Journal of Refugee Studies* 19:3 (2006): 287–307; Nicholas Maple, "Rights at Risk: A Thematic Investigation into How States Restrict the Freedom of Movement of Refugees on the African Continent," *New Issues in Refugee Research, Research Paper No. 281* (2016); Lama Mourad, "Brothers, Workers or Syrians? The Politics of Naming in Lebanese Municipali-

ties," *Journal of Refugee Studies* 34:2 (2021): 1387–1399; Khangelani Moyo and Franzisca Zanker, "No Hope for the 'Foreigners': The Conflation of Refugees and Migrants in South Africa," *Journal of Immigrant & Refugee Studies* 20:2 (2022): 253–265; Mehmet Gökay Özerim and Juliette Tolay, "Discussing the Populist Features of Anti-Refugee Discourses on Social Media: An Anti-Syrian Hashtag in Turkish Twitter," *Journal of Refugee Studies* 34:1 (2021): 204–218; and Katharina Natter, *The Politics of Immigration Beyond Liberal States: Morocco and Tunisia in Comparative Perspective* (New York: Cambridge University Press, 2023).

191 "Resettlement in the United States," *UNHCR*, January 2018, www.unhcr.org.
192 "Refugee Admissions by Region: Fiscal Year 1975 through May 31, 2018," *U.S. Department of State—Refugee Processing Center*, June 30, 2018, www.wrapsnet.org.
193 "U.S. Annual Refugee Resettlement Ceilings and Number of Refugees Admitted, 1980–Present."
194 Anastasia Brown and Todd Scribner, "Unfulfilled Promises, Future Possibilities: The Refugee Resettlement System in the United States," *Journal on Migration and Human Security* 2:2 (2014): 101–120, 102.
195 Daniel J. Tichenor, *Dividing Lines: The Politics of Immigration Control in America* (Princeton, NJ: Princeton University Press, 2002), 22.
196 Irfan, *Refuge and Resistance*, 10; Gil Loescher, *Refugees: A Very Short Introduction* (New York: Oxford University Press, 2021), 6, and "The International Refugee Regime: Stretched to the Limit?," *Journal of International Affairs* 47:2 (1994): 351–377; and Astri Suhrke and Adèle Garnier, "The Moral Economy of the Resettlement Regime," in Adèle Garnier, Liliana Lyra Jubilut, and Kristin Bergtora Sandvik, eds., *Refugee Resettlement: Power, Politics, and Humanitarian Governance* (New York: Berghahn Books, 2018), 244–252.
197 Gil Loescher and James Milner, "UNHCR and the Global Governance of Refugees," in Betts, ed., *Global Migration Governance*, 189–209, 202.
198 Ferris and Donato, *Refugees, Migration and Global Governance*, 2.
199 See Cameron, *Send Them Here*, 5, and Suhrke and Garnier, "The Moral Economy of the Resettlement Regime," 247.
200 Sabrineh Ardalan, "The Trump Administration, COVID-19, and the Continuing Assault on the Rights of Asylum Seekers and Refugees," *International Journal of Refugee Law* 32:4 (2020): 685–689; Coen, "International Order, the Rule of Law, and U.S. Departures from Refugee Protection"; and Fee and Arar, "What Happens When the United States Stops Taking in Refugees?."
201 See Julia Black and Zoe Sigman, "50,000 Lives Lost During Migration: Analysis of Missing Migrants Project Data 2014–2022," *International Organization for Migration*, 2022, https://missingmigrants.iom.int; Noah Coburn, "The Costs of Working with the Americans in Afghanistan: The United States' Broken Special Immigrant Visa Process," *Costs of War*, April 5, 2021, https://watson.brown.edu; and De León, *The Land of Open Graves*.
202 Glanville, *Sharing Responsibility*, 158.

203 See Charles B. Keely, "The International Refugee Regime(s): The End of the Cold War Matters," *International Migration Review* 31:1 (2001): 303-314, and Stephen Macekura, "'For Fear of Persecution': Displaced Salvadorans and U.S. Refugee Policy in the 1980s," *Journal of Policy History* 23:3 (2011): 357-380.
204 Gowayed, *Refuge*, 3.
205 Aihwa Ong, "Cultural Citizenship as Subject-Making," *Current Anthropology* 37:5 (1996): 737-762, 742.
206 This is not to suggest a complete absence of partisanship. Divisions among lawmakers during the Reagan administration regarding refugee admissions from Central America, for example, frequently unfolded along partisan lines. See Carl J. Bon Tempo, *Americans at the Gate: The United States and Refugees during the Cold War* (Princeton, NJ: Princeton University Press, 2008).
207 See Bon Tempo, *Americans at the Gate*; Rebecca Hamlin, *Let Me Be a Refugee: Administrative Justice and the Politics of Asylum in the United States, Canada, and Australia* (New York: Oxford University Press, 2014); Law, *The Immigration Battle in American Courts*; and Tichenor, *Dividing Lines*.
208 See Christopher H. Achen and Larry M. Bartels, *Democracy for Realists: Why Elections Do Not Produce Responsive Government* (Princeton, NJ: Princeton University Press, 2017); Philip Edward Jones and Paul R. Brewer, "Elite Cues and Public Polarization on Transgender Rights," *Politics, Groups, and Identities* 8:1 (2020): 71-85; McCoy and Somer, "Toward a Theory of Pernicious Polarization and How It Harms Democracies"; Stephen P. Nicholson, "Polarizing Cues," *American Journal of Political Science* 56:1 (2012): 52-66; Hans Noel, "Ideology and Its Discombobulations," *Journal of Politics* 81:3 (2019): e57-e61; and Sam Rosenfeld, *The Polarizers: Postwar Architects of Our Partisan Era* (Chicago: University of Chicago Press, 2017).
209 In the Turkish context, for example, Özerim and Tolay describe anti-refugee discourses animated by "leaderless" manifestations of populism. "Discussing the Populist Features of Anti-Refugee Discourses on Social Media." In the German context, Sadeghi finds that racialization dynamics are less intertwined with foreign policy and more connected to lingering German nationalism. See Sadeghi, *Conditional Belonging*.
210 In the British context, for instance, Statham and Geddes describe immigration politics as elite-led, highly institutionalized, and characterized by relatively weak civil society engagement. Paul Statham and Andrew Geddes, "Elites and the 'Organized Public': Who Drives British Immigration Politics and In Which Direction?," *West European Politics* 29:2 (2006): 248-269. In the context of Western Europe, a wide variety of choices in political parties and party system dynamics impact the manifestation of populist and nativist rhetoric. See Pontus Odmalm and Eve Hepburn, eds., *The European Mainstream and the Populist Radical Rights* (New York: Routledge, 2017).
211 See Fernando G. Nuñez-Mietz and Lucrecia García Iommi, "Can Transnational Norm Advocacy Undermine Internalization? Explaining Immunization against LGBT Rights in Uganda," *International Studies Quarterly* 61:1 (2017): 196-209, 201.

212 Labman, *Crossing Law's Border*, 160.
213 Cameron and Labman, "The Dynamics and Divergences of Executive Discretion in Refugee Resettlement."
214 See Joseph Kertes, "Second Country," in Nguyen, ed., *The Displaced*, 113–120, 119, and Eric Taylor Woods, "Beyond Multination Federalism: Reflections on Nations and Nationalism in Canada," *Ethnicities* 12:3 (2012): 270–292.
215 See Gruminder K. Bhambra, "On the Politics of Selective Memory in Europe," ch. 8 in Christopher Whitehead, Susannah Eckersley, Mads Daugbjerg, and Gönül Bozoglu, eds., *Dimensions of Heritage and Memory: Multiple Europes and the Politics of Crisis* (New York: Routledge, 2019), 172–181; William Chiu, "Refugees and Asylum," in Wayne Sandholtz and Kendall Stiles, eds., *International Norms and Cycles of Change* (Oxford, UK: Oxford University Press, 2009), 237–262, 256–257; Geddes, *Governing Migration*; Silja Klepp, "A Contested Asylum System: The European Union between Refugee Protection and Border Control in the Mediterranean Sea," *European Journal of Migration and Law* 12:1 (2010): 1–21; and David Owen, "Refugees, EU Citizenship and the Common European Asylum System: A Normative Dilemma for EU Integration," *Ethical Theory and Moral Practice* 22:2 (2019): 347–369.
216 See Sari Hanafi, "Forced Migration in the Middle East and North Africa," in Fiddian-Qasmiyeh et al., eds., *The Oxford Handbook of Refugee and Forced Migration Studies*, 585–598; Audie Klotz, "Borders and the Roots of Xenophobia in South Africa," *South Africa Historical Journal* 68: 2 (2016): 180–194; Mahmood Mamdani, *Citizen and Subject: Contemporary Africa and the Legacy of Late Colonialism* (Princeton, NJ: Princeton University Press, 1998/2018); and Sabelo Ndlovu-Gatsheni, "Africa for Africans or Africa for 'Natives' Only? 'New Nationalism' and Nativism in Zimbabwe and South Africa," *Africa Spectrum* 44:1 (2009): 61–78.
217 Sandholtz and Stiles, *International Norms*, 13–14.
218 Geddes notes, for example, the strong influence of the United States on regional repertoires of migration governance in North America. *Governing Migration*, 145. Relatedly, Bon Tempo and Diner point out that US immigration history is deeply intertwined with the country's historical status as a continental and overseas empire. *Immigration*, 8.
219 See Reece Jones, *Violent Borders: Refugees and the Right to Move* (New York: Verso, 2017), 68–69, and Daniel Ghezelbash, *Refuge Lost: Asylum Law in an Interdependent World* (New York: Cambridge University Press, 2018).
220 See John Haltiwanger, "Who Is Jair Bolsonaro? Meet Brazil's Version of Donald Trump," *Business Insider*, March 19, 2019, www.businessinsider.com, and Jared P. Van Ramshorts, "Anti-Immigrant Sentiment, Rising Populism, and the Oaxacan Trump," *Journal of Latin American Geography* 17:1 (2018): 253–256.
221 See Manuela Caiani, Donatella della Porta, and Claudius Wagemann, *Mobilizing on the Extreme Right: Germany, Italy, and the United States* (Oxford, UK: Oxford University Press, 2012); Marie Demker and Pontus Odmalm, "From Governmental Success to Governmental Breakdown: How a New Dimension of Conflict Tore Apart the Politics of Migration of the Swedish Centre-Right," *Journal of Ethnic*

and Migration Studies 48:2 (2021): 425–440; Pietro Castelli Gattinara, "The Far Right as Social Movement," *European Societies* 21:4 (2019): 447–462; Raffael Heiss and Jörg Matthes, "Stuck in a Nativist Spiral: Content, Selection, and Effects of Right-Wing Populists' Communication on Facebook," *Political Communication* 37:3 (2020): 303–328; Naoto Higuchi, *Japan's Ultra-Right* (Victoria, Australia: Trans Pacific Press, 2016); Catarina Kinnvall, "Populism, Ontological Insecurity and Hindutva: Modi and the Masculinization of Indian Politics," *Cambridge Review of International Affairs* 32:3 (2019): 283–302; and M. J. Tudor, "India's Nationalism in Historical Perspective: The Democratic Dangers of Ascendant Nativism," *India Politics and Policy* 1:1 (2018): 107–130.

222 See Clifford Bob, *The Global Right Wing and the Clash of World Politics* (New York: Cambridge University Press, 2012); Geddes, *Governing Migration*; and Alexander Betts, Fulya Memişoğlu, and Ali Ali, "What Difference Do Mayors Make? The Role of Municipal Authorities in Turkey and Lebanon's Response to Syrian Refugees," *Journal of Refugee Studies* 34:1 (2021): 491–519.

223 Steven L. B. Jensen, *The Making of International Human Rights: The 1960s, Decolonization and the Reconstruction of Global Values* (New York: Cambridge University Press, 2016), 22–23.

224 See Ghassan Hage, *Is Racism an Environmental Threat?* (Malden, MA: Polity Press, 2017).

225 See Randa Abdel-Fattah, "Islamophobia and Australian Muslim Political Consciousness in the War on Terror," *Journal of Intercultural Studies* 38:4 (2017): 397–411; Damian Breen and Nasar Meer, "Securing Whiteness? Critical Race Theory (CRT) and the Securitization of Muslims in Education," *Identities: Global Studies in Culture and Power* 26:5 (2019): 595–613; and Swati Parashar, "Terrorism and the Postcolonial 'State,'" in Olivia U. Rutazibwa and Robbie Shilliam, eds., *Routledge Handbook of Postcolonial Politics* (New York: Routledge, 2018), 110–125.

226 Melissa Schnyder and Noha Shawki, *Advocating for Refugees in the European Union: Norm Based Strategies by Civil Society Organizations* (Lanham, MD: Lexington Books, 2020).

227 See Ishan Ashutosh and Alison Mountz, "The Geopolitics of Migrant Mobility: Tracing State Relations Through Refugee Claims, Boats, and Discourses," *Geopolitics* 17:2 (2012): 335–354, 349; Christina Boswell and Andrew Geddes, *Migration and Mobility in the European Union* (New York: Palgrave Macmillan, 2011), 157–158; Fassin, *Humanitarian Reason*, 110; Alexandria J. Innes, "When the Threatened Become the Threat: The Construction of Asylum Seekers in British Media Narratives," *International Relations* 24:4 (2010): 456–477; Labman, *Crossing Law's Border*, 78; Eric Neumayer, "Bogus Refugees? The Determinants of Asylum Migration to Europe," *International Studies Quarterly* 49:3 (2005): 389–409; and Susan E. Zimmermann, "Reconsidering the Problem of 'Bogus' Refugees with 'Socio-Economic Motivations' for Seeking Asylum," in Nick Gill, Javier Caletrío, and Victoria Mason, eds., *Mobilities and Forced Migration* (New York: Routledge, 2014), 35–52.

228 See Jeffrey Crisp, "Mind the Gap! UNHCR, Humanitarian Assistance and the Development Process," *International Migration Review* 35:1 (2001): 168–191; Evan Easton-Calabria and Naohiko Omata, "Panacea for the Refugee Crisis? Rethinking the Promotion of 'Self-Reliance' for Refugees," *Third World Quarterly* 39:8 (2018): 1458–1474; Elena Fiddian-Qasmiyeh, "Paradoxes of Sahrawi Refugees' Educational Migration: Promoting Self-Sufficiency or Renewing Dependency," *Comparative Education* 47:4 (2011): 433–447; and Krause, *Difficult Life in a Refugee Camp*.

229 Klepp, for example, describes the ascendance of a migration control discourse in the 1990s disseminated by international organizations like the UNHCR and IOM as well as transnational NGOs, and Pécoud describes broader international migration narratives that emphasize the need for states to "manage" their borders and keep migration "under control." See Klepp, "A Contested Asylum System," 8, and Pécoud, "Narrating an Ideal Migration World," 24. See also FitzGerald's point that "security has become a master frame" for discussions of refugees and asylum in Europe. *Refuge Beyond Reach*, 13.

230 Constance MacIntosh, "Insecure Refugees: The Narrowing of Asylum-Seeker Rights to Freedom of Movement and Claims Determination Post 9/11 in Canada," *Review of Constitutional Studies* 16:2 (2012): 181–209, 182.

231 Rey Koslowski, *Migrants and Citizens: Demographic Change in the European State System* (Ithaca, NY: Cornell University Press, 2000), 161.

232 Ayten Gündogdu, *Rightlessness in an Age of Rights: Hannah Arendt and the Contemporary Struggles of Migrants* (Oxford, UK: Oxford University Press, 2015), 109.

233 See Roxanne Lynn Doty, "Immigration and the Politics of Security," *Security Studies* 8:2–3 (1998): 71–93; Alison Gerard, *The Securitization of Migration and Refugee Women* (New York: Routledge, 2014); Boswell and Geddes, *Migration and Mobility*, 163; and Peter E. Mulherin and Benjamin Isakhan, "The Abbott Government and the Islamic State: A Securitized and Elitist Foreign Policy Discourse," *Australian Journal of Political Science* 54:1 (2019): 82–98, 91.

234 Jeff Crisp, *The State of the World's Refugees: Crisis or Progress?* Presentation for the Blavatnik School of Government, University of Oxford, June 6, 2019. Copy shared with author June 19, 2019. See also Mayblin and Turner, *Migration Studies and Colonialism*, 2.

235 Chimni, "The Geopolitics of Refugee Studies." Racialized emphases on "unprecedented crisis" also perpetuate logics of colonial advantage embedded in international and bilateral agreements. See E. Tendayi Achiume, "Reimagining International Law for Global Migration: Migration as Decolonization," *American Society of International Law* 111 (2017): 142–146.

236 See Coen, "Localizing Refugeehood," and Geddes, *Governing Migration*, 170–171.

237 The extent to which post-9/11 declines in refugee admissions were an intended goal of the administrative restructuring is debatable, but it is noteworthy that the annual refugee admissions ceilings remained at 70,000 throughout those years.

238 See Tiffany Chu, "Hosting Your Enemy: Accepting Refugees from a Rival State and Respect for Human Rights," *Journal of Global Security Studies* 5:1 (2020): 4–24;

Marina Kaneti and H. Howell Williams, "Political, Ethnic, Religious, and Gender-Related Persecution," in James Ciment and John Radzilowski, eds., *American Immigration: An Encyclopedia of Political, Social, and Cultural Change* (New York: Routledge, 2014): 32–39; Keely, "The International Refugee Regime(s)"; Nicholas R. Micinski, "Refugee Policy as Foreign Policy: Iraqi and Afghan Refugee Resettlements to the United States," *Refugee Survey Quarterly* 37:3 (2018): 253–278, and "Threats, Deportability and Aid: The Politics of Refugee Rentier States and Regional Stability," *Security Dialogue* (2021), DOI: 10.1177/09670106211027464; Larry Nackerud et al., "The End of the Cuban Contradiction in U.S. Refugee Policy," *International Migration Review* 33:1 (1999): 176–192; and Norman L. Zucker and Naomi Flink Zucker, "The Uneasy Troika in US Refugee Policy: Foreign Policy, Pressure Groups, and Resettlement Costs," *Journal of Refugee Studies* 2:3 (1989): 359–372.

239 See David S. FitzGerald and David Cook-Martín, *Culling the Masses: The Democratic Origins of Racist Immigration Policy in the Americas* (Cambridge, MA: Harvard University Press, 2014); Jeremy Hein, *States and International Migrants: The Incorporation of Indochinese Refugees in the United States and France* (New York: Routledge, 1993); Eszter Kovács, "The Power of Second-Generation Diaspora: Hungarian Ethnic Lobbying in the United States in the 1970s–1980s," *Diaspora Studies* 11:2 (2018): 171–188; and Zucker and Zucker, "The Uneasy Troika."

240 Rebecca Hamlin and Philip E. Wolgin, "Symbolic Politics and Policy Feedback: The United Nations Protocol Relating to the Status of Refugees and American Refugee Policy in the Cold War," *International Migration Review* 46:3 (2012): 596–624.

241 See García, *The Refugee Challenge*, and Lipman, *In Camps*.

242 See Cameron and Labman, "The Dynamics and Divergences of Executive Discretion in Refugee Resettlement"; Franz Eder, "Making Concurrence-Seeking Visible: Groupthink, Discourse Networks, and the 2003 Iraq War," *Foreign Policy Analysis* 15:1 (2019): 21–42; Rebecca Hamlin, "Illegal Refugees: Competing Policy Ideas and the Rise of the Regime of Deterrence in American Asylum Politics," *Refugee Survey Quarterly* 31:2 (2012): 33–53, 40; and Wadhia, *Banned*, 100.

243 Bon Tempo, *Americans at the Gate*, 2.

244 Note that Bon Tempo offers an important exploration of how refugees were understood through anticommunist identity conceptualizations and Cameron offers a valuable analysis of how religious groups elevated humanitarian discourse around refugees. See Bon Tempo, *Americans at the Gate*, and Cameron, *Send Them Here*.

245 See Monika Gosin, *The Racial Politics of Division: Interethnic Struggles for Legitimacy in Multicultural Miami* (Ithaca, NY: Cornell University Press, 2019), and Mayblin and Turner, *Migration Studies and Colonialism*, 65.

246 See Maria Eriksson Baaz and Judith Verweijen, "Confronting the Colonial: The (Re)production of 'African' Exceptionalism in Critical Security and Military Studies," *Security Dialogue* 49:1–2 (2018): 57–69, 59, and Homi K. Bhabha, *The Location of Culture* (New York: Routledge, 1994).

247 See Benjamin R. Banta, "Just War Theory and the 2003 Iraq War Forced Displacement," *Journal of Refugee Studies* 21:3 (2008): 261–284; Michael Barutciski and

Astri Suhrke, "Lessons from the Kosovo Refugee Crisis: Innovations in Protection and Burden-Sharing," *Journal of Refugee Studies* 14: 2 (2001): 95–134; Alexander Betts and Jean-Francois Durieux, "Convention Plus as a Norm-Setting Exercise," *Journal of Refugee Studies* 20:3 (2007): 509–535; Jamie Draper, "Domination and Misframing in the Refugee Regime," *Critical Review of International Social and Political Philosophy* 25:7 (2022): 939–962; Gibney, "Refugees and Justice"; Kritzman-Amir, "Not In My Backyard"; Owen, *What Do We Owe To Refugees?*; and James Souter, "Towards a Theory of Asylum as Reparation for Past Injustice," *Political Studies* 62:2 (2014): 326–342.

248 See Alexander Betts, "Public Goods Theory and the Provision of Refugee Protection: The Role of the Joint-Product Model in Burden-Sharing Theory," *Journal of Refugee Studies* 16:3 (2003): 274–296; Anja Klug, "Strengthening the Protection of Migrants and Refugees in Distress at Sea through International Cooperation and Burden-Sharing," *International Journal of Refugee Law* 26:1 (2014): 48–64; Gregor Noll, "Risky Games? A Theoretical Approach to Burden-Sharing in the Asylum Field," *Journal of Refugee Studies* 16:3 (2003): 236–252; W. Courtland Robinson, "The Comprehensive Plan of Action for Indochinese Refugees, 1989–1997: Sharing the Burden and Passing the Buck," *Journal of Refugee Studies* 17:3 (2004): 319–333; Suhrke, "Burden-Sharing during Refugee Emergencies"; Eiko R. Thielemann, "Between Interests and Norms: Explaining Burden-Sharing in the European Union," *Journal of Refugee Studies* 16:3 (2003): 253–273; and Emek M. Ucarer, "Burden-Shirking, Burden-Shifting, and Burden-Sharing in the Emergent European Asylum Regime," *International Politics* 43:2 (2006): 219–240.

249 See FitzGerald, *Refuge Beyond Reach*, and Ghezelbash, *Refuge Lost*.

250 See Abdelaaty, *Discrimination and Delegation*, and "Rivalry, Ethnicity, and Asylum Admissions Worldwide," *International Relations* 47:2 (2020): 346–373; Micinski, "Threats, Deportability and Aid"; and Zeynep Şahin-Mencütek and Gerasimos Tsourapas, "When Do States Repatriate Refugees? Evidence from the Middle East," *Journal of Global Security Studies* 8:1 (2023): 1–18.

251 See, for example, Laura Barnett, "Global Governance and the Evolution of the International Refugee Regime," *International Journal of Refugee Law* 14:2/3 (2002): 238–262; Alexander Betts, "The Refugee Regime Complex," *Refugee Survey Quarterly* 29:1 (2010): 12–37; and Bimal Ghosh, ed., *Managing Migration: Time for a New International Regime?* (New York: Oxford University Press, 2000).

252 See Banerjee and Smith, eds., *Migration Governance in North America*, and Geddes, *Governing Migration*.

253 John G. Ruggie, "Global Governance and 'New Governance Theory': Lessons from Business and Human Rights," *Global Governance* 20:1 (2014): 5–17, 8–10. Note that Acharya emphasizes normative frameworks as "bottom-up processes." See Amitav Acharya, "Norm Subsidiarity and Regional Orders: Sovereignty, Regionalism, and Rule-Making in the Third World," *International Studies Quarterly* 55:1 (2011): 95–123.

254 See Christina Boswell, "Burden-Sharing in the European Union: Lessons from the German and UK Experience," *Journal of Refugee Studies* 16:3 (2003): 316–335;

Sieglinde Rosenberger and Alexadra König, "Welcoming the Unwelcome: The Politics of Minimum Reception Standards for Asylum Seekers in Austria," *Journal of Refugee Studies* 25:4 (2011): 537–554; and Joanne Thorburn, "Transcending Boundaries: Temporary Protection and Burden-Sharing in Europe," *International Journal of Refugee Law* 7:3 (1995): 459–480.

255 See Cameron, *Send Them Here*; Meryll Dean and Miki Nagashima, "Sharing the Burden: The Role of Government and NGOs in Protecting and Providing for Asylum Seekers and Refugees in Japan," *Journal of Refugee Studies* 20:3 (2007): 481–508; Jessica Eby, Erika Iverson, Jennifer Smyers, and Erol Kekic, "The Faith Community's Role in Refugee Resettlement in the United States," *Journal of Refugee Studies* 24:3 (2011): 586–605; and Hamlin and Wolgin, "Symbolic Politics." The role of domestic parliamentary debates in generating support for refugees is also briefly addressed by Amanda Cellini in "The Resettlement of Hungarian Refugees in 1956," *Forced Migration Review* 54 (2017): 6–8.

256 See Cynthia Gorman, "Redefining Refugees: Interpretive Control and the Bordering Work of Legal Categorization in U.S. Asylum Law," *Political Geography* 58 (2017): 36–45, and Emma Haddad, *The Refugee in International Society: Between Sovereigns* (New York: Cambridge University Press, 2008).

257 It is noteworthy that Ilgit and Klotz explore discursive representations of refugees in the context of securitization and collective identity, focusing primarily on German national identity. Asli Ilgit and Audie Klotz, "Refugee Rights or Refugees as Threats? Germany's New Asylum Policy," *BJPIR* 20:3 (2018): 613–631. See also an exploration of how memories of migration have shaped the "rewriting" of Turkish national identity narratives in Juliette Tolay, "Rewriting National Narratives through the Study of Past Migrations: Turkey's History of Migrations," *Ethnopolitics* 17:2 (2018): 201–221.

258 See Errol A. Henderson, "Hidden in Plain Sight: Racism in International Relations Theory," *Cambridge Review of International Affairs* 26:1 (2013): 71–92, and Robert Vitalis, *White World Order, Black Power Politics: The Birth of American International Relations* (Ithaca, NY: Cornell University Press, 2015). See also Sankaran Krishna, "Race, Amnesia, and the Education of International Relations," *Alternatives* 26:4 (2001): 401–424.

259 Coen, "Can't Be Held Responsible."

260 For a foundational theory of norms in IR, see Martha Finnemore and Kathryn Sikkink, "International Norm Dynamics and Political Change," *International Organization* 52:4 (1998): 887–917. For subsequent critiques of this model and efforts to unpack the fluidity and non-linear evolution of norms, see Amitav Acharya, "How Ideas Spread: Whose Norms Matter? Norm Localization and Institutional Change in Asian Regionalism," *International Organization* 58:2 (2004): 239–275; Betts and Orchard, eds., *Implementation and World Politics*; Matthew J. Hoffmann, "Norms and Social Constructivism in International Relations," in Robert Denemark et al., eds., *International Studies Encyclopedia* (Oxford, UK: Wiley-Blackwell, 2010/2017), 1–23; Mona Lena Krook and Jacqui True, "Rethinking the Life Cycles of Interna-

tional Norms: The United Nations and the Global Promotion of Gender Equality," *European Journal of International Relations* 18:1 (2010): 103–27, 107; and Antje Wiener, *A Theory of Contestation* (New York: Springer, 2014).

261 See Kiran Banerjee and Craig Damian Smith, "International Relations and Migration: Mobility as Norm Rather Than Exception," in Jamie Levin, ed., *Nomad–State Relationships in International Relations: Before and After Borders* (Cham, CH: Palgrave Macmillan, 2020), 265–281, and Chimni, "The Birth of a 'Discipline.'"

262 See Fiona B. Adamson, "Pushing the Boundaries: Can We 'Decolonize' Security Studies?," *Journal of Global Security Studies* 5:1 (2020): 129–135, 131, and Persaud, "Situating Race in International Relations," 79.

263 See Matthew J. Gibney, *The Ethics and Politics of Asylum: Liberal Democracy and the Response to Refugees* (New York: Cambridge University Press, 2004). See also Micinski's discussion of the literature on how liberal democracies respond to refugees in "Threats, Deportability and Aid."

264 See Ted Brader, Nicholas A. Valentino, and Elizabeth Suhay, "What Triggers Public Opposition to Immigration? Anxiety, Group Cues, and Immigration Threat," *American Journal of Political Science* 52:4 (2008): 959–978; Victoria M. Esses, Leah K. Hamilton, and Danielle Gaucher, "The Global Refugee Crisis: Empirical Evidence and Policy Implications for Improving Public Attitudes and Facilitating Refugee Resettlement," *Social Issues and Policy Review* 11:1 (2017): 78–123, 104–105; René Flores, "Can Elites Shape Public Attitudes Toward Immigrants? Evidence from the 2016 U.S. Presidential Election," *Social Forces* 96:4 (2018): 1649–1690; Halabi, *Radical Hospitality*; and Innes, "When the Threatened Become the Threat."

265 Jocelyn Vaughn and Tim Dunne, "Leading from the Front: America, Libya and the Localisation of R2P," *Cooperation and Conflict* 50:1 (2015): 29–49, 31.

266 See, for example, Michael J. Boyle, "The Coming Illiberal Order," *Global Politics and Strategy* 58:2 (2016): 35–66, and Tim Dunne, "Liberalism, International Terrorism, and Democratic Wars," *International Relations* 23:1 (2009): 107–114.

267 See Elspeth Guild, Kees Groenendijk, and Sergio Carrera, eds., *Illiberal Liberal States: Immigration, Citizenship and Integration in the EU* (New York: Routledge, 2009). See also the discussion of the "liberal paradox" wherein illiberal asylum policies are enacted by "liberal democracies" in Sandra Lavenex, "Common Market, Normative Power or Super State? Conflicting Political Identities in EU Asylum and Immigration Policy," *Comparative European Politics* 17:4 (2019): 567–584.

268 See Thomas Gammeltoft-Hansen, *Access to Asylum: International Refugee Law and the Globalization of Migration Control* (New York: Cambridge University Press, 2011), and Haddad, *The Refugee in International Society*.

269 See Koslowski, *Migrants and Citizens*, 15, and *International Migration and Globalization of Domestic Politics* (New York: Routledge, 2005), 25. See also Abdelaaty's point that refugees inhabit "the intersection of domestic and international politics." Abdelaaty, *Discrimination and Delegation*, 11.

270 Broader disciplinary silos further inhibit our understandings of refugee policy, but the book's attention to the role of partisan identity in particular highlights the need to bridge refugee regime scholarship with work on political polarization.
271 Katalin Sárváry, "No Place for Politics? Truth, Progress and the Neglected Role of Diplomacy in Wendt's Theory of History," in Stefano Guzzini and Anna Leander, eds., *Constructivism and International Relations: Alexander Wendt and His Critics* (New York: Routledge, 2006), 158–177, 160.
272 See Edward G. Carmines, Michael J. Ensley, and Michael W. Wagner, "Who Fits the Left-Right Divide? Partisan Polarization in the American Electorate?," *American Behavioral Scientist* 56:12 (2012): 1631–1653; McCoy and Somer, "Toward a Theory of Pernicious Polarization and How It Harms Democracies"; and Noel, "Ideology and Its Discombobulations."
273 See Emilia Justyna Powell and Jeffrey K. Staton, "Domestic Judicial Institutions and Human Rights Treaty Violation," *International Studies Quarterly* 53:1 (2009): 149–174, 167.
274 See Alexander Anievas, Nivi Machanda, and Robbie Shilliam, "Confronting the Global Color Line: An Introduction," in Alexander Anievas, Nivi Machanda, and Robbie Shilliam, eds., *Race and Racism in International Relations* (New York: Routledge, 2015), 1–15; Adom Getachew, *Worldmaking After Empire: The Rise and Fall of Self-Determination* (Princeton, NJ: Princeton University Press, 2019); Vitalis, *White World Order, Black Power Politics*; and Zuckerman, ed., *The Social Theory of W.E.B. Du Bois*.
275 As Sadeghi notes, even those with formal legal citizenship might be rendered "perpetually foreign" with regard to social belonging through processes of racialization. See *Conditional Belonging*, 17.
276 See Amitav Acharya, "Race and Racism in the Founding of the Modern World Order," *International Affairs* 98:1 (2022): 23–43; Jasmine K. Gani, "From Discourse to Practice: Orientalism, Western Policy and the Arab Uprisings," *International Affairs* 98:1 (2022): 45–65; Persaud, "Situating Race in International Relations"; and Robbie Shilliam, "Race and Research Agendas," *Cambridge Review of International Affairs* 26:1 (2013): 152–158.
277 See Lila Abu-Lughod, *Do Muslim Women Need Saving* (Cambridge, MA: Harvard University Press, 2013); R. Charli Carpenter, *"Innocent Women and Children": Gender, Norms and the Protection of Civilians* (Burlington, VT: Ashgate, 2006); Errol A. Henderson, "Hidden in Plain Sight: Racism in International Relations Theory," in Anievas, Machanda, and Shilliam, eds., *Race and Racism in International Relations*, 19–43, 20; and Meghana Nayak, "Orientalism and 'Saving' US State Identity After 9/11," *International Feminist Journal of Politics* 8:1 (2006): 42–61.
278 For examples of scholarship within IR pursuing these questions, see Alexander Barder, *Global Race War: International Politics and Racial Hierarchy* (New York: Oxford University Press, 2021); Doty, *Imperial Encounters*; Chowdhry and Nair, "Introduction"; Persaud, "Situating Race in International Relations"; and Shilliam, *Race and the Undeserving Poor*. For examples within Sociology, see Gowayed,

"Resettled and Unsettled"; Neda Maghbouleh, *The Limits of Whiteness: Iranian Americans and the Everyday Politics of Race* (Stanford, CA: Stanford University Press, 2017); Sadeghi, *Conditional Belonging*; and Uzma Quraishi, *Redefining the Immigrant South: Indian and Pakistani Immigration to Houston During the Cold War* (Chapel Hill: University of North Carolina Press, 2020).

CHAPTER 2. BIPARTISAN LOGICS OF REFUGEE RESPONSIBILITY-SHARING

1 María Cristina García, *The Refugee Challenge in Post-Cold War America* (New York: Oxford University Press, 2017), 206.
2 Examples include Sen. Spencer Abraham (R-MI), Rep. Chris Smith (R-NJ), Sen. Sam Brownback (R-KS), and Rep. Ileana Ros-Lehtinen (R-FL).
3 See, for example, Sen. Ted Kennedy (D-MA), *The Congressional Record*, May 2, 2002, S3845, and "International Rescue Committee Laments Passage of House Bill That Would Restrict Syrian & Iraqi Refugee Resettlement," *International Rescue Committee*, November 19, 2015, www.rescue.org.
4 See Thomas Gammeltoft-Hansen, "International Refugee Law and Refugee Policy: The Case of Deterrence Policies," *Journal of Refugee Studies* 27:4 (2014): 1–22; Rebecca Hamlin, "Illegal Refugees: Competing Policy Ideas and the Rise of the Regime of Deterrence in American Asylum Politics," *Refugee Survey Quarterly* 31:2 (2012): 33–53; Reece Jones, *Violent Borders: Refugees and the Right to Move* (New York: Verso, 2017); Reece Jones and Corey Johnson, "Border Militarization and the Re-Articulation of Sovereignty," *Transactions of the Institute of British Geographers* 41:2 (2016): 187–200; and Charles B. Keely, "The International Refugee Regime(s): The End of the Cold War Matters," *International Migration Review* 31:1 (2001): 303–314.
5 This phrasing is borrowed from Roxanne Lynn Doty, *Imperial Encounters: The Politics of Representation in North-South Relations* (Minneapolis: University of Minnesota Press, 1996), 18.
6 See Carl J. Bon Tempo, *Americans at the Gate: The United States and Refugees during the Cold War* (Princeton, NJ: Princeton University Press, 2008); David S. FitzGerald and David Cook-Martín, *Culling the Masses: The Democratic Origins of Racist Immigration Policy in the Americas* (Cambridge, MA: Harvard University Press, 2014); Rebecca Hamlin and Philip Wolgin, "Symbolic Politics and Policy Feedback: *The United Nations Protocol Relating to the Status of Refugees* and American Refugee Policy in the Cold War," *International Migration Review* 46:3 (2012): 586–624; Jeremy Hein, *States and International Migrants: The Incorporation of Indochinese Refugees in the United States and France* (New York: Routledge, 1993); Eszter Kovács, "The Power of Second-Generation Diaspora: Hungarian Ethnic Lobbying in the United States in the 1970s–1980s," *Diaspora Studies* 11:2 (2018): 171–188; Jana K. Lipman, *In Camps: Vietnamese Refugees, Asylum Seekers, and Repatriates* (Oakland: University of California Press, 2020); Gil Loescher and John A. Scanlan, *Calculated Kindness: Refugees and America's Half-Open Door,*

1945 to the Present (New York: Free Press, 1986); Daniel J. Tichenor, *Dividing Lines: The Politics of Immigration Control in America* (Princeton, NJ: Princeton University Press, 2002), 15; and Norman L. Zucker and Naomi Flink Zucker, "The Uneasy Troika in U.S. Refugee Policy: Foreign Policy, Pressure Groups, and Resettlement Costs," *Journal of Refugee Studies* 2:3 (1989): 359–372.

7   See Alexander Betts, "North-South Cooperation in the Refugee Regime: The Role of Linkages," *Global Governance* 14:2 (2008): 157–178, 169–170; María Cristina García, *Havana USA: Cuban Exiles and Cuban Americans in South Florida, 1959–1994* (Berkeley: University of California Press, 1996); and Emma Haddad, *The Refugee in International Society: Between Sovereigns* (Cambridge, UK: Cambridge University Press 2008), 143.

8   President George W. Bush began using the phrase "war on terrorism" in the days immediately following the September 11, 2001 attacks. In May 2013, President Obama announced that the War on Terror was over, pointing to policy shifts in dismantling extremist networks.

9   Michael Goodhart, "Reverting to Form: American Exceptionalism and International Human Rights," in Michael Goodhart and Anja Mihr, eds., *Human Rights in the 21st Century: Continuity and Change since 9/11* (New York: Palgrave Macmillan, 2011), 65–85, 68.

10 See Bernard Bailyn, *The Ideological Origins of the American Revolution* (Cambridge, MA: Harvard University Press, 1992). Krebs and Lobasz describe American exceptionalism as one of the most stable and sustainable "identity narratives" shaping debates over foreign policy. Ronald R. Krebs and Jennifer K. Lobasz, "Fixing the Meaning of 9/11: Hegemony, Coercion, and the Road to War in Iraq," *Security Studies* 16:3 (2007): 409–451, 429.

11 "George Washington—Proclamation of January 1, 1795," *The Avalon Project: Documents in Law, History and Diplomacy*, 2008, https://avalon.law.yale.edu.

12 Nathaniel Cadle, "America as 'World-Salvation,'" in Sylvia Söderlind and James Taylor Carson, eds., *American Exceptionalisms: From Winthrop to Winfrey* (Albany: State University of New York Press, 2011), 125–146.

13 Thomas Paine, *Common Sense*, 1776, https://billofrightsinstitute.org.

14 Oliver Turner, "Frontiering International Relations: Narrating US Policy in the Asia Pacific," *Foreign Policy Analysis* 18:2 (2022): 1–20, 7.

15 John Higham, *Strangers in the Land: Patterns of American Nativism 1860–1925* (New York: Antheneum, 1963), 23.

16 Ryan T. O'Leary, "From Anglo-Saxon Nativism to Executive Order: Civil Religion and Anti-Immigration Rhetoric," *Politics and Religion* 9:4 (2016): 771–793.

17 Mae M. Ngai, "The Architecture of Race in American Immigration Law: A Reexamination of the Immigration Act of 1924," *Journal of American History* 86:1 (1999): 67–92, 75.

18 Carl J. Bon Tempo, "American Exceptionalism and Immigration Debates in the Modern United States," in Söderlind and Carson, eds., *American Exceptionalisms*, 147–165.

19 "Whom We Shall Welcome," *President's Commission on Immigration and Naturalization*, 1953, https://archive.org, pp. xii.
20 "President George W. Bush's Inaugural Address," *The White House*, January 20, 2001, https://georgewbush-whitehouse.archives.gov.
21 Sylvia Söderlind, "The Shining of America," in Söderlind and Carson, eds., *American Exceptionalisms*, 1.
22 "Republican Party Platform of 1956," *The American Presidency Project*, August 20, 1956, www.presidency.ucsb.edu.
23 "Republican Party Platform of 1960," *The American Presidency Project*, July 25, 1960, www.presidency.ucsb.edu.
24 Evyn Lê Espiritu Gandhi, *Archipelago of Resettlement: Vietnamese Refugee Settlers and Decolonization across Guam and Israel-Palestine* (Oakland: University of California Press, 2022), 3. See also Demmer's discussion of the Ford administration and members of Congress supporting the resettlement of evacuees from South Vietnam as part of a "selective amnesia process" to divert attention away from the destructiveness of the US military during the Vietnam War and to transform the US role "from aggressor to patron." Amanda C. Demmer, *After Saigon's Fall: Refugees and US-Vietnamese Relations, 1975–2000* (New York: Cambridge University Press, 2021), 47.
25 Quoted in Michael S. Teitelbaum, "Immigration, Refugees, and Foreign Policy," *International Organization* 38:3 (1984): 429–450, 439.
26 Robert Vitalis, *White World Order, Black Power Politics: The Birth of American International Relations* (Ithaca, NY: Cornell University Press, 2015), 179.
27 See García, *The Refugee Challenge*; Lipman, *In Camps*; and Loescher and Scanlan, *Calculated Kindness*.
28 See Alexander Barder, *Global Race War: International Politics and Racial Hierarchy* (New York: Oxford University Press, 2021), 25, and Julia Gaffield, "The Racialization of International Law after the Haitian Revolution: The Holy See and National Sovereignty," *American Historical Review* 125:3 (2020): 841–868, 845.
29 Kristina Shull, *Detention Empire: Reagan's War on Immigrations & the Seeds of Resistance* (Chapel Hill: University of North Carolina Press, 2022), 2.
30 Adom Getachew, *Worldmaking After Empire: The Rise and Fall of Self-Determination* (Princeton, NJ: Princeton University Press, 2019), 46.
31 Geoffrey Cameron, *Send Them Here: Religion, Politics, and Refugee Resettlement in North America* (Chicago: McGill-Queen's University Press, 2021), 62.
32 See Kevin Kenny, *The Problem of Immigration in a Slaveholding Republic: Policing Mobility in the 19th-Century United States* (New York: Oxford University Press, 2023).
33 For additional examples of Cuban refugees weaving themselves into American identity narratives, see Shull, *Detention Empire*, 49.
34 Frank D. Bean, Georges Vernez, and Charles B. Keely, *Opening and Closing the Doors: Evaluating Immigration Reform and Control* (Santa Monica, CA: RAND, 1989), 91–93.

35 Rhetoric around a "profound moral obligation" to evacuate and resettle South Vietnamese allies became mainstreamed by President Gerald Ford and this logic persisted for decades across various refugee policy actors. See Demmer, *After Saigon's Fall*.
36 Gov. Ray used his influence within the National Governors Association and testimony before congressional committees to present these arguments to federal authorities. See Matthew R. Walsh, *The Good Governor: Robert Ray and the Indochinese Refugees of Iowa* (Jefferson, NC: McFarland & Company, 2017).
37 "Democratic Party Platform of 1980," *The American Presidency Project*, August 11, 1980, www.presidency.ucsb.edu.
38 "Republican Party Platform of 1980," *The American Presidency Project*, July 15, 1980, www.presidency.ucsb.edu.
39 For FY1980, the admissions ceiling was 231,700 and the number of refugees admitted was 207,116. "U.S. Annual Refugee Resettlement Ceilings and Number of Refugees Admitted, 1980–Present," *Migration Policy Institute*, www.migrationpolicy.org.
40 Bean et al., *Opening and Closing the Doors*, 93.
41 "Republican Party Platform of 1984," *The American Presidency Project*, August 20, 1984, www.presidency.ucsb.edu.
42 Elizabeth A. Oldmixon and Nicholas Drummond, "Religion and Realism: U.S. Foreign Policy in the Twentieth Century," in Barbara A. McGraw, ed., *The Wiley Blackwell Companion to Religion and Politics in the U.S.* (Malden, MA: Wiley, 2016), 369–382, 378.
43 William Jefferson Clinton, "Address Before a Joint Session of the Congress on the State of the Union," *The Presidency Project*, February 4, 1997, www.presidency.ucsb.edu.
44 *The Congressional Record*, November 17, 1999, S14702.
45 *The Congressional Record*, May 15, 2002, S4384.
46 "Thomas Jefferson, December 8, 1801, Annual Message," *Library of Congress*, n.d., http://memory.loc.gov.
47 Barbara Franz, *Uprooted and Unwanted: Bosnian Refugees in Austria and the United States* (College Station: Texas A&M University Press, 2005), 114.
48 See Du Bois' use of this phrasing in "The Souls of White Folk" in Phil Zuckerman, ed., *The Social Theory of W.E.B. Du Bois* (Thousand Oaks, CA: Sage, 2004), 36.
49 See Madeline O. Campbell, *Interpreters of Occupation: Gender and the Politics of Belonging in an Iraqi Refugee Network* (Syracuse, NY: Syracuse University Press, 2016), 152. It is noteworthy that between 2001 and 2016, the United States resettled far more Iraqis than Afghans—more than 143,000 compared with less than 30,000, respectively—through both formal refugee admissions as well as Special Immigrant Visa (SIV) programs established for translators and other local civilians employed by the US government. See Nicholas R. Micinski, "Refugee Policy as Foreign Policy: Iraqi and Afghan Refugee Resettlements to the United States," *Refugee Survey Quarterly* 37:3 (2018): 253–278.

50 *The Congressional Record*, September 17, 2008, H8300.
51 During the 2004–2010 years, refugee ceilings were normalized between 70,000 and 80,000. Actual admissions fluctuated between 41,000 and 74,000. "U.S. Annual Refugee Resettlement Ceilings and Number of Refugees Admitted, 1980–Present."
52 See Oula Kadhum, "Nation-Destroying, Emigration and Iraqi Nationhood after the 2003 Intervention," *International Affairs* 99:2 (2023): 587–604.
53 Campbell, *Interpreters of Occupation*, 150.
54 Sen. Ted Kennedy (D-MA), *The Congressional Record*, July 23, 2007, S9769.
55 Sen. Sam Brownback (R-KS), *The Congressional Record*, November 17, 1999, S14703.
56 The ceiling was increased up from 125,000, including an additional 10,000 Soviet refugees. Andrew Rosenthal, "U.S. Will Allow 6,000 More Refugees Next Year," *New York Times*, October 16, 1990, www.nytimes.com.
57 George H. W. Bush, "Proclamation 6219—Refugee Day, 1990," *The American Presidency Project*, October 30, 1990, www.presidency.ucsb.edu.
58 "International Rescue Committee: US Commitment to Accept up to 8,000 Syrians Not Enough," *International Rescue Committee*, September 2, 2015, www.rescue.org.
59 "A Brief History of the Presidential Determination," *HIAS*, August 7, 2017, www.hias.org.
60 The United States supported the formation of the International Refugee Organization (the predecessor to the UNHCR), played a prominent role in the drafting of the Universal Declaration of Human Rights, and admitted nearly one-third of the 1.3 million individuals in post-war displacement camps in Europe. See Phil Orchard, *A Right to Flee: Refugees, States, and the Construction of International Cooperation* (New York: Cambridge University Press, 2014), and Astri Suhrke, "Burden-Sharing during Refugee Emergencies: The Logic of Collective versus National Action," *Journal of Refugee Studies* 11:4 (1998): 396–415.
61 Maddalena Marinari, *Unwanted: Italian and Jewish Mobilization against Restrictive Immigration Laws, 1882–1965* (Chapel Hill: University of North Carolina Press, 2020), 107.
62 James Ciment and John Radzilowski, eds., *American Immigration: An Encyclopedia of Political, Social, and Cultural Change* (New York: Routledge, 2014), 942.
63 Hamlin, "Illegal Refugees," 40.
64 Alexander Betts, Gil Loescher, and James Milner, *UNHCR: The Politics and Practice of Refugee Protection, Second Edition* (New York: Routledge, 2012), 14, and Nevzat Soguk, *States and Strangers: Refugees and Displacements of Statecraft* (Minneapolis: University of Minnesota Press, 1999), 172.
65 See Steven L. B. Jensen, *The Making of International Human Rights: The 1960s, Decolonization and the Reconstruction of Global Values* (New York: Cambridge University Press, 2016); Gil Loescher, "UNHCR's Origins and Early History: Agency, Influence, and Power in Global Refugee Policy," *Refuge: Canada's Journal*

on Refugees 33:1 (2017): 77–86; Derrick M. Nault, *Africa and the Shaping of International Human Rights* (New York: Oxford University Press, 2021); and William A. Schabas, ed., *The Universal Declaration of Human Rights: The Travaux Préparatoires* (New York: Cambridge University Press, 2013).

66 See E. Tendayi Achiume, "Syria, Cost-Sharing, and the Responsibility to Protect Refugees," *Minnesota Law Review* 100:2 (2015): 687–761; B. S. Chimni, "The Geopolitics of Refugee Studies: A View from the South," *Journal of Refugee Studies* 11:4 (1998): 350–374; Ayten Gündogdu, *Rightlessness in an Age of Rights: Hannah Arendt and the Contemporary Struggles of Migrants* (New York: Oxford University Press, 2015); Haddad, *The Refugee in International Society*; Sari Hanafi, "Forced Migration in the Middle East and North Africa," in Elena Fiddian-Qasmiyeh et al., eds., *The Oxford Handbook of Refugee and Forced Migration Studies* (New York: Oxford University Press, 2014), 585–598; Lucy Mayblin, "Colonialism, Decolonization, and the Right to Be Human: Britain and the 1951 Geneva Convention on the Status of Refugees," *Journal of Historical Sociology* 27:3 (2014): 423–441; and Ulrike Krause, "Colonial Roots of the 1951 Refugee Convention and Its Effects on the Global Refugee Regime," *Journal of International Relations and Development* 24:3 (2021): 599–626.

67 Kenneth D. Brill, "The Endless Debate: Refugees Law and Policy and the 1980 Refugee Act," *Cleveland State Law Review* 32:1 (1983): 117–174, 124.

68 Roger P. Winter, "The International Refugee Protection System," in Alan E. Nash, ed., *Human Rights and the Protection of Refugees Under International Law: Proceedings of a Conference Held in Montreal, November 29–December 2, 1987* (Quebec: Institute for Research on Public Policy, 1988), 37–42, 40–41.

69 "2000 Republican Party Platform," *The American Presidency Project*, July 31, 2000, www.presidency.ucsb.edu.

70 "President George W. Bush's Inaugural Address."

71 Sen. Ted Kennedy (D-MA), *The Congressional Record*, June 29, 2001, S7261.

72 Sen. Sam Brownback (R-KS), *The Congressional Record*, June 18, 2004, S7051.

73 Campbell, *Interpreters of Occupation*, 157.

74 See Anne Scheinfeldt, "Current Development: Legislative Branch Developments: Bipartisan Refugee Caucus," *Georgetown Immigration Law Journal* 17:739 (2003): 739–740. See also Melanie Nezer, "An Overview of Pending Asylum and Refugee Legislation in the U.S. Congress," *Journal on Migration and Human Security* 2:2 (2014): 121–143.

75 "Assessing the New Normal: Liberty and Security for the Post-September 11 United States," *Lawyers Committee for Human Rights*, 2003, 45.

76 "U.S. Annual Refugee Resettlement Ceilings and Number of Refugees Admitted, 1980–Present."

77 Rep. Ileana Ros-Lehtinen (R-FL), *The Congressional Record*, June 23, 2010, H4706.

78 Rep. Sheila Jackson-Lee (D-NY), *The Congressional Record*, June 23, 2010, H4706.

79 Rep. Diane Watson (D-CA), *The Congressional Record*, June 23, 2010, H4705.

80 "2012 Republican Party Platform," *The American Presidency Project*, August 27, 2012, www.presidency.ucsb.edu.

81 Michelle Nichols, "U.S. Says Some 360,000 Refugee Spots Pledged at United Nations," *Reuters*, September 20, 2016, www.reuters.com.
82 Andrew Geddes, *Governing Migration beyond the State: Europe, North America, South America, and Southeast Asia in a Global Context* (New York: Oxford University Press, 2021), 35.
83 See Shauna Labman, *Crossing Law's Border: Canada's Refugee Resettlement Program* (Toronto: UBC Press, 2019), 6, and "UNHCR Projected Global Resettlement Needs," *UNHCR*, 2015, www.unhcr.org.
84 García notes that Sweden outpaced the United States in the resettlement of Iraqi refugees in 2007, for example. See García, *The Refugee Challenge*, 146.
85 See David S. FitzGerald, *Refuge Beyond Reach: How Rich Democracies Repel Asylum Seekers* (New York: Oxford University Press, 2019); David Owen, *What Do We Owe To Refugees?* (Medford, MA: Polity Press, 2020), 98; Lipman, *In Camps*; and Volker Türk and Rebecca Dowd, "Protection Gaps," ch. 22 in Fiddian-Qasmiyeh et al., *The Oxford Handbook*, 278–289, 284.
86 See Micinski, "Refugee Policy as Foreign Policy."
87 See Carl J. Bon Tempo, "Refugees and Human Rights in the Post-World War II United States," in A. G. Roeber, ed., *Human v. Religious Rights? German and U.S. Exchanges and Their Global Implications* (Göttingen: Vandenhoeck & Ruprecht, 2020), 77–84; García, *The Refugee Challenge*; Anna O. Law, "The Diversity Visa Lottery: A Cycle of Unintended Consequences in United States Immigration Policy," *Journal of American Ethnic History* 21:4 (2002): 3–29; Lipman, *In Camps*; and Loescher and Scanlan, *Calculated Kindness*.
88 Orchard points out that President Truman was a refugee protection norm entrepreneur who successfully helped "reframe domestic understandings" of refugees in terms of Cold War "strategic and security considerations," for example, rather than extensions of immigration policy. Phil Orchard, "The Dawn of International Refugee Protection: States, Tacit Cooperation and Non-Extradition," *Journal of Refugee Studies* 30:2 (2017): 282–300, 157.
89 Chandran Kukathas, *Immigration and Freedom* (Princeton, NJ: Princeton University Press, 2021), 195.
90 Ciment and Radzilowski, *American Immigration*, 942.
91 For further exploration of how refugees were positioned within anticommunist identity juxtapositions, see Bon Tempo, *Americans at the Gate*.
92 "Republican Party Platform of 1980."
93 "Republican Party Platform of 1984."
94 Hamlin, "Illegal Refugees," 41.
95 "U.S. Annual Refugee Resettlement Ceilings and Number of Refugees Admitted, 1980–Present."
96 It is important to note that these pockets of opposition to refugee admissions were ideologically diverse. See Bon Tempo, *Americans at the Gate*, 168–169.
97 "Republican Party Platform of 1984."

98 Joseph Kertes, "Second Country," in Viet Thanh Nguyen, ed., *The Displaced: Refugee Writers on Refugee Lives* (New York: Abrams Press, 2018), 113–120, 116.
99 "Whom We Shall Welcome," see pp. 25 and 46.
100 Jonathan H. L'Homedieu, "Baltic Exiles and the U.S. Congress: Investigations and Legacies of the House Select Committee, 1953–1955," *Journal of American Ethnic History* 31:2 (2012): 41–67, 61.
101 See Gerardo Martí, "White Christian Libertarianism and the Trump Presidency," in Grace Yukich and Penny Edgell, eds., *Religion Is Raced* (New York: New York University Press, 2020), 19–39.
102 Jeanett Castellanos and Alberta M. Gloria, "Cuban Americans: From Golden Exiles to Dusty Feet—Freedom, Hope, Endurance, and the American Dream," in Patricia Arredondo, ed., *Latinx Immigrants: Transcending Acculturation and Xenophobia* (Cham, CH: Springer, 2018), 75–94, 82.
103 Cheris Brewer Current, "Normalizing Cuban Refugees," *Ethnicities* 8:1 (2008): 42–67.
104 Shull, *Detention Empire*, see pp. 71 and 74.
105 See Stephen M. Caliendo and Charlton D. McIlwain, *The Routledge Companion to Race and Ethnicity* (New York: Routledge, 2011), 173.
106 Min Zhou, "Are Asian Americans Becoming 'White'?," *Context* 3:1 (2004): 29–37, 32.
107 See Jason E. Pierce, *Making the White Man's West: Whiteness and the Creation of the American West* (Boulder: University of Colorado Press, 2016), and Anthony A. Soliman, "Historicizing Whiteness and White Supremacy," *The Forum: Journal of History* 10:1 (2018): 3–15.
108 Uzma Quraishi, *Redefining the Immigrant South: Indian and Pakistani Immigration to Houston During the Cold War* (Chapel Hill: University of North Carolina Press, 2020), 111.
109 Lipman, *In Camps*, 16.
110 Aihwa Ong, "Cultural Citizenship as Subject-Making: Immigrants Negotiate Racial and Cultural Boundaries in the United States," *Current Anthropology* 37:5 (1996): 737–762.
111 Viet Thanh Nguyen, "Introduction," in Nguyen, ed., *The Displaced*, 16.
112 "Republican Party Platform of 1980."
113 "Republican Party Platform of 1988," *The American Presidency Project*, August 16, 1988, www.presidency.ucsb.edu.
114 Paul Pierson, *Dismantling the Welfare State? Reagan, Thatcher, and the Politics of Retrenchment* (New York: Cambridge University Press, 1994).
115 Miguel de Oliver, "Nativism and the Obsolescence of Grand Narrative: Comprehending the Quandary of Anti-Immigration Groups in the Neoliberal Era," *Journal of Ethnic and Migration Studies* 37:7 (2011): 977–997, 988.
116 Rep. Burt L. Talcott (R-CA), quoted in Yến Lê Espiritu, *Body Count: The Vietnam War and Militarized Refuge(es)* (Oakland: University of California Press, 2014), 34.

117 Sharad Chari and Katherine Verdery, "Thinking Between the Posts: Postcolonialism, Postsocialism, and Ethnography after the Cold War," *Comparative Studies in Society and History* 51:1 (2009): 6–34, 18. For more on the infusion of "modernity" with racial whiteness, see Vitalis, *White World Order*.
118 President Truman, quoted in William Inboden III, *Religion and American Foreign Policy, 1945–1960: The Soul of Containment* (New York: Cambridge University Press, 2008), 114.
119 See Erin C. Cassese and Mirya R. Holman, "Religion, Gendered Authority, and Identity in American Politics," *Politics and Religion* 10:1 (2017): 31–56, 33, and James Hunter, *Culture Wars: The Struggle to Define America* (New York: Basic Books, 1991).
120 See Norman L. Zucker and Naomi Flink Zucker, *Desperate Crossings: Seeking Refuge in America* (New York: M.E. Sharpe, 1996). Note that Nicaraguan asylum-seekers whose claims were accepted tended to be of higher socioeconomic status and tended to be pro-capitalism and conservative in ways that affirmed the Reagan administration's identity narratives. See Shull, *Detention Empire*, 133.
121 Hon. Bob Livingston, "A Nicaraguan Refugee Family's Plea for Help," *Bound Congressional Record*, April 2, 1985, 7525.
122 See Robert E. Lewis, Mark W. Fraser, and Peter J. Pecora, "Religiosity among Indochinese Refugees in Utah," *Journal for the Scientific Study of Religion* 27:2 (1988): 272–283, and Peter C. Phan, "Vietnamese Catholics in the United States: Christian Identity between the Old and the New," *U.S. Catholic Historian* 18:1 (2000): 19–35.
123 David W. Haines, *Safe Haven? A History of Refugees in America* (Sterling, VA: Kumarian Press, 2010), 69.
124 Nancy Foner and Richard Alba, "Immigrant Religion in the U.S. and Western Europe: Bridge or Barrier to Inclusion?," *International Migration Review* 42:2 (2008): 360–392, 365.
125 Rep. Jerry Weller (R-IL), *The Congressional Record*, September 17, 2008, H8301.
126 Sen. Gordon Smith (R-OR), *The Congressional Record*, July 8, 2004, S7836.
127 Ruth Igielnik and Jens Manuel Krogstad, "Where Refugees to the U.S. Come From," *Pew Research Center*, February 3, 2017, www.pewresearch.org.
128 Michel Agier, *Managing the Undesirables: Refugee Camps and Humanitarian Government* (Malden, MA: Polity Press, 2011), 11.
129 Lipman, *In Camps*, 194.
130 Rep. Jerry Weller (R-IL), *The Congressional Record*, September 17, 2008, H8301.
131 Sen. Sam Brownback (R-KS), *The Congressional Record*, June 18, 2004, S7051.
132 Sen. Orrin Hatch (R-UT), *The Congressional Record*, July 8, 2009, S7242.
133 Reyna Grande, "The Parent Who Stays," in Nguyen, ed., *The Displaced*, 81–89, 86.
134 See David Forsythe, "U.S. Foreign Policy and Human Rights," *Journal of Human Rights* 1:4 (2010): 501–521, 511, and Jensen, *The Making of International Human Rights*, 26.
135 "History," *Tom Lantos Human Rights Commission*, n.d., https://humanrightscommission.house.gov.

136 See García, *The Refugee Challenge*, 20, and Rasmus Sinding Søndergaard, "The Right to Leave: Soviet Jewish Emigration," in *Reagan, Congress, and Human Rights: Contesting Morality in U.S. Foreign Policy* (New York: Cambridge University Press, 2020), 118–163.
137 Reagan officials collaborated with Congress to earmark more than half of annual resettlement slots for Indochinese refugees, for example. See Demmer, *After Saigon's Fall*, 99.
138 "U.S. Annual Refugee Resettlement Ceilings and Number of Refugees Admitted, 1980–Present."
139 "Iranian Refugees: The Many Faces of Persecution," *U.S. Committee for Refugees Issue Paper*, December 1984, 19.
140 Michael H. Hunt, *Ideology and U.S. Foreign Policy* (New Haven, CT: Yale University Press, 2009), 186.
141 Cameron, *Send Them Here*, 123.
142 Lipman, *In Camps*, 8.
143 Jensen, *The Making of International Human Rights*, 269.
144 The United States ratified the International Covenant on Civil and Political Rights (ICCPR) in 1992, and both the Convention on the Elimination of All Forms of Racial Discrimination (CERD) and the Convention against Torture (CAT) in 1994.
145 "U.S. Annual Refugee Resettlement Ceilings and Number of Refugees Admitted, 1980–Present."
146 See David Chandler, "The Road to Military Humanitarianism: How the Human Rights NGOs Shaped a New Humanitarian Agenda," *Human Rights Quarterly* 23:3 (2001): 678–700.
147 Roxanne Lynn Doty, "Bare Life: Border-Crossing Deaths and Spaces of Moral Alibi," *Environment and Planning D: Society and Space* 29:4 (2011): 599–612.
148 William Jefferson Clinton, "Address Before a Joint Session of the Congress on the State of the Union," *The Presidency Project*, January 23, 1996, www.presidency.ucsb.edu.
149 "Remarks on Signing the Human Rights Proclamation," *U.S. Government Publishing Office*, December 5, 1995, www.govinfo.gov.
150 Anthony Zurcher, "America's 'Invisible' Muslims," *BBC*, October 30, 2016, www.bbc.com.
151 Goodhart, "Reverting to Form," 79.
152 Stephen Hopgood, *The Endtimes of Human Rights* (Ithaca, NY: Cornell University Press, 2013), 97.
153 Jensen, *The Making of International Human Rights*, 13.
154 Geddes, *Governing Migration*, 171.
155 See "Human Rights, Refugee, and Other Foreign Relations Provisions Act of 1996," *The Congressional Record*, September 25, 1996, H11126–H11129.
156 See H.R. 4036—Human Rights, Refugee, and Other Foreign Relations Provisions Act of 1996, *Congress.gov*, 1996, www.congress.gov.

157 "U.S. Annual Refugee Resettlement Ceilings and Number of Refugees Admitted, 1980–Present."
158 Rep. Cynthia McKinney (D-GA), *The Congressional Record*, July 19, 1999, H5769.
159 Rep. Benjamin Gilman (R-NY), *The Congressional Record*, July 19, 1999, H5769.
160 See Louis Henkin, "U.S. Ratification of Human Rights Conventions: The Ghost of Senator Bricker," *American Journal of International Law* 89:2 (1995): 341–350; Jamie Mayerfeld, *The Promise of Human Rights: Constitutional Government, Democratic Legitimacy, and International Law* (Philadelphia: University of Pennsylvania Press, 2016), 116; and Kelebogile Zvobgo, "Human Rights versus National Interests: Shifting U.S. Public Attitudes on the International Criminal Court," *International Studies Quarterly* 63:4 (2019): 1065–1078.
161 Alaina Kaus, "Liberal Humanitarianism: Obscuring U.S. Culpability in James Disco and Susan Clark's *Echoes of the Lost Boys of Sudan* and Dave Egger's *What Is the What*," *Contemporary Literature* 60:1 (2019): 198–226.
162 Keneshia N. Grant, *The Great Migration and the Democratic Party: Black Voters and the Realignment of American Politics in the 20th Century* (Philadelphia: Temple University Press, 2020), 121.
163 García, *The Refugee Challenge*, 112.
164 See Sara L. McKinnon, "Unsettling Resettlement: Problematizing 'Lost Boys of Sudan' Resettlement and Identity," *Western Journal of Communication* 72:4 (2008): 397–414, and Melinda B. Robins, "'Lost Boys' and the Promised Land: U.S. Newspaper Coverage of Sudanese Refugees," *Journalism* 4:1 (2003): 29–49.
165 Sen. Spencer Abraham (R-MI), *The Congressional Record*, September 10, 1997, S9091.
166 Sen. Ted Kennedy (D-MA), *The Congressional Record*, September 10, 1997, S9091.
167 See Maria Eriksson Baaz and Judith Verweijen, "Confronting the Colonial: The (Re)production of 'African' Exceptionalism in Critical Security and Military Studies," *Security Dialogue* 49:1–2 (2018): 57–69, 59, and Homi K. Bhabha, *The Location of Culture* (New York: Routledge, 1994).
168 Tahseen Shams, *Here, There, and Elsewhere: The Making of Immigrant Identities in a Globalized World* (Stanford, CA: Stanford University Press, 2020), 21.
169 Gandhi, *Archipelago of Resettlement*, 79.
170 Sen. Ted Kennedy (D-MA), *The Congressional Record*, May 2, 2002, S3845.
171 Sean Gill, "Path to Refugee Status Easing," *Los Angeles Times*, February 2, 2002, www.latimes.com.
172 Sen. Jim Bunning (R-KY), *The Congressional Record*, May 15, 2002, S4384.
173 Sen. Sam Brownback (R-KS), *The Congressional Record*, June 18, 2004, S7051.
174 Scheinfeldt, "Current Development."
175 Gil Loescher and James Milner, *Protracted Refugee Situations: Domestic and International Security Implications* (New York: Routledge, 2005), 7.
176 National Defense Authorization Act for Fiscal Year 2008, *The Congressional Record*, December 3, 2007, S12646.

177 "U.S. Annual Refugee Resettlement Ceilings and Number of Refugees Admitted, 1980–Present."
178 Lila Abu-Lughod, *Do Muslim Women Need Saving?* (Cambridge, MA: Harvard University Press, 2013), 62. Emphasis in original.
179 See Micinski, "Refugee Policy as Foreign Policy."
180 Rep. Sheila Jackson-Lee (D-TX), *The Congressional Record*, June 6, 2007, H6052–53.
181 Rep. Henry Hyde (R-IL), *The Congressional Record*, July 15, 2003, H6725–26.
182 Rep. Mark Kirk (R-IL), *The Congressional Record*, July 9, 2009, H7878.
183 Rep. Connie Morella (R-MD), *The Congressional Record*, November 27, 2001, H8350.
184 Rep. Ileana Ros-Lehtinen (R-FL), *The Congressional Record*, November 27, 2001, H8350.
185 Rep. J. C. Watts (R-OK), *The Congressional Record*, June 13, 2001, H3103.
186 George W. Bush, "Address Before a Joint Session of the Congress on the State of the Union," *The American Presidency Project*, January 28, 2003, www.presidency.ucsb.edu.
187 See Rashid Khalidi, *Resurrecting Empire: Western Footprints and America's Perilous Path in the Middle East* (Boston: Beacon Press, 2004); Matthew Leep, *Cosmopolitan Belongingness and War: Animals, Loss, and Spectral-Poetic Moments* (Albany: State University of New York Press, 2021); Shadi Mokhtari, *After Abu Ghraib: Exploring Human Rights in America and the Middle East* (New York: Cambridge University Press, 2009); and Jeremy Pressman, "Power Without Influence: The Bush Administration's Foreign Policy Failure in the Middle East," *International Security* 33:4 (2009): 149–179.
188 Rep. Joe Knollenberg (R-MI), *The Congressional Record*, June 8, 2006, H3527.
189 George W. Bush, "Address Before a Joint Session of the Congress on the State of the Union," *The American Presidency Project*, January 31, 2006, www.presidency.ucsb.edu.
190 Sen. Patrick Leahy (D-VT), *The Congressional Record*, April 2, 2008, S2338.
191 Sen. Ted Kennedy (D-MA), *The Congressional Record*, July 23, 2007, S9769.
192 See Campbell, *Interpreters of Occupation*, and Micinski, "Refugee Policy as Foreign Policy."
193 "Address by President Gerald R. Ford Before a Joint Session of the Congress Reporting on United States Foreign Policy," *Gerald R. Ford Presidential Library & Museum*, April 10, 1975, www.fordlibrarymuseum.gov.
194 See the testimony of Dr. Lawrence Fuchs, *Domestic and Foreign Policy Implications of U.S. Immigration and Refugee Resettlement Policy* (Washington, DC: House Committee on Foreign Affairs, 1982), 169, and William M. LeoGrande, *Our Own Backyard: The United States in Central America, 1977–1992* (University of North Carolina Press, 1998), 583.
195 See Sen. Judd Gregg (R-NH), *The Congressional Record*, April 20, 1999, S3893.

196 See the speech by Sen. Bob Kerrey (D-NE), *The Congressional Record*, May 3, 2000, H2420, shared by Rep. Doug Bereuter (R-NE).
197 Yên Lê Espiritu, *Home Bound: Filipino American Lives across Cultures, Communities, and Countries* (Berkeley: University of California Press, 2003), 207.
198 Rep. Jim Bunning (R-KY), *The Congressional Record*, May 15, 2002, S4384.
199 Branwen Gruffydd Jones, "'Good Governance' and 'State Failure:' The Pseudo-Science of Statesmen in Our Times," in Alexander Anievas, Nivi Machanda, and Robbie Shilliam, eds., *Race and Racism in International Relations* (New York: Routledge, 2015), 62–80.
200 See Adam Goodman, *The Deportation Machine: America's Long History of Expelling Immigrants* (Princeton, NJ: Princeton University Press, 2020); S. Deborah Kang, *The INS on the Line: Making Immigration Law on the US-Mexico Border, 1917–1954* (New York: Oxford University Press, 2017), 170; and Elliot Young, *Forever Prisoners: How the United States Made the World's Largest Immigrant Detention System* (New York: Oxford University Press, 2021).
201 Hamlin, "Illegal Refugees," 35.
202 Meghana Nayak, *Who Is Worthy of Protection? Gender-Based Asylum and U.S. Immigration Politics* (New York: Oxford University Press, 2015), 38.
203 Hamlin, "Illegal Refugees," 38.
204 "Republican Party Platform of 1984."
205 See Bill Ong Hing, *American Presidents, Deportations, and Human Rights Violations: From Carter to Trump* (New York: Cambridge University Press, 2019).
206 "1996 Democratic Party Platform," *The American Presidency Project*, August 26, 1996, www.presidency.ucsb.edu.
207 "Republican Party Platform of 1988."
208 Clinton, "Address Before a Joint Session of the Congress on the State of the Union."
209 Justin Peter Steil and Ion Bogdan Vasi, "The New Immigration Contestation: Social Movements and Local Immigration Policy Making in the United States, 2000–2011," *American Journal of Sociology* 119:4 (2014), 1104–1155.
210 Hinda Seif, "'Tired of Illegals': Immigrant Driver's Licenses, Constituent Letters, and Shifting Restrictionist Discourse in California," in Monica W. Varsanyi, ed., *Taking Local Control: Immigration Policy Activism in U.S. Cities and States* (Stanford, CA: Stanford University Press, 2010), 275–294, 284.
211 Nick Dragojlovic, "Listening to Outsiders: The Impact of Messenger Nationality on Transnational Persuasion in the United States," *International Studies Quarterly* 59:1 (2015): 73–85, 81.
212 Sen. Sam Brownback (R-KS), *The Congressional Record*, June 18, 2004, S7051.
213 Orchard, *A Right to Flee*, 213.
214 Rep. Jerry Weller (R-IL), *The Congressional Record*, September 17, 2008, H8301.
215 Sen. Pat Leahy (D-VT), *The Congressional Record*, March 21, 2013, S2150.
216 See Emily M. Farris and Heather Silber Mohamed, "Picturing Immigration: How the Media Criminalizes Immigrants," *Politics, Groups, and Identities* 6:4 (2018):

814–824, and Efrén O. Pérez, *Unspoken Politics: Implicit Attitudes and Political Thinking* (New York: Cambridge University Press, 2016).
217 Rebecca Hamlin, *Crossing: How We Label and React to People on the Move* (Stanford, CA: Stanford University Press, 2021), 74–75.
218 Alan I. Abramowitz, *The Disappearing Center: Engaged Citizens, Polarization, and American Democracy* (New Haven, CT: Yale University Press, 2010), 37.
219 Søndergaard, "The Right to Leave," 18.
220 See Pratheepan Gulasekaram and S. Karthick Ramakrishnan, *The New Immigration Federalism* (New York: Cambridge University Press, 2015), 111, and Jeffrey S. Lantis and Patrick Homan, "Factionalism and U.S. Foreign Policy: A Social Psychological Model of Minority Influence," *Foreign Policy Analysis* 15:2 (2019): 157–175.
221 See Sen. Richard Blumenthal (D-CT), *The Congressional Record*, July 23, 2014, S4846–4847.
222 H.R. 5230, *GovTrack*, August 1, 2014, www.govtrack.us.
223 Rev. Eusebio Elizondo used this phrase in his letter expressing the opposition of the U.S. Conference of Catholic Bishops (USCCB) to H.R. 5230. See *The Congressional Record*, August 1, 2014, H7213.
224 Rep. Nancy Pelosi, *The Congressional Record*, August 1, 2014, H7224.
225 See Rep. Lucille Royal-Allard (D-CA), *The Congressional Record*, August 1, 2014, H7228.
226 Rep. Chaka Fattah (D-PA), *The Congressional Record*, July 31, 2014, H7165.
227 See Bon Tempo, *Americans at the Gate*, and LeoGrande, *Our Own Backyard*.
228 *The Congressional Record*, August 1, 2014, H7198.
229 Espiritu, *Home Bound*, 7–8.
230 Abramowitz, *The Disappearing Center*, 36.
231 Chimni, "The Geopolitics of Refugee Studies," 351.
232 Rep. Sheila Jackson-Lee (D-TX), *The Congressional Record*, June 6, 2007, H6052–6053.
233 See Alise Coen, "Capable and Culpable? The United States, RtoP, and Refugee Responsibility-Sharing," *Ethics & International Affairs* 31:1 (2017): 71–92; Espiritu, *Body Count*; Jacqueline L. Hazelton, *Bullets Not Ballots: Success in Counterinsurgency Warfare* (Ithaca, NY: Cornell University Press, 2021); LeoGrande, *Our Own Backyard*; and Gilburt Loescher and John Scanlan, "Human Rights, U.S. Foreign Policy, and Haitian Refugees," *Journal of Interamerican Studies and World Affairs* 26:3 (1984): 313–356.
234 See E. Tendayi Achiume, "Migration as Decolonization," *Stanford Law Review* 71:6 (2019): 1509–1574; Gurminder K. Bhambra, "The Current Crisis of Europe: Refugees, Colonialism, and the Limits of Cosmopolitanism," *European Law Journal* 23:5 (2017): 395–405; Lucy Mayblin and Joe Turner, *Migration Studies and Colonialism* (Medford, MA: Polity Press, 2021); and Encarnación Gutiérrez Rodríguez, "The Coloniality of Migration and the 'Refugee Crisis': On the Asylum-Migration Nexus, the Transatlantic White European Settler Colonialism-Migration and Racial Capitalism," *Refuge: Canada's Journal on Refugees* 34:1 (2018): 16–28.

CHAPTER 3. NATIVIST PRISMS OF CULTURAL THREAT

1 See Douglas S. Massey and Magaly Sánchez, *Brokered Boundaries: Creating Immigrant Identity in Anti-Immigrant Times* (New York: Russell Sage, 2010), 69; Paulina Ochoa Espejo, *On Borders: Territories, Legitimacy, & The Rights of Place* (New York: Oxford University Press, 2020), 65; and Michael Pugh, "Drowning Not Waving: Boat People and Humanitarianism at Sea," *Journal of Refugee Studies* 17:1 (2004): 50–69, 54.
2 Donald Trump (@realDonaldTrump), "Refugees from Syria are now pouring into our great country. Who knows who they are—some could be ISIS. Is our president insane?" Twitter, November 17, 2015, 7:54am, https://twitter.com/realdonaldtrump/status/666615398574530560.
3 See Dany Bahar, "How Economics Could Solve the Refugee Crisis," *Brookings Institution*, June 16, 2016, www.brookings.edu.
4 Katie Oxx, *The Nativist Movement in America: Religious Conflict in the Nineteenth Century* (New York: Routledge, 2013), 16.
5 Joe R. Feagin, "Old Poison in New Bottles: The Deep Roots of Modern Nativism," in Juan F. Perea, ed., *Immigrants Out! The New Nativism and the Anti-Immigrant Impulse in the United States* (New York: New York University Press, 1997), 13–43, 13.
6 John Higham, *Strangers in the Land: Patterns of American Nativism, 1860–1925* (New York: Antheneum, 1963), 24.
7 Phil Zuckerman, ed., *The Social Theory of W.E.B. Du Bois* (Thousand Oaks, CA: Sage, 2004), 25.
8 Julia Gaffield, "The Racialization of International Law after the Haitian Revolution: The Holy See and National Sovereignty," *American Historical Review* 125:3 (2020): 841–868, 843.
9 See Srdjan Vucetic, "A Racialized Peace? How Britain and the U.S. Made Their Relationship Special," *Foreign Policy Analysis* 7:4 (2011): 403–421.
10 Beyond the US context, Kaya points to broader "re-homogenization" efforts wherein governments "ethnicize" migration policies by restricting entries along ethnic and religious lines. Ayhan Kaya, *Islam, Migration and Integration: The Age of Securitization* (New York: Palgrave Macmillan, 2012), 4.
11 See Tomás Alaguer, *Racial Fault Lines: The Historical Origins of White Supremacy in California* (Berkeley: University of California Press, 2009); Jack Citrin and David O. Sears, *American Identity and the Politics of Multiculturalism* (New York: Cambridge University Press, 2014); Kevin Kenny, *The Problem of Immigration in a Slaveholding Republic: Policing Mobility in the 19th-Century United States* (New York: Oxford University Press, 2023); and Jia Lynn Yang, *One Mighty and Irresistible Tide* (New York: W.W. Norton, 2020).
12 Nour Halabi, *Radical Hospitality: American Policy, Media, and Immigration* (New Brunswick, NJ: Rutgers University Press, 2023), 142.
13 Elizabeth Theiss-Morse, *Who Counts as an American? The Boundaries of National Identity* (New York: Cambridge University Press, 2009), 13.

14 Randolph B. Persaud, "Situating Race in International Relations: The Dialectics of Civilizational Security in American Immigration," in Geeta Chowdhry and Sheila Nair, eds., *Power, Postcolonialism and International Relations: Reading Race, Gender and Class* (New York: Routledge, 2022), 56–81, 73.
15 Robbie Shilliam, "Colonial Architecture or Relatable Hinterlands? Locke, Nandy, Fanon, and the Bandung Spirit," *Constellations* 23:3 (2016): 425–435.
16 Halabi, *Radical Hospitality*, 31.
17 See José Casanova, "Immigration and the New Religious Pluralism: A European Union/United States Comparison," in Thomas Banchoff, ed., *Democracy and the New Religious Pluralism* (New York: Oxford University Press, 2007), 74; Noel Ignatiev, *How the Irish Became White* (New York: Routledge, 1995), 151; and John R. Mulkern, *The Know-Nothing Party in Massachusetts: The Rise and Fall of a People's Movement* (Boston: Northeastern University Press, 1990), 95.
18 Nazli Kibria, Cara Bowman, and Megan O'Leary, *Race and Immigration* (Cambridge, UK: Polity Press, 2014), 31.
19 Maddalena Marinari, *Unwanted: Italian and Jewish Mobilization against Restrictive Immigration Laws, 1882–1965* (Chapel Hill: University of North Carolina Press, 2020), 99.
20 Marina Espinoza, "State Terrorism: Orientalism and the Drone Programme," *Critical Studies on Terrorism* 11:2 (2018): 376–393, 380.
21 Feagin, "Old Poison in New Bottles."
22 Perceptions of Syrian Muslims as racially non-white, for example, intensified following the rebirth of the Ku Klux Klan in the domestic politics of the 1920s, and also varied widely by location. The racialization of Iranians shifted in US domestic identity narratives based on changing foreign policy contexts and local interpretations of external events such as the Iranian Revolution and hostage crisis. See Edward E. Curtis IV, *Muslims of the Heartland: How Syrian Immigrants Made a Home in the American Midwest* (New York: New York University Press, 2022), and Sahar Sadeghi, *Conditional Belonging: The Racialization of Iranians in the Wake of Anti-Muslim Politics* (New York: New York University Press, 2023).
23 Robert P. Jones, *The End of White Christian America* (New York: Simon & Schuster, 2016), 92. Note also Ferris and Donato's point that immigration has become the central driver of US population growth. Elizabeth G. Ferris and Katharine M. Donato, *Refugees, Migration and Global Governance* (New York: Routledge, 2020), 5.
24 See Christopher A. Bail, *Terrified: How Anti-Muslim Fringe Organizations Became Mainstream* (Princeton, NJ: Princeton University Press, 2014); Heidi Beirich and Mark Potok, "The Nativist Lobby," *Southern Poverty Law Center*, February 2009, www.splcenter.org; and Jean Stefancic, "Funding the Nativist Agenda," in Perea, ed., *Immigrants Out*, 119–135.
25 Sahar Aziz, "Orientalism, Empire, and The Racial Muslim," in Tamara Sonn, ed., *Overcoming Orientalism: Essays in Honor of John L. Esposito* (New York: Oxford University Press, 2021), 221–244, 231.

26 Sarah Gualtieri, *Between Arab and White: Race and Ethnicity in the Early Syrian American Diaspora* (Berkeley: University of California Press, 2009), 4, 56.
27 Sarah Gualtieri, "Becoming 'White': Race, Religion, and the Foundations of Syrian/Lebanese Ethnicity in the United States," *Journal of American Ethnic History* 20:4 (2001): 29–58, 36.
28 See Neda Maghbouleh, *The Limits of Whiteness: Iranian Americans and the Everyday Politics of Race* (Stanford, CA: Stanford University Press, 2017); Sadeghi, *Conditional Belonging*; and Uzma Quraishi, *Redefining the Immigrant South: Indian and Pakistani Immigration to Houston During the Cold War* (Chapel Hill: University of North Carolina Press, 2020).
29 See Curtis, *Muslims of the Heartland*, 13, and David R. Roediger, *Working Toward Whiteness: How America's Immigrants Became White* (New York: Basic Books, 2005), 51.
30 Aihwa Ong, *Buddha Is Hiding: Refugees, Citizenship, the New America* (Berkeley: University of California Press, 2003), 84.
31 Edward W. Said, *Orientalism* (New York: Vintage Books 1979/1994).
32 Sunaina Maira, "Islamophobia and the War on Terror: Youth, Citizenship, and Dissent," in John Esposito and Ibrahim Kalin, eds., *Islamophobia: The Challenge of Pluralism in the 21st Century* (Oxford, UK: Oxford University Press, 2011), 109–110.
33 Salim Kerboua, "From Orientalism to Neo-Orientalism: Early and Contemporary Constructions of Islam and the Muslim World," *Intellectual Discourse* 24:1 (2016): 7–34, 18–19.
34 See Alise Coen, "Securitization, Normalization, and Representations of Islam in Senate Discourse," *Politics & Religion* 10:1 (2017): 111–136; Fawaz Gerges, "Islam and Muslims in the Mind of America: Influences on the Making of U.S. Policy," *Journal of Palestine Studies* 26:2 (1997): 68–80; Peter Gottschalk and Gabriel Greenberg, "From Muhammad to Obama: Caricatures, Cartoons, and Stereotypes of Muslims," in Esposito and Kalin, *Islamophobia*; and Jack Shaheen, "Reel Bad Arabs: How Hollywood Vilifies a People," *American Academy of Political and Social Science* 588:1 (2003): 171–193.
35 John M. Hobson, *The Eurocentric Conception of World Politics: Western International Theory, 1760–2010* (New York: Cambridge University Press, 2012), 6.
36 Gowayed notes that the racialization of Syrians as "Arab" often implicates religion (Islam). Heba Gowayed, "Resettled and Unsettled: Syrian Refugees and the Intersection of Race and Legal Status in the United States," *Ethnic and Racial Studies* 43:2 (2020): 275–293, 280.
37 Syrian Christian inclusion in American whiteness on the basis of shared religious group membership emerged in early twentieth-century debates over Syrian naturalization. Gualtieri, "Becoming White," 42.
38 Zoltán I. Búzás, "The Color of Threat: Race, Threat Perception, and the Demise of the Anglo-Japanese Alliance (1902–1923)," *Security Studies* 22:4 (2014): 573–606, 578.
39 Mohamed Nimer, ed., *Anti-Americanism and Islamophobia: Causes and Remedies* (Beltsville, MD: Amana Publications, 2007), 15–16.

40 See Jacob Neusner and Tamara Sonn, *Comparing Religions through Law: Judaism and Islam* (New York: Routledge, 1999).
41 Joshua L. Mitchell and Brendan Toner, "Exploring the Foundations of U.S. State-Level Anti-Sharia Initiatives," *Politics and Religion* 9:4 (2016): 720–743, 722.
42 Karen Lugo, *Mosques in America: A Guide to Accountable Permit Hearings and Continuing Citizen Oversight* (Washington, DC: The Center for Security Policy, 2016), 1.
43 David Neiwert, "Anti-Refugee Campaign Reaches Full Boil After Paris Attacks as Governors Try to Halt Flow," *Southern Poverty Law Center*, November 17, 2015, www.splcenter.org.
44 Joel Gunter, "Trump's 'Muslim Lockdown': What Is the Center for Security Policy?," *BBC*, December 8, 2015, www.bbc.com.
45 *The Congressional Record*, June 16, 2016, H3960.
46 See Catalina Amuedo-Dorantes, Cynthia Bansak, and Susan Pozo, "Refugee Admissions and Public Safety: Are Refugee Settlement Areas More Prone to Crime?," *International Migration Review* 55:1 (2020): 135–165.
47 See Patrick Thaddeus Jackson, *Civilizing the Enemy: German Reconstruction and the Invention of the West* (Ann Arbor: University of Michigan Press, 2006), 72.
48 See Robert Vitalis, *White World Order, Black Power Politics: The Birth of American International Relations* (Ithaca, NY: Cornell University Press, 2015), 34–40.
49 See, for example, Amira K. Bennison, *The Great Caliphs: The Golden Age of the Abbasid Empire* (New Haven, CT: Yale University Press, 2009); Dimitri Gutas, *Greek Thought, Arabic Culture: The Graeco-Arabic Translation Movement in Baghdad and Early Abbasid Society* (New York: Routledge, 1998); Jonathan Lyons, *The House of Wisdom: How the Arabs Transformed Western Civilization* (New York: Bloomsbury Press, 2008); Scott L. Montgomery, *Science in Translation: Movements of Knowledge through Cultures and Time* (Chicago: University of Chicago Press, 2000); and Nayef R. F. Al-Rodhan, ed., *The Role of the Arab-Islamic World in the Rise of the West* (London: Palgrave Macmillan, 2012).
50 See Eric O. Hanson, *Religion and Politics in the International System Today* (New York: Cambridge University Press, 2006), and John M. Hobson, *The Origins of Western Civilization* (New York: Cambridge University Press, 2004).
51 Gruminder K. Bhambra, "On the Politics of Selective Memory in Europe," in Christopher Whitehead, Susannah Eckersley, Mads Daugbjerg, and Gönül Bozoglu, eds., *Dimensions of Heritage and Memory: Multiple Europes and the Politics of Crisis* (New York: Routledge, 2019), 172–181, 175.
52 S. Jonathon O'Donnell, "Islamophobic Conspiracism and Neoliberal Subjectivity: The Inassimilable Society," *Patterns of Prejudice* 52:1 (2018): 1–23, 4–5.
53 Eric M. Eisenberg, "Building a Mystery: Toward a New Theory of Communication and Identity," *Journal of Communication* 51:3 (2001): 534–552, 541.
54 Fiona de Londras, "Can Counter-Terrorist Internment Ever Be Legitimate?," *Human Rights Quarterly* 33:3 (2011): 593–619, 607.
55 "Act for America," *The Southern Poverty Law Center*, n.d., www.splcenter.org.

56 "About Us," *ACT for America*, n.d., www.actforamerica.org.
57 "ACT Policy Statement: Non-Discrimination and Anti-Violence Policy," *ACT for America*, n.d., www.actforamerica.org.
58 Brigitte Gabriel, *Rise: In Defense of Judeo-Christian Values and Freedom* (Lake Mary, FL: Charisma House, 2018).
59 "Refugee Resettlement," *ACT for America*, n.d., www.actforamerica.org.
60 Alexander Anievas, Nivi Machanda, and Robbie Shilliam, "Confronting the Global Color Line," in Anievas et al., eds., *Race and Racism in International Relations* (New York: Routledge, 2015), 1–15, 11.
61 "Populations At Risk," *Global Centre for the Responsibility to Protect*, www.globalr2p.org.
62 ACT president Brigitte Gabriel was a particularly important figure in speaking against Syrian refugee resettlement on Fox News programs such as *The Neil Cavuto Show*.
63 Shereen Marisol Meraji, "Refugee Resettlement Evokes Fear, Debate in Montana," *NPR*, October 17, 2016, www.npr.org.
64 Nathan Brown, "Act Head Calls for Action in Twin Falls before Muslims 'Take Over,'" *Magicvalley.com*, August 5, 2016, https://magicvalley.com.
65 O'Donnell, "Islamophobic Conspiracism," 14.
66 Stephanie Dickrell, "Fact-Checking Refugee Resettlement Activist," *SC Times*, April 23, 2015, www.sctimes.com.
67 "Refugee Resettlement Watch," April 26, 2015, https://refugeeresettlementwatch.wordpress.com.
68 It is noteworthy that Corcoran was invited to present at a 2016 conference organized by CSP founder Frank Gaffney, where she met then-candidate Trump and discussed the dangers of the United States accepting Muslim refugees. Jared Goyette, "How an Environmental Lobbyist Became an Influential Anti-Refugee Blogger," *The World*, April 1, 2016, https://theworld.org.
69 "CAIR Publishes List of American 'Islamophobes,'" *Refugee Resettlement Watch*, November 8, 2014, https://refugeeresettlementwatch.wordpress.com.
70 Michael Patrick Leahy, "Twenty-Three Syrian Refugees Have Been Resettled in Nevada During the First 25 Days of FY 2017," *Breitbart.com*, October 26, 2016, www.breitbart.com.
71 "Syrian Refugee Numbers to Soar in Nevada in FY2017," *Refugee Resettlement Watch*, October 28, 2016, https://refugeeresettlementwatch.wordpress.com.
72 "It is all about a ready supply of cheap labor!," *Refugee Resettlement Watch*, July 25, 2016, https://refugeeresettlementwatch.wordpress.com.
73 This logic parallels the "nostalgic return to origins" associated with earlier US immigration quota legislation in the 1920s. See Elizabeth Cohen, *The Political Value of Time: Citizenship, Duration, and Democratic Justice* (New York: Cambridge University Press, 2018), 45.
74 Jens Rydgren, "Is Extreme Right-Wing Populism Contagious? Explaining the Emergence of a New Party Family," *European Journal of Political Research* 44:3 (2005): 413–437, 427.

75 See Matthew J. Lindsay, "Immigration as Invasion: Sovereignty, Security, and the Origins of the Federal Immigration Power," *Harvard Civil Rights-Civil Liberties Law Review* 45:1 (2010): 1–56, and Ediberto Román, *Those Damned Immigrants: America's Hysteria over Undocumented Immigration* (New York: New York University Press, 2013).

76 Cultural difference frames tend to emphasize "irreconcilable problems" resulting from "the cohabitation of established native populations with new, culturally distinct immigrant groups." Such language has enabled political actors to appeal to members of the public who do not perceive themselves to be explicitly racist or xenophobic but nonetheless favor curtailing immigration to preserve the ethnocultural character of their societies. See David Art, *Inside the Radical Right: The Development of Anti-Immigrant Parties in Western Europe* (New York: Cambridge University Press, 2011), 32.

77 See Leo R. Chavez, *The Latino Threat: Constructing Immigrants, Citizens, and the Nation, Second Edition* (Stanford, CA: Stanford University Press, 2013).

78 Samuel P. Huntington, *Who Are We? America's Great Debate* (New York: Simon & Schuster, 2004), 139, 146.

79 *The Congressional Record*, April 2, 2004, H2147.

80 *The Congressional Record*, April 2, 2004, H2147.

81 Regina Branton, Erin C. Cassese, Bradford S. Jones, and Chad Westerland, "All Along the Watchtower: Acculturation Fear, Anti-Latino Affect, and Immigration," *Journal of Politics* 73:2 (2011): 664–679, 664.

82 Steve King (@SteveKingIA), "@FraukePetry Wishing you successful vote. Cultural suicide by demographic transformation must end. @geertwilderspvv," Twitter, September 18, 2016, 1:01pm, https://twitter.com/SteveKingIA/status/777568225538088960.

83 "Rep. Steve King: U.S. Doesn't Need 'Somebody Else's Babies,'" PBS, March 13, 2017, www.pbs.org.

84 Paul Spickard, *Almost All Aliens: Immigration, Race, and Colonialism in American History and Identity* (New York: Routledge, 2009), 12.

85 Jones, *The End of White Christian America*, 203.

86 *The Congressional Record*, January 20, 2016, S115–16.

87 Quraishi, *Redefining the Immigrant South*, 32, 35. See also Sadeghi, *Conditional Belonging*.

88 Chavez, *The Latino Threat*, ix.

89 *The Congressional Record*, January 20, 2016, S115–16.

90 Coats self-identified as "the son of a Swedish immigrant." Dan Coats (@SenDanCoats), "As the son of a Swedish immigrant, I welcome IKEA to Indiana. My allen wrench stands ready to assemble," Twitter, November 10, 2015, 9:53am, https://twitter.com/SenDanCoats/status/664108534276227073?s=20.

91 Christina M. Knopf, "Those Who Bear the Heaviest Burden: Warfare and American Exceptionalism in the Age of Entitlement," in Jason A. Edwards and David Weiss, eds., *The Rhetoric of American Exceptionalism: Critical Essays* (Jefferson, NC: McFarland & Co., 2011), 171–188, 185.

92 Sara Ahmed, "A Phenomenology of Whiteness," *Feminist Theory* 8:2 (2007): 149–168, 159.
93 These themes resonate within a broader history of US political elites constructing threats around racial change to generate fear among white citizens. See Keneshia N. Grant, *The Great Migration and the Democratic Party: Black Voters and the Realignment of American Politics in the 20th Century* (Philadelphia: Temple University Press, 2020), 91.
94 *The Congressional Record*, April 27, 2016, H2060.
95 See Katrina Rebecca Bloch, "'Anyone Can Be an Illegal': Color-Blind Ideology and Maintaining Latino/Citizen Borders," *Critical Sociology* 40:1 (2014): 47–65, 58, and Roxanne Lynn Doty, *Anti-Immigrantism in Western Democracies: Statecraft, Desire, and the Politics of Exclusion* (New York: Routledge, 2003), 18, 20.
96 *The Congressional Record*, April 27, 2016, H2060–61.
97 Huntington, *Who Are We*, xvii.
98 Joel Perlmann and Roger Waldinger, "Second Generation Decline? Children of Immigrants, Past and Present—A Reconsideration," *International Migration Review* 31:4 (1997): 893–922, 917.
99 Charles Jaret, "Troubled by Newcomers: Anti-Immigrant Attitudes and Actions during Two Eras of Mass Immigration to the United States," *Journal of American Ethnic History* 18:3 (1999): 9–39, 29.
100 *The Congressional Record*, November 18, 2015, S8147.
101 *The Congressional Record*, November 18, 2015, H8285–86.
102 Stephen Piggott, "Anti-Immigrant Groups Decry Trump's 'Amnesty' Plan, but Have Pushed for Many of Its Tenets for Decades," *Southern Poverty Law Center*, January 31, 2018, www.splcenter.org.
103 See Elizabeth Cohen, *Illegal: How America's Lawless Immigration Regime Threatens Us All* (New York: Basic Books), 152–153.
104 "Quotes from Contemporary Public Officials," *Federation for American Immigration Reform*, n.d., https://fairus.org.
105 Mark Krikorian, "The Security Costs of Immigration," *Center for Immigration Studies*, February 1, 2003, https://cis.org.
106 "About," *Refugee Resettlement Watch*, April 26, 2015, https://refugeeresettlementwatch.wordpress.com.
107 See, for example, Mark Krikorian, "The Syrian Refugee Crisis and Its Impact on the Security of the U.S. Refugee Admissions Program: Hearing before the U.S. House of Representatives Judiciary Committee Subcommittee on Immigration and Border Security," *Center for Immigration Studies*, November 19, 2015, https://cis.org.
108 Daniel J. Tichenor, *Dividing Lines: The Politics of Immigration Control in America* (Princeton, NJ: Princeton University Press, 2002).
109 "FAIR Presses Obama Administration Regarding Syrian Refugees," *ImmigrationReform.com*, March 11, 2016, https://immigrationreform.com.
110 "Paris Massacre Must Lead Washington to Reconsider Mass Resettlement of Migrants," *ImmigrationReform.com*, November 17, 2015, https://immigrationreform.com.

111 "FAIR's Statement on Donald Trump's Muslim Immigration Comments," *Federation for American Immigration Reform*, December 8, 2015, https://fairus.org.
112 "National Security and Refugee Resettlement from 'High Risk' Countries," *Federation for American Immigration Reform*, August 2016, https://fairus.org.
113 "Protecting Refugees: Questions and Answers," *UNHCR*, February 1, 2002, www.unhcr.org.
114 "Muslim Assimilation Failed in France. Is It Failing Here, Too?," *Center for Immigration Studies*, December 3, 2015, https://cis.org.
115 Jones, *The End of White Christian America*, 2–3.
116 Roxanne Lynn Doty, *The Law Into Their Own Hands: Immigration and the Politics of Exceptionalism* (Tucson: University of Arizona Press, 2009), 57–58.
117 See Ron Dudai, "Entryism, Mimicry and Victimhood Work: The Adoption of Human Rights Discourse by Right-Wing Groups in Israel," *International Journal of Human Rights* 21:7 (2017): 866–888; Daniel Sullivan et al., "Competitive Victimhood as a Response to Accusations of Ingroup Harm Doing," *Journal of Personality and Social Psychology* 102:4 (2012): 778–795; and Isaac F. Young and Daniel Sullivan, "Competitive Victimhood: A Review of the Theoretical and Empirical Literature," *Current Opinion in Psychology* 11 (2016): 30–34.
118 "About EBI," *Evangelicals for Biblical Immigration*, n.d., https://evangelicalsforbiblicalimmigration.com.
119 Erwin Lutzer, "Our Spiritual Walls Must Be Rebuilt," *Billy Graham Evangelistic Association*, October 4, 2016, https://billgraham.org.
120 Evangelicals for Biblical Immigration—EBI. "God loves us all . . ." *Facebook*, September 24, 2016, www.facebook.com.
121 Peter Coates, *American Perceptions of Immigrant and Invasive Species: Strangers on the Land* (Berkeley: University of California Press, 2006), 169.
122 See, for example, Mark J. Rozell and Clyde Wilcox, eds., *God at the Grass Roots: The Christian Right in the 1994 Elections* (Lanham, MD: Rowman & Littlefield, 1995); William Martin, "The Christian Right and American Foreign Policy," *Foreign Policy* 114 (1999): 66–80; and Mark D. Regnerus, David Sikkink, and Christian Smith, "Voting with the Christian Right: Contextual and Individual Patterns of Electoral Influence," *Social Forces* 77:4 (1999): 1375–1401.
123 "About Us," *Christian Coalition*, n.d., www.cc.org.
124 "Order Your Christian Coalition of America Decal," *Christian Coalition*, n.d., www.cc.org.
125 Earl Cox, "Refugee or Infiltrator? Who's to Say?," *Christian Coalition*, December 11, 2015, www.cc.org.
126 Timothy J. Demy and Paul R. Shockley, eds., *Evangelical America: An Encyclopedia of Contemporary American Religious Culture* (Santa Barbara, CA: ABC-CLIO, 2017), 153–154.
127 "Vision and Mission Statements," *Family Research Council*, n.d., www.frc.org.
128 "Haven Forbid? U.S. Debates Refugee Crisis," *Family Research Council*, November 19, 2015, www.frc.org.

129 See Andreas Bandak, "Performing the Nation: Syrian Christians on the National Stage," in Christa Salamandra and Leif Stenberg, eds., *Syria from Reform to Revolt, Volume 2* (Syracuse, NY: Syracuse University Press, 2015), and Ibrahim Zabad, *Middle Eastern Minorities: The Impact of the Arab Spring* (New York: Routledge, 2017).

130 "Haven Forbid?"

131 *The Congressional Record*, November 19, 2015, S8116.

132 *The Congressional Record*, October 28, 2015, H7325.

133 Doris Buss and Didi Herman, *Globalizing Family Values: The Christian Right in International Politics* (Minneapolis: University of Minnesota Press, 2003), 34.

134 See Philip Jenkins, *The Next Christendom: The Coming of Global Christianity*, Third Edition (New York: Oxford University Press, 2011).

135 Ong, *Buddha Is Hiding*, 27.

136 Arun Kundnani, *The Muslims Are Coming! Islamophobia, Extremism, and the Domestic War on Terror* (New York: Verso, 2014), 41.

137 Robbie Shilliam, *Race and the Undeserving Poor* (Newcastle upon Tyne: Agenda Publishing 2018), 7.

138 Vu Tran, "A Refugee Again," in Viet Thanh Nguyen, ed., *The Displaced: Refugee Writers on Refugee Lives* (New York: Abrams Press, 2018), 165–171, 168.

139 See Dina Nayeri, *The Ungrateful Refugee: What Immigrants Never Tell You* (New York: Catapult, 2019), 62.

140 See Stephen Hopgood, *The Endtimes of Human Rights* (Ithaca, NY: Cornell University Press, 2013), 2–3.

141 Halabi, *Radical Hospitality*, 139.

142 See Patricia Anne Simpson and Helga Druxes, eds., *Digital Media Strategies of the Far Right in Europe and the United States* (New York: Lexington Books, 2015), 2, and Sean M. Eddington, "The Communicative Constitution of Hate Organizations Online: A Semantic Network Analysis of 'Make America Great Again,'" *Social Media + Society* 4:3 (2018): 1–12.

143 Barbara Perry and Ryan Scrivens, "White Pride Worldwide: Constructing Global Identities Online," in Jennifer Schweppe and Mark Austin Walters, eds., *The Globalisation of Hate: Internationalising Hate Crime?* (Oxford, UK: Oxford University Press, 2016), 65–78.

144 Bhambra notes that "working class" has become a rhetorical device used to account for white *middle class* support for nativist politics surrounding Brexit and Trump's candidacy. Gurminder K. Bhambra, "Brexit, Trump, and 'Methodological Whiteness': On the Misrecognition of Race and Class," *British Journal of Sociology* 61:1 (2017): 214–232, 226.

145 John M. Hobson, "Re-Embedding the Global Color Line within Post-1945 International Theory," in Anievas et al., eds., *Race and Racism in International Relations*, 81–97.

CHAPTER 4. TERRORIST INFILTRATORS, GENDERED THREAT, AND THE SPECTER OF 9/11

1 Chas Sisk, "Tennessee Lawmaker Calls for National Guard to Round Up Syrian Refugees," *NPR*, November 19, 2015, www.npr.org.
2 Natalie DiBlasio, "Mayor: Japanese Internment Camps Justify Rejecting Refugees," *USA Today*, November 19, 2015, www.usatoday.com.
3 Franz Eder, "Making Concurrence-Seeking Visible: Groupthink, Discourse Networks, and the 2003 Iraq War," *Foreign Policy Analysis* 15:1 (2019): 21–42, 30.
4 Porochista Khakpour, *Brown Album: Essays on Exile and Identity* (New York: Vintage Books, 2020), 161.
5 "President Bush Addresses the Nation," *Washington Post*, September 20, 2001, www.washingtonpost.com.
6 See Alise Coen, "Securitization, Normalization, and Representations of Islam in Senate Discourse," *Politics and Religion* 10:1 (2017): 111–136; Sara de Jong, "Resettling Afghan and Iraqi Interpreters Employed by Western Armies: The Contradictions of the Migration-Security Nexus," *Security Dialogue* 53:3 (2022): 220–237; Uzma Jamil, "Reading Power: Muslims in the War on Terror Discourse," *Islamophobia Studies Journal* 2:2 (2014): 29–42; Erin M. Kearns, Alison E. Betus, and Anthony F. Lemieux, "Why Do Some Terrorist Attacks Receive More Media Attention Than Others?," *Justice Quarterly* 36:6 (2019): 985–1022; Charles Kimball, "The War on Terror and Its Effects on American Muslims," in Jane I. Smith and Yvonne Yazbeck Haddad, eds., *The Oxford Handbook of American Islam* (New York: Oxford University Press, 2015), 490–506; and Mahmood Monshipouri, *The War on Terror and Muslims in the West* (New York: Routledge, 2009).
7 See Wayne A. Cornelius, "Controlling 'Unwanted' Immigration: Lessons from the United States, 1993-2004," *Journal of Ethnic and Migration Studies* 31:4 (2005): 775–794, 789; Jennifer S. Holmes and Linda Camp Keith, "Does the Fear of Terrorists Trump the Fear of Persecution in Asylum Outcomes in the Post-September 11 Era?," *PS: Political Science and Politics* 43:3 (2010): 431–436; Daniel J. Hopkins, "Politicized Places: Explaining Where and When Immigrants Provoke Local Opposition," *American Political Science Review* 104:1 (2010): 40–60, 51; and Reece Jones, *Border Walls: Security and the War on Terror in the United States, India, and Israel* (New York: Zed Books, 2012).
8 Amy Zalman and Jonathan Clarke, "The Global War on Terror: A Narrative in Need of a Rewrite," *Ethics & International Affairs* 23:2 (2009): 101–113, 106.
9 See Marina Espinoza, "State Terrorism: Orientalism and the Drone Programme," *Critical Studies on Terrorism* 11:2 (2018): 376–393, 379. See also E. Tendayi Achiume, "Reimagining International Law for Global Migration: Migration as Decolonization," *American Society of International Law* 111 (2017): 142–146; Lucy Mayblin, "Colonialism, Decolonisation, and the Right to Be Human: Britain and the 1951 Geneva Convention on the Status of Refugees," *Journal of Historical So-*

ciology 27:3 (2014): 423–441; and Lucy Mayblin and Joe Turner, *Migration Studies and Colonialism* (Medford, MA: Polity Press, 2021).

10 Tina Managhan, "We All Dreamed It: The Politics of Knowing and Unknowing the 'War on Terror,'" *Critical Studies on Terrorism* 10:1 (2017): 22–43, 23.

11 See Akbar Ahmed, *The Thistle and the Drone: How America's War on Terror Became a Global War on Tribal Islam* (Washington, DC: Brookings, 2013); Bill Ong Hing, *American Presidents, Deportations, and Human Rights Violations: From Carter to Trump* (New York: Cambridge, 2019), 231; Satvinder S. Juss, ed., *Human Rights and America's War on Terror* (New York, Routledge, 2019); and Dirk Nabers, "Filling the Void of Meaning: Identity Construction in U.S. Foreign Policy After September 11, 2001," *Foreign Policy Analysis* 5:2 (2009): 191–214, 209.

12 See Mubarak Altwaiji, "Neo-Orientalism and the Neo-Imperialism Thesis: Post-9/11 U.S. and Arab World Relationship," *Arab Studies Quarterly* 36:4 (2014): 313–323, and Salim Kerboua, "From Orientalism to Neo-Orientalism: Early and Contemporary Constructions of Islam and the Muslim World," *Intellectual Discourse* 24:1 (2016): 7–34.

13 See Caron E. Gentry and Kathryn Whitworth, "The Discourse of Desperation: The Intersections of Neo-Orientalism, Gender and Islam in the Chechen Struggle," *Critical Studies on Terrorism* 4:2 (2011): 145–161, 161, and Edward W. Said, *Orientalism* (New York: Vintage Books, 1979/1994), 40.

14 Deepa Kumar, "Framing Islam: The Resurgence of Orientalism During the Bush II Era," *Journal of Communication Inquiry* 34:3 (2010): 254–277.

15 See Mayblin and Turner, *Migration Studies and Colonialism*, 126, and Aurora Vergara-Figueroa, *Afrodescendant Resistance to Deracination in Colombia: Massacre at Bellavista-Bojayá-Chocó* (Cham, CH: Palgrave Macmillan, 2018).

16 Mollie Reilly, "Republican Candidates Want to Block Syrian Refugees After Paris Attacks," *Huffington Post*, November 16, 2015, www.huffingtonpost.com.

17 *The Congressional Record*, November 17, 2015, S8022.

18 Rep. Hal Rogers (R-KY), *The Congressional Record*, November 19, 2015, S8384.

19 Rep. Marsha Blackburn (R-TN), *The Congressional Record*, October 6, 2015, H6800.

20 See Constance Duncombe, "Foreign Policy and the Politics of Representation: The West and Its Other," *Global Change, Peace & Security* 23:1 (2011): 31–46, 36, and Stuart Hall, "The West and the Rest: Discourse and Power," in Tania Das Gupta, Carl E. James, and Chris Andersen, eds., *Race and Racialization: Essential Readings, Second Edition* (Toronto: Canadian Scholars, 2018), 85–93.

21 See Benjamin R. Banta, "Just War Theory and the 2003 Iraq War Forced Displacement," *Journal of Refugee Studies* 21:3 (2008): 261–284, and Alise Coen, "Capable and Culpable? The United States, RtoP, and Refugee Responsibility-Sharing," *Ethics & International Affairs* 31:1 (2017): 71–92.

22 *The Congressional Record*, October 28, 2015, H7323.

23 *The Congressional Record*, November 19, 2015, H8398.

24 *The Congressional Record*, January 20, 2016, S101.

25 The effects of the Iraq War, for example, were linked with the initial outbreak of the Syrian conflict and the development of new iterations of Salafi militant strategies that made the conflict more lethal and intractable. See Ranj Alaaldin, "Shia Ascendancy in Iraq and the Sectarian Polarization of the Middle East," in Benjamin Isakhan, ed., *The Legacy of Iraq: From the 2003 War to the "Islamic State"* (Edinburgh, UK: Edinburgh University Press, 2015), 192; Colin P. Kelley et al., "Climate Change in the Fertile Crescent and Implications of the Recent Syrian Drought," *PNAS* 112:11 (2015): 3245; Thomas Hegghammer, "Global Jihadism after the Iraq War," *Middle East Journal* 60:1 (2006): 11–32; and Jessica Stern, "The Continuing Cost of the Iraq War: The Spread of Jihadi Groups Throughout the Region," *Costs of War*, February 18, 2014, https://watson.brown.edu.

26 Espinoza, "State Terrorism," 5.

27 See Charlotte Heath-Kelly, "Counter-Terrorism and the Counterfactual: Producing the 'Radicalisation' Discourse and the UK PREVENT Strategy," *International Relations* 15:3 (2013): 394–415, and Arun Kundnani, *The Muslims Are Coming! Islamophobia, Extremism, and the Domestic War on Terror* (New York: Verso, 2014), 40.

28 See Jones, *Border Walls*, 32, and Nabers, "Filling the Void," 203–204.

29 *The Congressional Record*, November 19, 2015, H8398.

30 *The Congressional Record*, November 19, 2015, H8384.

31 Harmonie Toros, "'9/11 Is Alive and Well' Or How Critical Terrorism Studies Has Sustained the 9/11 Narrative," *Critical Studies on Terrorism* 10:2 (2017): 203–219, 205.

32 Meghana Nayak, "Orientalism and 'Saving' US State Identity After 9/11," *International Feminist Journal of Politics* 8:1 (2006): 42–61, 48.

33 Madeline O. Campbell, *Interpreters of Occupation: Gender and the Politics of Belonging in an Iraqi Refugee Network* (Syracuse, NY: Syracuse University Press, 2016), 63.

34 Laleh Khalili, "Gendered Practices of Counterinsurgency," *Review of International Studies* 37:4 (2011): 1471–1491, 1480.

35 Gentry and Whitworth, "The Discourse of Desperation," 156.

36 See Dana L. Cloud, "'To Veil the Threat of Terror': Afghan Women and the Clash of Civilizations in the Imagery of the U.S. War on Terrorism," *Quarterly Journal of Speech* 90:3 (2004): 285–306; Maryam Khalid, "Gender, Orientalism and Representations of the 'Other' in the War on Terror," *Global Change, Peace & Security* 23:1 (2011): 15–29; Nicola Pratt, "Weaponizing Feminism for the 'War on Terror,' Versus Employing Strategic Silence," *Critical Studies on Terrorism* 6:2 (2013): 327–331; and Laura J. Shepherd, "Veiled References: Constructions of Gender in the Bush Administration Discourse on the Attacks on Afghanistan Post-9/11," *International Feminist Journal of Politics* 8:1 (2006): 19–41.

37 Lila Abu-Lughod, *Do Muslim Women Need Saving* (Cambridge, MA: Harvard University Press, 2013), 6–7.

38 Sara de Jong, "Segregated Brotherhood: The Military Masculinities of Afghan Interpreters and Other Locally Employed Civilians," *International Feminist Journal of Politics* 24:2 (2022): 243–263, 245.

39 R. Charli Carpenter, *"Innocent Women and Children": Gender, Norms and the Protection of Civilians* (Burlington, VT: Ashgate, 2006), 46.
40 Cynthia Enloe, *The Morning After: Sexual Politics at the End of the Cold War* (Berkeley: University of California Press, 1993), 166.
41 *The Congressional Record*, November 19, 2015, H8382.
42 Rep. Ted Lieu (D-CA), *The Congressional Record*, November 19, 2015, H8389.
43 Rep. Zoe Lofgren (D-CA), *The Congressional Record*, November 19, 2015, H8383.
44 See Lewis Turner, "The Politics of Labeling Refugee Men as 'Vulnerable,'" *Social Politics: International Studies in Gender, State & Society* 28:1 (2021): 1–23.
45 See Jennifer Hyndaman and Wenona Giles, "Waiting for What? The Feminization of Asylum in Protracted Situations," *Gender, Place & Culture* 18:3 (2011): 361–379, and Heather L. Johnson, "Click to Donate: Visual Images, Constructing Victims and Imagining the Female Refugee," *Third World Quarterly* 32:6 (2011): 1015–1037.
46 See Hyndman and Giles, "Waiting for What"; Mike Lebson, "Why Refugees Rebel: Towards a Comprehensive Theory of Refugee Militarization," *International Migration* 51:5 (2013): 133–148; and Lewis Turner, "Syrian Refugee Men as Objects of Humanitarian Care," *International Feminist Journal of Politics* 21:4 (2019): 595–616.
47 Rep. Thompson (D-MI), *The Congressional Record*, November 19, 2015, H8398.
48 Nayak, "Orientalism," 55.
49 Rep. Jackson Lee, *The Congressional Record*, November 19, 2015, H8396.
50 *The Congressional Record*, November 19, 2015, H8394.
51 Carpenter, *Innocent Women and Children*, 32–33.
52 Cynthia Enloe, *Bananas, Beaches and Bases: Making Feminist Sense of International Politics, Second Edition* (Berkeley: University of California Press, 2014), 87.
53 Abu-Lughod, *Do Muslim Women Need Saving*, 70.
54 Enloe, *The Morning After*, 46.
55 Espinoza, "State Terrorism," 8.
56 Turner, "Syrian Refugee Men," 608.
57 Campbell, *Interpreters of Occupation*, 16.
58 Stephanie J. Nawyn, "Refugees in the United States and the Politics of Crisis," in Cecilia Menjívar, Marie Ruiz, and Immanuel Ness, eds., *The Oxford Handbook of Migration Crises* (New York: Oxford University Press, 2018), 163–180, 164–165.
59 See Elisabeth Olivius, "Constructing Humanitarian Selves and Refugee Others: Gender Equality and the Global Governance of Refugees," *International Feminist Journal of Politics* 18:2 (2016): 270–290, 282–283.
60 "Presidential Candidate Donald Trump in Keene, New Hampshire," *C-SPAN*, September 30, 2015, www.c-span.org.
61 See Brooks Jackson, "False GOP Theme: 'Unvetted' Refugees," *FactCheck.Org*, August 4, 2016, www.factcheck.org, and "Voters Who Fail to Fact Check Ads May Be Fooled This Election," *WINK News*, August 8, 2016, www.winknews.com.
62 Carpenter, *Innocent Women and Children*, 18–19.
63 *The Congressional Record*, November 19, 2015, H8383.

64 Rep. Sandy Levin (D-MI), *The Congressional Record*, November 19, 2015, H8395. Note that Rep. Jackson Lee similarly referred to the 2 percent statistic in terms of "combat age males." *The Congressional Record*, November 19, 2015, H8396.
65 "Refugees From War Aren't the Enemy," *New York Times*, November 18, 2015. See also references to the article by Rep. Conyers in *The Congressional Record*, November 19, 2015, H8390.
66 Turner, "Syrian Refugee Men," 597.
67 See the stories of Mohammad (Alaa) Aljaleel, who came to be known as "The Cat Man of Aleppo" for his work rescuing cats and other animals during the war; Dr. Mohammad Abo-Hilal, who established Syria Bright Future as an NGO offering mental health services in the Za'atari Refugee camp; and Hosam Katan, a journalist and photographer who was nearly killed from a sniper's bullet while covering the conflict in Aleppo.
68 Lewis Turner, "Who Will Resettle Single Syrian Men?," *Forced Migration Review* 54 (February 2017): 29–31.
69 Carpenter, *Innocent Women and Children*, 88.
70 "Representative Matt Salmon on Vetting Syrian Refugees," *C-SPAN*, November 17, 2015, www.c-span.org.
71 "Presidential Candidate Donald Trump Rally in Las Vegas," *C-SPAN*, February 22, 2016, www.c-span.org.
72 Carpenter, *Innocent Women and Children*, 88.
73 *The Congressional Record*, December 2, 2015, H8965.
74 *The Congressional Record*, December 2, 2015, H8967.
75 Jack Shaheen, *Guilty: Hollywood's Verdict on Arabs after 9/11* (Northampton, MA: Olive Branch Press, 2008).
76 Sam Frizell, "Chris Christie Defends Call to Bar Syrian Orphans," *TIME*, December 15, 2015, https://time.com.
77 Alice Martini, "Making Women Terrorists into 'Jihadi Brides': An Analysis of Media Narratives on Women Joining ISIS," *Critical Studies on Terrorism* 11:3 (2018): 458–477, 461.
78 See Alexander Anievas, Nivi Machanda, and Robbie Shilliam, eds., *Race and Racism in International Relations* (New York: Routledge, 2015); Roxanne Lynn Doty, *Imperial Encounters: The Politics of Representation in North-South Relations* (Minneapolis: University of Minnesota Press, 1996); Denise Ferreira Da Silva, *Toward a Global Idea of Race* (Minneapolis: University of Minnesota Press, 2007); Errol A. Henderson, "Hidden in Plain Sight: Racism in International Relations Theory," *Cambridge Review of International Affairs* 26:1 (2013): 71–92; Robert Vitalis, *White World Order, Black Power Politics: The Birth of American International Relations* (Ithaca, NY: Cornell University Press, 2015); and Kelebogile Zvobgo and Meredith Loken, "Why Race Matters in International Relations," *Foreign Policy*, June 19, 2020, https://foreignpolicy.com.
79 Sarah May Patrick, "Framing Terrorism: Geography-Based Media Coverage Variations of the 2004 Commuter Train Bombings in Madrid and the 2009 Twin

Suicide Car Bombings in Baghdad," *Critical Studies on Terrorism* 7:3 (2014): 379–393, 380.
80 Lucy Taylor, "Decolonizing International Relations: Perspectives from Latin America," *International Studies Review* 14:3 (2012): 386–400, 388.
81 Yến Lê Espiritu, *Home Bound: Filipino American Lives across Cultures, Communities, and Countries* (Berkeley: University of California Press, 2003), 6.
82 *The Congressional Record*, November 17, 2015, S7993.
83 Nayak, "Orientalism," 45.
84 *The Congressional Record*, November 18, 2015, H8350.
85 Parallel themes were present in French constructions of terrorism during the 1930s. See Chris Millington, "Immigrants and Undesirables: 'Terrorism' and the 'Terrorist' in 1930s France," *Critical Studies on Terrorism* 12:1 (2018): 40–59.
86 *The Congressional Record*, November 19, 2015, H8384.
87 Aziz Douai and Sharon Lauricella, "The 'Terrorism' Frame in 'Neo-Orientalism': Western News and the Sunni-Shia Muslim Sectarian Relations After 9/11," *International Journal of Media & Cultural Politics* 10:1 (2014): 7–24, 16.
88 See Victoria M. Esses, Leah K. Hamilton, and Danielle Gaucher, "The Global Refugee Crisis: Empirical Evidence and Policy Implications for Improving Public Attitudes and Facilitating Refugee Resettlement," *Social Issues and Policy Review* 11:1 (2017): 78–123, 82–83.
89 Dina Nayeri, *The Ungrateful Refugee: What Immigrants Never Tell You* (New York: Catapult, 2019), 151. For more on the emotional, physical, and psychological costs imposed on those awaiting resettlement, see Molly Fee, "Lives Stalled: The Costs of Waiting for Refugee Resettlement," *Journal of Ethnic and Migration Studies* 48:11 (2022): 2659–2677.
90 *The Congressional Record*, November 19, 2015, H8382.
91 Managhan, "We All Dreamed It," 37.
92 Duncombe, "Foreign Policy," 44.
93 *The Congressional Record*, December 2, 2015, H8968.
94 "Creeping Sharia" or "Stealth Sharia" conspiracies became widespread among Republicans and conservatives after 2010 and were accompanied by efforts to pass "anti-Shariah" bills at the state and local levels. See John L. Esposito and Natana J. Delong-Bas, *Shariah: What Everyone Needs to Know* (New York: Oxford University Press, 2018), 10–11.
95 S. Jonathon O'Donnell, "Islamophobic Conspiracism and Neoliberal Subjectivity: The Inassimilable Society," *Patterns of Prejudice* 52:1 (2018): 1–23, 3.
96 Sara Ahmed, "A Phenomenology of Whiteness," *Feminist Theory* 8:2 (2007): 149–168, 159.
97 See "Representative Matt Salmon on Vetting Syrian Refugees."
98 Jackson, "False GOP Theme."
99 See, for example, Rep. Richard Hudson (R-NC), *The Congressional Record*, November 19, 2015, H8383; Rep. Jeb Hensarling (R-TX), *The Congressional Record*, November 19, 2015, H8386; Rep. Brad Ashford (R-NE), *The Congressional Record*,

November 19, 2015, H8388; and Rep. Trey Gowdy (R-SC), *The Congressional Record*, November 19, 2015, H8393.
100 Gov. Sam Brownback, quoted in Brian Dulle, "Kansas Governor: Kansas Will Not Accept Syrian Refugees," *KSNT*, November 16, 2015, www.ksnt.com.
101 "Gov. Greg Abbott Says Texas Will Not Accept Any Syrian Refugees," *ABC13*, November 16, 2015, https://abc13.com.
102 Gov. Butch Otter (R-ID) offered this logic in calling on the Obama administration to halt not only Syrian refugees but the Refugee Resettlement Program as a whole. "Gov. Otter Calls for Halt to Refugee Resettlement Effort," *KHQ* (November 16, 2015), www.khq.com.
103 "Representative McCaul on Syrian Refugees," *CSPAN*, November 22, 2015, www.c-span.org.
104 Michael McCaul, *Failures of Imagination: The Deadliest Threats to Our Homeland* (New York: Crown Forum/Penguin Random House, 2016), 2.
105 "President Bush Addresses the Nation."
106 McCaul, *Failures of Imagination*, 5.
107 Rep. Louie Gohmert (R-TX), *The Congressional Record*, December 2, 2015, H8968.
108 Sen. Dan Coats (R-IN), *The Congressional Record*, January 20, 2016, S115.
109 Douai and Lauricella, "The 'Terrorism' Frame," 11.
110 Rep. Steven Palazzo (R-MS), *The Congressional Record*, November 19, 2015, H8388.
111 "Statement from Governor Doug Ducey," *Office of the Governor Doug Ducey*, November 16, 2015, https://azgovernor.gov.
112 See Coen, "Securitization," 124, and Juan Cole, "Islamophobia and American Foreign Policy Rhetoric: The Bush Years and After," in John Esposito and Ibrahim Kalin, eds., *Islamophobia: The Challenge of Pluralism in the 21st Century* (Oxford, UK: Oxford University Press, 2011), 127–142, 130.
113 See Juliane Hamer and Omid Safi, eds., *The Cambridge Companion to American Islam* (New York: Cambridge University Press, 2013); M. A. Muqtedar Khan, *Islam and Good Governance: A Political Philosophy of Ihsan* (New York: Palgrave Macmillan, 2019); Charles Kurzman and Didem Türkoglu, "Do Muslims Vote Islamic Now?," *Journal of Democracy* 26:4 (2015): 100–109; Seyyed Hossein Nasr and Oliver Leaman, eds., *History of Islamic Philosophy* (New York: Routledge, 2005); and Quintan Wiktorowicz, "Anatomy of the Salafi Movement," *Studies in Conflict & Terrorism* 29:3 (2006): 207–239.
114 Managhan, "We All Dreamed It," 32.
115 "Presidential Candidate Donald Trump Rally in Las Vegas," *C-SPAN*, February 22, 2016, www.c-span.org.
116 "Republican National Convention, Day 4," *C-SPAN*, July 21, 2016, www.c-span.org.
117 "2nd Presidential Debate—Letting Refugees into the U.S.," *C-SPAN*, October 9, 2016, www.c-span.org.
118 Robbie Shilliam, "Race and Research Agendas," *Cambridge Review of International Affairs* 26:1 (2013): 152–158, 153.

119 See Hobson, "Re-Embedding the Global Color Line within Post-1945 International Theory," 82–83.
120 "Republican National Convention, Day 4."
121 Nayak, "Orientalism," 44.
122 See Ronald R. Krebs and Jennifer K. Lobasz, "Fixing the Meaning of 9/11: Hegemony, Coercion, and the Road to War in Iraq," *Security Studies* 16:3 (2007): 409–451.
123 Patrick, "Framing Terrorism," 385.
124 Barbara Franz, *Uprooted and Unwanted: Bosnian Refugees in Austria and the United States* (College Station: Texas A&M University Press, 2005), 120.
125 See Janet L. Langlois, "'Celebrating Arabs': Tracing Legend and Rumor Labyrinths in Post-9/11 Detroit," *Journal of American Folklore* 118:468 (2005): 219–236.
126 Maggie Haberman, "Donald Trump Calls for Surveillance of 'Certain Mosques' and a Syrian Refugee Database," *New York Times*, November 21, 2015, www.nytimes.com.
127 Imtiyaz Delawala, "What ABC News Footage Shows of 9/11 Celebrations," *ABC News*, December 4, 2015, https://abcnews.go.com.
128 *The Congressional Record*, June 16, 2016, H3963.
129 *The Congressional Record*, June 15, 2016, H3911.
130 *The Congressional Record*, June 15, 2016, H3912.
131 See Ronald R. Krebs and Jennifer Lobasz, "The Sound of Silence: Rhetorical Coercion, Democratic Acquiescence, and the Iraq War," in A. Trevor Thrall and Jane K. Cramer, eds., *American Foreign Policy and the Politics of Fear: Threat Inflation Since 9/11* (New York: Routledge, 2009), 117–134, 124, 128.
132 Toros, "9/11 Is Alive and Well."
133 *The Congressional Record*, January 20, 2016, S108.
134 Rep. Michael McCaul (R-TX), *The Congressional Record*, November 19, 2015, H8382.
135 Sen. John Thune (R-SD), *The Congressional Record*, November 17, 2015, S8008.
136 Nabers, "Filling the Void," 205.
137 Jill Carle, "Climate Change Seen as Top Global Threat," *Pew Research Center*, July 14, 2015, www.pewresearch.org.
138 *The Congressional Record*, November 19, 2015, H8382.
139 Nawyn, "Refugees in the United States," 164. Emphasis in the original.
140 See, respectively, Rep. Zoe Lofgren (D-CA), *The Congressional Record*, November 19, 2015, H8382, and Rep. Xavier Becerra (D-CA), *The Congressional Record*, November 19, 2015, H8389.
141 Sen. David Vitter (R-LA), *The Congressional Record*, November 17, 2015, S8022.
142 *The Congressional Record*, November 17, 2015, S7994–95.
143 Shoba Sivaprasad Wadhia, *Banned: Immigration Enforcement in the Time of Trump* (New York: New York University Press, 2019), 101.
144 James B. Comey, "Worldwide Threats and Homeland Security Challenges: Hearing Before the Committee on Homeland Security," *Congress.Gov*, October 21, 2015, www.congress.gov.

145 Hing, *American Presidents*, 235.
146 "Statement of Governor LePage Opposing the Settlement of Syrian Refugees in Maine," *Governor Paul R. LePage*, November 16, 2015, www.maine.gov.
147 See Managhan, "We All Dreamed It," 32–34.
148 Nabers, "Filling the Void," 208.
149 Similarly, Lipman points out that Vietnamese refugees were largely portrayed "through images of children" in US discourse during the Cold War to graft "a generic innocence and 'new life' onto their bodies." Jana K. Lipman, *In Camps: Vietnamese Refugees, Asylum Seekers, and Repatriates* (Oakland: University of California Press, 2020), 33.
150 Abu-Lughod, *Do Muslim Women Need Saving*, 70.
151 See Turner, "The Politics of Labeling Refugee Men as 'Vulnerable.'"
152 Rep. Brendan Boyle (D-PA), *The Congressional Record*, November 19, 2015, H8389.
153 Rep. Zoe Lofgren (D-CA), *The Congressional Record*, November 19, 2015, H8382.
154 The bill passed in the House 289–137. While 47 Democrats voted with Republicans to pass the bill, only two Republicans voted against it. "H.R. 4038: American SAFE Act of 2015," *GovTrack*, November 19, 2015, www.govtrack.us.
155 Mirya R. Holman, Jennifer L. Merolla, and Elizabeth J. Zechmeister, "Terrorist Threat, Male Stereotypes, and Candidate Evaluations," *Political Research Quarterly* 69:1 (2016): 134–147.

CHAPTER 5. REFUGEES AS PARTISAN SYMBOLS

1 See remarks by Senators Ben Cardin (D-MD), Dick Durbin (D-IL), and Pat Leahy (D-VT), *The Congressional Record*, June 18, 2015, S403, and July 23, 2015, S5534.
2 "International Rescue Committee: US Commitment to Accept Up to 8,000 Syrians Not Enough," *International Rescue Committee*, September 2, 2015, www.rescue.org.
3 Rebecca Kaplan, "Hillary Clinton: U.S. Should Take 65,000 Syrian Refugees," *CBS News*, September 20, 2015, www.cbsnews.com.
4 Elise Foley, "Donald Trump Uses New Ad to Scare Everyone about Refugees and Immigrants," *Huffington Post*, August 19, 2016, www.huffingtonpost.com.
5 Patrick Thaddeus Jackson, *Civilizing the Enemy: German Reconstruction and the Invention of the West* (Ann Arbor: University of Michigan Press, 2006), 47.
6 "Sen. Ted Cruz Discusses Syrian Refugees with Greg Palkot," *U.S. Senator for Texas Ted Cruz*, Feb. 12, 2014, www.cruz.senate.gov.
7 Juliet Eilperin and Carol Morello, "President Obama Directs Administration to Accept at Least 10,000 Syrian Refugees in the Next Fiscal Year," *Washington Post*, September 10, 2015, www.washingtonpost.com.
8 David Weigel, "Republican Candidates and Voters Wrestle with the Refugee Question," *Washington Post*, September 10, 2015, www.washingtonpost.com.
9 Elizabeth Landers, "Marco Rubio Open to Allowing 'Some' Refugees into U.S.," *CNN*, September 8, 2015, www.cnn.com.

10 Bill Trott and Matt Spetalnick, "Critics Push U.S. to Help Europe By Taking More Refugees," *Reuters*, September 6, 2015, www.reuters.com.
11 "Transcript: National Press Club Luncheon with Senator Lindsey Graham," *The National Press Club*, September 8, 2015, www.press.org.
12 Mollie Reilly, "Republican Candidates Want to Block Syrian Refugees After Paris Attacks," *Huffington Post*, November 16, 2015, www.huffingtonpost.com.
13 Christopher H. Achen and Larry M. Bartels, *Democracy for Realists* (Princeton, NJ: Princeton University Press, 2016), 250.
14 See John C. Green, Lyman A. Kellstedt, Corwin E. Smidt, and James L. Guth, "How the Faithful Voted: Religious Communities and the Presidential Vote," in David E. Campbell, ed., *A Matter of Faith: Religion in the 2004 Presidential Election* (Washington, DC: Brookings Institution, 2007), 15–36; Shento Iyengar, Gaurav Sood, and Yptach Lelkes, "Affect, Not Ideology: A Social Identity Perspective on Polarization," *Public Opinion Quarterly* 76:3 (2012): 405–431; Maurice Mangum, "The Racial Underpinnings of Party Identification and Political Ideology," *Social Science Quarterly* 94:5 (2013): 1222–1244; and Matthew Levendusky, *The Partisan Sort: How Liberals Became Democrats and Conservatives Became Republicans* (Chicago: University of Chicago Press, 2009).
15 Grossman and Hopkins note that most Republican Party leaders and elected officials proudly identify themselves as members of the conservative movement. Matt Grossman and David A. Hopkins, *Asymmetric Politics: Ideological Republicans and Group Interest Democrats* (New York: Oxford University Press, 2016), 72. See also Alan Abramowitz, *The Disappearing Center: Engaged Citizens, Polarization, and American Democracy* (New Haven, CT: Yale University Press, 2010); Andrew Gelman and Julia Azari, "19 Things We Learned from the 2016 Election," *Statistics and Public Policy* 4:1 (2017): 1–10; and Lilliana Mason, "'I Disrespectfully Agree': The Differential Effects of Partisan Sorting on Social and Issue Polarization," *American Journal of Political Science* 59:1 (2015): 128–145.
16 See Achen and Bartels, *Democracy for Realists*, 253, and Leonie Huddy, Lilliana Mason, and Lene Aarøe, "Expressive Partisanship: Campaign Involvement, Political Emotion, and Partisan Identity," *American Political Science Review* 109:1 (2015): 1–17.
17 See Katherine Cramer, *The Politics of Resentment: Rural Consciousness in Wisconsin and the Rise of Scott Walker* (Chicago: University of Chicago Press, 2016); Michael C. Dawson, *Behind the Mule: Race and Class in African-American Politics* (Princeton, NJ: Princeton University Press, 1995); Vincent Hutchings and Hakeem Jefferson, "Out of Options? Blacks and Support for the Democratic Party," *World Congress of the International Political Science Association* (2014); and Lilliana Mason and Julie Wronski, "One Tribe to Bind Them All: How Our Social Group Attachments Strengthen Partisanship," *Political Psychology* 39:S1 (2018): 257–277.
18 See Iyengar et al., "Affect, Not Ideology," 421, and Ben M. Tappin and Ryan T. McKay, "Moral Polarization and Out-Party Hostility in the U.S. Political Context," *Journal of Social and Political Psychology* 7:1 (2019): 213–245, 214.

19 See Abramowitz, *The Disappearing Center*, and Aaron C. Weinschenk, "Polarization, Ideology, and Vote Choice in U.S. Congressional Elections," *Journal of Elections, Public Opinion and Parties* 24:1 (2014): 73–89.
20 Shanto Iyenger and Sean J. Westwood, "Fear and Loathing across Party Lines: New Evidence on Group Polarization," *American Journal of Political Science* 59:3 (2015): 690–707, 691. See also Alan Abramowitz and Steven Webster, "The Rise of Negative Partisanship and the Nationalization of U.S. Elections in the 21st Century," *Electoral Studies* 41:1 (2016): 12–22, and Lilliana Mason, "A Cross-Cutting Calm: How Social Sorting Drives Affective Polarization," *Public Opinion Quarterly* 80:S1 (2016): 351–377.
21 Erin C. Cassese, "Partisan Dehumanization in American Politics," *Political Behavior* 43:1 (2021): 29–50.
22 Nathan P. Kalmoe and Lilliana Mason, "Partisanship, Violence, & American Democracy," University of Chicago Press book launch event for *Radical American Partisanship*, May 13, 2021, Zoom webinar.
23 Mason distinguishes identity-based/symbolic ideology from issue-based/operational ideology, wherein a set of policy attitudes can be categorized on more liberal or conservative ends of a spectrum. This is an important distinction insofar as the sense of belonging within and feeling connected to an identity community called "conservatives" does not necessarily require fidelity to conservative policy principles. Lilliana Mason, *Uncivil Agreement: How Politics Became Our Identity* (Chicago: University of Chicago Press, 2018), 18, 21–22. For additional insights on distinguishing ideology and partisan identity, see Donald R. Kinder and Nathan P. Kalmoe, *Neither Liberal Nor Conservative: Ideological Innocence in the American Public* (Chicago: University of Chicago Press, 2017).
24 Cara J. Wong, *Boundaries of Obligation in American Politics: Geographic, National, and Racial Communities* (New York: Cambridge University Press, 2010), 16. See also Elizabeth Theiss-Morse, *Who Counts as an American? The Boundaries of National Identity* (New York: Cambridge University Press, 2009); Abigail Fisher Williamson, "Mechanisms of Declining Intra-Ethnic Trust in Newly Diverse Immigrant Destinations," *Journal of Ethnic and Migration Studies* 41:11 (2015): 1725–1745; and Nira Yuval-Davis, *The Politics of Belonging: Intersectional Contestations* (London: Sage, 2011).
25 Matthew J. Hoffmann, "Norms and Social Constructivism in International Relations," *Oxford Research Encyclopedia of International Studies* (2010/2017), DOI: 10.1093/acrefore/9780190846626.013.60, 1–22, 15.
26 See Jeremy Pressman, *The Sword Is Not Enough: Arabs, Israelis, and the Limits of Military Force* (Manchester, UK: Manchester University Press, 2020), and Ty Soloman, *The Politics of Subjectivity in American Foreign Policy Discourses* (Ann Arbor: University of Michigan Press, 2015).
27 See Jennifer McCoy and Murat Somer, "Toward a Theory of Pernicious Polarization and How It Harms Democracies: Comparative Evidence and Possible

Remedies," *ANNALS of the American Academy of Political and Social Science* 681:1 (2019): 234–271.

28 Mason, *Uncivil Agreement*, 14.

29 For further discussion of how embedding issues in "cultural conflict" during legislative debates renders them nonnegotiable, see Elizabeth A. Oldmixon, *Uncompromising Positions: God, Sex, and the U.S. House of Representatives* (Washington, DC: Georgetown University Press, 2005), 143. Research on polarization also suggests that when political elites become polarized on policy issues, those issues tend to be perceived with higher levels of certainty and lower levels of critical reflection. See Jon C. Rogowski and Joseph L. Sutherland, "How Ideology Fuels Affective Polarization," *Political Behavior* 38:2 (2016): 485–508, 488, and James N. Druckman, Erik Peterson, and Rune Slothuus, "How Elite Partisan Polarization Affects Public Opinion Formation," *American Political Science Review* 107:1 (2013): 57–79.

30 Tappin and McKay, "Moral Polarization and Out-Party Hostility," 215.

31 See Matthew Feinberg and Robb Willer, "From Gulf to Bridge: When Do Moral Arguments Facilitate Political Influence?," *Personality and Social Psychology Bulletin* (2015): 1–17; Jesse Graham, Jonathan Haidt, and Brian A. Nosek, "Liberals and Conservatives Rely on Different Sets of Moral Foundations," *Journal of Personality and Social Psychology* 96:5 (2009): 1029–1046; Jonathan Haidt and Jesse Graham, "When Morality Opposes Justice: Conservatives Have Moral Intuitions that Liberals May Not Recognize," *Social Justice Research* 20:1 (2007): 98–115; Dan P. McAdams et al., "Family Metaphors and Moral Intuitions: How Conservatives and Liberals Narrate Their Lives," *Journal of Personality and Social Psychology* 95:4 (2008): 978–990; and Aaron C. Weinschenk and Christopher T. Dawes, "Moral Foundations, System Justification, and Support for Trump in the 2016 Presidential Election," *The Forum* 17:2 (2019): 195–208.

32 See Erin C. Cassese and Mirya R. Holman, "Religion, Gendered Authority, and Identity in American Politics," *Politics and Religion* 10:1 (2017): 31–56; Scott Clifford, "Compassionate Democrats and Tough Republicans: How Ideology Shapes Partisan Stereotypes," *Political Behavior* 42:4 (2020): 1269–1293; Damon C. Roberts and Stephen M. Utych, "Linking Gender, Language, and Partisanship: Developing a Database of Masculine and Feminine Words," *Political Research Quarterly* 73:1 (2020): 40–50; and Nicholas J. G. Winter, "Masculine Republicans and Feminine Democrats: Gender and Americans' Explicit and Implicit Images of the Political Parties," *Political Behavior* 32:4 (2010): 587–618.

33 See Erin C. Cassese and Mirya R. Holman, "Party and Gender Stereotypes in Campaign Attacks," *Political Behavior* 40:3 (2018): 785–807; Danny Hayes, "Candidate Qualities Through a Partisan Lens: A Theory of Trait Ownership," *American Journal of Political Science* 49:4 (2005): 908–923; Matthew Leep, "(Ac)Counting (for) Their Dead: Responsiveness to Iraqi Civilian Casualties in the U.S. House of Representatives," *International Politics* 52:1 (2015): 45–65, and "Partisan Discourse, Polarization, and the Politics of Military Fatalities in Iraq," *Democracy and Security* 11:4 (2015): 329–352; and Winter, "Masculine Republicans and Feminine Democrats."

34 Halabi suggests such tropes have been powerful tools for mobilizing support of expanding immigration hospitality not only among policymakers but also among activists, journalists, and members of the public. See Nour Halabi, *Radical Hospitality: American Policy, Media, and Immigration* (New Brunswick, NJ: Rutgers University Press, 2023), 162.
35 "2016 Democratic Party Platform," *The American Presidency Project*, July 21, 2016, www.presidency.ucsb.edu.
36 "2016 Democratic Party Platform."
37 See A. Burcu Bayram, "Aiding Strangers: Generalized Trust and the Moral Basis of Public Support for Foreign Development Aid," *Foreign Policy Analysis* 13:1 (2017): 133–153; Peter Hays Gries, *The Politics of American Foreign Policy: How Ideology Divides Liberals and Conservatives over Foreign Affairs* (Stanford, CA: Stanford University Press, 2014), 10–11; Peter H. Ditto and Spassena P. Koleva, "Moral Empathy Gaps and the American Culture War," *Emotion Review* 3:3 (2011): 331–332; and Brian C. Rathbun, "Does One Right Make a Realist? Conservatism, Neoconservatism, and Isolationism in the Foreign Policy Ideology of American Elites," *Political Science Quarterly* 123:2 (2008): 271–299.
38 See Gov. Jack A. Markell (D-DE), "Why My State Won't Turn Refugees Away," *CNN*, November 18, 2015, www.cnn.com.
39 Rep. Zoe Lofgren (D-CA), *The Congressional Record*, November 19, 2015, H8383.
40 See, for example, Sen. Ben Cardin (D-MD), *The Congressional Record*, January 20, 2016, S125.
41 Rep. Eddie Bernice Johnson (D-TX), *The Congressional Record*, November 19, 2015, H8394.
42 See the letter to President Obama supporting refugee admissions authored by former DHS Secretaries Janet Napolitano and Michael Chertoff and shared by Democratic members of Congress. *The Congressional Record*, November 19, 2015, H8385.
43 *The Congressional Record*, November 19, 2015, H8394.
44 *The Congressional Record*, November 19, 2015, H8387.
45 *The Congressional Record*, November 19, 2015, H8383.
46 Rep. Danny K. Davis (D-IL), *The Congressional Record*, November 19, 2015, H8394-95.
47 *The Congressional Record*, November 17, 2015, S8001-02.
48 Rep. John Conyers (D-MI), *The Congressional Record*, November 19, 2015, H8382.
49 Gov. Gary Herbert (D-VT). See "Shumlin: I Have Faith in Syrian Refugee Screening Process," *Burlington Free Press*, November 18, 2015, www.burlingtonfreepress.com.
50 Carl J. Bon Tempo, "American Exceptionalism and Immigration Debates in the Modern United States," in Sylvia Söderlind and James Taylor Carson, eds., *American Exceptionalisms: From Winthrop to Winfrey* (Albany: State University of New York Press, 2011), 147–165, 148.
51 Jason A. Edwards, "Review: An Exceptional Debate: The Championing of and Challenge to American Exceptionalism," *Rhetoric and Public Affairs* 15:2 (2012): 351–367.

52 Stephen M. Walt, "The Myth of American Exceptionalism," *Foreign Policy*, October 11, 2011.
53 Rep. Danny K. Davis (D-IL), *The Congressional Record*, November 19, 2015, H8394–8395.
54 Tamara Keith, "How 'Stronger Together' Became Clinton's Response to 'Make America Great Again,'" *NPR*, August 8, 2016, www.npr.org.
55 "2nd Presidential Debate—Letting Refugees into the U.S.," *C-SPAN*, November 2, 2016, www.c-span.org.
56 Rep. Jim McDermott (D-WA), *The Congressional Record*, November 19, 2015, H8386.
57 Rep. John Conyers (D-MI), *The Congressional Record*, November 19, 2015, H8382.
58 "2nd Presidential Debate."
59 Nick Gass, "Sanders: We Will Not Turn Our Backs on Syrian Refugees," *Politico*, November 17, 2015, www.politico.com.
60 "Transcript: Washington Governor Inslee Welcomes Syrian Refugees to Settle in His State," *NPR*, November 18, 2015, www.npr.org.
61 "2016 Democratic Party Platform."
62 This partisan labeling continued after H.R. 4038 was passed in the House during debates over other immigration restriction measures. See, for example, congressional deliberation over the "Visa Waiver Program Improvement and Terrorist Travel Prevention Act of 2015," *The Congressional Record*, December 8, 2015, H9047–H9061.
63 Rep. Betty McCollum (DFL-MN), *The Congressional Record*, November 19, 2015, H8394.
64 Rep. Jerry Nadler (D-NY), *The Congressional Record*, November 19, 2015, H8383.
65 Mason, *Uncivil Agreement*, 77.
66 Rep. John Conyers (D-MI), *The Congressional Record*, November 19, 2015, H8382.
67 *The Congressional Record*, January 20, 2016, S125.
68 Rep. Zoe Lofgren (D-CA), *The Congressional Record*, November 19, 2015, H8383.
69 *The Congressional Record*, November 17, 2015, S8001–8002.
70 Rep. Bennie Thompson (D-MS), *The Congressional Record*, November 19, 2015, H8385.
71 Rep. Ted Lieu (D-CA), *The Congressional Record*, November 19, 2015, H8389.
72 *The Congressional Record*, November 19, 2015, H8384.
73 *The Congressional Record*, November 19, 2015, H8383.
74 "Gov. Pence Tells State Agencies to Stop Resettling Syrian Refugees," *Chicago Tribune*, November 17, 2015, www.chicagotribune.com.
75 R. Scott Carey, "Hoosier Whiteness and the Indiana Pacers: Racialized Strategic Change and the Politics of Organizational Sensemaking," *Sport in Society: Cultures, Commerce, Media, Politics* 16:5 (2013): 631–653, 637.

76 "2016 Republican Party Platform," *The American Presidency Project*, July 18, 2016, www.presidency.ucsb.edu.
77 Rep. Matt Salmon (R-AZ), "Representative Matt Salmon on Vetting Syrian Refugees," *C-SPAN*, November 17, 2015, www.c-span.org.
78 Rep. Brad Ashford (R-NE), for example, claimed that the SAFE Act did not "diminish" that American legacy because it did not entirely "shut down the refugee asylum process." *The Congressional Record*, November 19, 2015, H8388.
79 Achen and Bartels, *Democracy for Realists*, 269.
80 See Hans Noel, *Political Ideologies and Political Parties in America* (New York: Cambridge University Press, 2014), 158, and Uzma Quraishi, *Redefining the Immigrant South: Indian and Pakistani Immigration to Houston During the Cold War* (Chapel Hill: University of North Carolina Press, 2020), 108–109.
81 Gries, *The Politics of American Foreign Policy*, 10–11.
82 Ty Solomon, "Time and Subjectivity in World Politics," *International Studies Quarterly* 58:4 (2014): 671–681, 675.
83 Bill O'Reilly, *Culture Warrior* (New York: Broadway Books, 2006), 194.
84 O'Reilly, *Culture Warrior*, 110.
85 *The Congressional Record*, November 19, 2015, H8388–89.
86 This quote by Christian Whiton, a former adviser in the George W. Bush administration, appeared in a September 2016 *Washington Examiner* article and was also entered into *The Congressional Record* by Sen. John Cornyn (R-TX). Whiton went on to become a senior adviser for the Trump administration. *The Congressional Record*, September 20, 2016, S5997.
87 *The Congressional Record*, January 20, 2016, S101.
88 Rep. Bob Goodlatte (R-VA), *The Congressional Record*, November 19, 2015, H8381.
89 Sen. Chuck Grassley (R-IA), *The Congressional Record*, January 19, 2016, S82–S83.
90 Richard Feldstein, *Political Correctness: A Response from the Cultural Left* (Minneapolis: University of Minnesota Press, 1996), 3.
91 Arlie Russell Hochschild, *Strangers in Their Own Land: Anger and Mourning on the American Right* (New York: New Press, 2018), 138–139.
92 Sen. Ted Cruz, *The Congressional Record*, June 16, 2016, S4279–4280.
93 *The Congressional Record*, October 28, 2015, H7323–7325.
94 *The Congressional Record*, November 17, 2015, S7994.
95 "Full Text: Trump Values Voter Summit Remarks," *Politico*, September 9, 2016, www.politico.com.
96 Arnie Seipel, "Sweeping Reactions from Politicians Over Syrian Refugees in U.S.," *NPR*, November 16, 2015, www.npr.org.
97 Rep. Michael McCaul (R-TX), *The Congressional Record*, November 19, 2015, H8382.
98 Sen. John McCain (R-AZ), *The Congressional Record*, November 17, 2015, S7994.
99 "Presidential Candidate Donald Trump Rally in Las Vegas," *C-SPAN*, February 22, 2016, www.c-span.org.

100 "2016 Republican Party Platform."
101 Achen and Bartels, *Democracy for Realists*, 266.
102 See "The Parties on the Eve of the 2016 Election: Two Coalitions, Moving Further Apart," *Pew Research Center*, September 13, 2016, www.pewresearch.org; Danielle Kurtzleben, "Why Don't We Hear More About the Christian Left," *NPR*, October 6, 2016, www.npr.org; and Amelia Thomson-Deveau and Laura Bronner, "Why Democrats Struggle to Mobilize a 'Religious Left,'" *FiveThirtyEight*, May 29, 2019, https://fivethirtyeight.com.
103 Elizabeth A. Oldmixon and Nicholas Drummond, "Religion and Realism: U.S. Foreign Policy in the Twentieth Century," in Barbara A. McGraw, ed., *The Wiley Blackwell Companion to Religion and Politics in the U.S.* (Malden, MA: Wiley, 2016), 369–382, 373.
104 Bernhard Weidinger, "Equal before God, and God Alone: Cultural Fundamentalism, (Anti-)Egalitarianism, and Christian Rhetoric in Nativist Discourse from Austria and the United States," *Journal of Austrian-American History* 1:1 (2017): 40–68, 46.
105 *The Congressional Record*, November 19, 2015, H8391.
106 *The Congressional Record*, November 19, 2015, H8393.
107 See Ronald M. Peters, Jr. and Cindy Simon Rosenthal, *Speaker Nancy Pelosi and the New American Politics* (New York: Oxford University Press, 2010).
108 *The Congressional Record*, November 19, 2015, H8387.
109 "Syrian Refugee Crisis: 7 Things You Can Do to Help," *Catholic Relief Services*, 2016, www.crs.org.
110 "Monthly Prayer Archives," *Catholic Relief Services*, March 2016, www.crs.org.
111 "Catholic Charities Prepares to Receive Syrian Refugees," *The Catholic Sun*, September 10, 2015, www.catholicsun.org.
112 Rep. Sheila Jackson Lee (D-TX), for instance, challenged the SAFE Act by posing the question, "Where is our mercy?." *The Congressional Record*, November 19, 2015, H8384.
113 Ted Jelen, "Religion and Foreign Policy Attitudes: Exploring the Effects of Denomination and Doctrine," *American Politics Quarterly* 22:3 (1994): 382–400, 384.
114 Weidinger, "Equal Before God," 51–53.
115 *The Congressional Record*, November 19, 2015, H8389.
116 *The Congressional Record*, November 19, 2015, H8389.
117 "Family Research Council," *Southern Poverty Law Center*, n.d., www.splcenter.org.
118 "Full Text: Trump Values Voter Summit Remarks."
119 "Donald Trump Remarks in Orlando, Florida," *C-SPAN*, August 11, 2016, www.c-span.org.
120 David J. Bier, "Refugee Program Admits More Christians Than Muslims," *CATO Institute*, July 29, 2016, www.cato.org.
121 Elliot Abrams, "The United States Bars Christian, Not Muslim, Refugees from Syria," *The Council on Foreign Relations*, September 9, 2016, www.cfr.org.
122 Jon Ward, "Transcript: Donald Trump's Closed Door Meeting with Evangelical Leaders," *Yahoo News*, June 22, 2016, www.yahoo.com.

123 "2016 Republican Party Platform."
124 *The Congressional Record*, November 19, 2015, H8388.
125 See, for example, Zack Beauchamp, "Let Us Not Make the Same Mistake: A Letter from More Than 1,000 Rabbis on Refugees," *Vox*, December 5, 2015, www.vox.com, and Rachel Nusbaum, "The World Gathers to Confront the Refugee Crisis: Here's What You Need to Know," *HIAS*, September 14, 2016, www.hias.org.
126 *The Congressional Record*, June 16, 2016, H3959.
127 *The Congressional Record*, June 16, 2016, H3962–3963.
128 *The Congressional Record*, November 19, 2015, S8116.
129 Elizabeth Bruenig, "Is Donald Trump Sparking a Conservative Culture War?," *The New Republic*, January 26, 2016, https://newrepublic.com.
130 David Gibson, "Trump to Top Evangelicals: 'I'm on Your Side,'" *Religious News Service*, June 21, 2016, https://religionnews.com.
131 Dragojlovic, for example, observes partisan differences in responses to transnational advocacy regarding refugee policy, with Democrats more supportive of increasing refugee admissions when foreign allies encourage doing so. Nick Dragojlovic, "Listening to Outsiders: The Impact of Messenger Nationality on Transnational Persuasion in the United States," *International Studies Quarterly* 59:1 (2015): 73–85.
132 See, for example, Oldmixon, *Uncompromising Positions*, 143; Jamie Mayerfeld, *The Promise of Human Rights: Constitutional Government, Democratic Legitimacy, and International Law* (Philadelphia: University of Pennsylvania Press, 2016), 116; Rathbun, "Does One Right Make a Realist," 276; Markku Ruotsila, *The Origins of Christian Anti-Internationalism: Conservative Evangelicals and the League of Nations* (Washington, DC: Georgetown University Press, 2008); and Elliot A. Rosen, *The Republican Party in the Age of Roosevelt: Sources of Anti-Government Conservatism in the United States* (Charlottesville: University of Virginia Press, 2014).
133 Gries, *The Politics of American Foreign Policy*, 13.
134 See Steven L. B. Jensen, *The Making of International Human Rights: The 1960s, Decolonization and the Reconstruction of Global Values* (New York: Cambridge University Press, 2016), 117, and Oldmixon and Drummond, "Religion and Realism," 375.
135 Noel similarly illustrates the dynamics of partisan justification with regard to shifting stances on abortion within the Republican Party. See *Political Ideologies*, 162–163.
136 Rep. Zoe Lofgren (D-CA), *The Congressional Record*, November 19, 2015, H8383.
137 Alexander Betts, *Survival Migration: Failed Governance and the Crisis of Displacement* (Ithaca, NY: Cornell University Press, 2013), 175.
138 See, for example, Peter Gatrell, *A Whole Empire Walking: Refugees in Russia during World War I* (Bloomington: Indiana University Press, 2005), 33, and Are Knudsen, "Widening the Protection Gap: The 'Politics of Citizenship' for Palestinian Refugees in Lebanon, 1948–2008," *Journal of Refugee Studies* 22:1 (2009): 51–73.

139 Noelle Brigden, *The Migrant Passage: Clandestine Journeys from Central America* (Ithaca, NY: Cornell University Press, 2018), 18.

140 Lucy Taylor, "Decolonizing International Relations: Perspectives from Latin America," *International Studies Review* 14:3 (2012): 386–400, 386.

CHAPTER 6. ENDURING AND EVOLVING IDENTITY NARRATIVES

1 See Matthew Coen Leep, "The Affective Production of Others: United States Policy towards the Israeli-Palestinian Conflict," *Cooperation and Conflict* 45:3 (2010): 331–352, 336, and Antje Wiener, "Enacting Meaning-in-Use: Qualitative Research on Norms and International Relations," *Review of International Studies* 35:1 (2009): 175–193, 189.

2 See Lamis Elmy Abdelaaty, *Discrimination and Delegation: Explaining State Responses to Refugees* (New York: Oxford University Press, 2021), 185; Claire L. Adida, Adeline Lo, and Melina R. Platas, "Perspective Taking Can Promote Short-Term Inclusionary Behavior towards Syrian Refugees," *PNAS* 115:38 (2018): 9521–9526; and Alexander Betts, "International Relations and Forced Migration," ch. 5 in Elena Fiddian-Qasmiyeh, Gil Loescher, Katy Long, and Nando Sigona, eds., *The Oxford Handbook of Refugee and Forced Migration Studies* (Oxford, UK: Oxford University Press, 2014), 60–73, 61.

3 See Maja Zehfux, "Constructivism and Identity: A Dangerous Liaison," in Stefano Guzzini and Anna Leander, eds., *Constructivism and International Relations: Alexander Wendt and His Critics* (New York: Routledge, 2006), 92–116, and Rebecca Adler-Nissen, "The Social Self in International Relations: Identity, Power and the Rediscovery of Constructivism's Symbolic Interactionist Roots," *European Review of International Studies* 3:3 (2017): 27–39.

4 Hage relatedly notes that "Islamophobic classifications vaguely and continuously fluctuate between the Arab, the Muslim, and 'Islam,'" such that "it is unclear where the Arab and the Muslim begin and end." Ghassan Hage, *Is Racism an Environmental Threat?* (Malden, MA: Polity Press, 2017), 8.

5 Jessica Taylor, "Trump Calls for 'Total and Complete Shutdown of Muslims Entering' U.S.," *NPR*, December 7, 2015, www.npr.org.

6 Tracy Wilkinson, "Trump Moves to Middle in His Speech on 'America First' Approach to Foreign Policy," *Los Angeles Times*, April 27, 2016, www.latimes.com.

7 "Executive Order 13769 of January 27, 2017," *The Federal Register*, February 1, 2017.

8 Ted Hesson, "Trump Targets 11 Nations in Refugee Order," *Politico*, October 24, 2017, www.politico.com.

9 See Samantha Smith, "Young People Less Likely to View Iraq, Syrian Refugees as Major Threat to U.S.," *Pew Research Center*, February 3, 2017, www.pewresearch.org.

10 Greg Bluestein, "Syrian Refugees in the Sixth Become a Focus of GOP Attack on Jon Ossoff," *Atlanta Journal-Constitution*, June 1, 2017, www.ajc.com.

11 When questioned about the fundraising email, Handel denied affiliation with the PAC sending the messages. Sam Levine, "GOP Congressional Candidate Will

'End Muslim Immigration,' Fundraising Email Says," *Huffington Post*, February 21, 2017, www.huffpost.com.
12. "Global Trends: Forced Displacement in 2018," *UNHCR*, 2018, www.unhcr.org.
13. "World Refugee Day: Celebrating Refugees on the Front Lines of the Pandemic and Economic Recovery," *International Rescue Committee*, June 20, 2020, www.rescue.org.
14. "Syria Regional Refugee Response," *UNHCR*, October 11, 2018, https://data2.unhcr.org.
15. The onset of the COVID-19 pandemic in the spring of 2020 further diminished refugee admissions for FY2020 (11,814). See "U.S. Annual Refugee Resettlement Ceilings and Number of Refugees Admitted, 1980–Present," *Migration Policy Institute*, n.d., www.migrationpolicy.org.
16. Damir Utrzan, Elizabeth Wieling, and Timothy Piehler, "A Needs and Readiness Assessment of the United States Refugee Resettlement Program: Focus on Syrian Asylum-Seekers and Refugees," *International Migration* 57:1 (2019): 127–144, 136–137.
17. Conor Finnegan and Ben Gittleson, "Trump 'Decimated' Refugee Program Hampering Biden's Historic Goal: Advocates," *ABC News*, February 18, 2021, https://abcnews.go.com.
18. See Molly Fee and Rawan Arar, "What Happens When the United States Stops Taking in Refugees?," *Context* 18:2 (2019): 18–23, 22.
19. The Biden administration raised annual refugee admissions ceilings from 18,000 (FY2020) to 62,500 (FY2021) and then up to 125,000 for FY2022 and FY2023. However, formal refugee admissions remained very low (below 12,000 in 2021 and just over 25,000 in 2022) in part due to the slow rebuilding of the domestic resettlement infrastructure. "U.S. Annual Refugee Resettlement Ceilings and Number of Refugees Admitted, 1980–Present."
20. See Brian R. Calfano, Nazita Lajevardi, and Melissa R. Michelson, "Evaluating Resistance toward Muslim American Political Integration," *Politics and Religion* 14:3 (2020): 512–525, and Nazita Lajevardi, *Outsiders at Home: The Politics of American Islamophobia* (New York: Cambridge University Press, 2020).
21. See Katayoun Kishi, "Anti-Muslim Assaults Reach 9/11-Era Levels, FBI Data Show," *Pew Research Center*, November 21, 2016, www.pewresearch.org, and "Assaults against Muslims in the U.S. Surpass 2001 Level," *Pew Research Center*, November 15, 2017, www.pewresearch.org.
22. Janice A. Iwama, "Understanding Hate Crimes against Immigrants: Considerations for Future Research," *Sociology Compass* 12:3 (2018): e12565.
23. Paula Ioanide, *The Emotional Politics of Racism: How Feelings Trump Facts in an Era of Colorblindness* (Stanford, CA: Stanford University Press, 2015), 48.
24. Porochista Khakpour, *Brown Album: Essays on Exile and Identity* (New York: Vintage Books, 2020), 128. See also Porochista Khakpour, *Sick: A Memoir* (New York: Harper, 2018), 167.

25 See Cameron Easley, "Biden's Move to Expand Refugee Admissions Is His Most Unpopular Executive Action So Far," *Morning Consult*, February 10, 2021, https://morningconsult.com, and Michael Lipka, "Most Americans Express Support for Taking in Refugees, But Opinions Vary by Party and Other Factors," *Pew Research Center*, September 19, 2022, www.pewresearch.org.

26 "A Letter from Faith Leaders and Evangelicals for Biblical Immigration," *Evangelicals for Biblical Immigration*, September 4, 2017, https://evangelicalsforbiblicalimmigration.com. Note that NumbersUSA also republished the letter on their website. "EBI: 'The Bible Does Not Teach Open Borders,'" *NumbersUSA*, September 5, 2017, www.numbersusa.org.

27 See David L. Chappell, "Religious Ideas of the Segregationists," *Journal of American Studies* 32:2 (1998): 237–262.

28 Paulina Ochoa Espejo, *On Borders: Territories, Legitimacy, & the Rights of Place* (New York: Oxford University Press, 2020), 35.

29 See S. Jonathon O'Donnell, "Antisemitism Under Erasure: Christian Zionist Anti-Globalism and the Refusal of Cohabitation," *Ethnic and Racial Studies* 44:1 (2021): 39–57, and Thorsten Wojczewski, "Trump, Populism, and American Foreign Policy," *Foreign Policy Analysis* 16:3 (2020): 292–311. See also Rep. Dana Rohrabacher's (R-CA) juxtaposition of American "patriots" with threatening "globalists" in *The Congressional Record*, March 4, 2010, H1155–1160.

30 "Immigration, the United Nations and the New Globalism," *Focus on the Family*, January 8, 2017, https://dailycitizen.focusonthefamily.com.

31 "Making America Great Again: Immigration," *Trump 2020 Campaign Website*, n.d., www.promiseskept.com.

32 See Andrew Geddes, *Governing Migration beyond the State: Europe, North America, South America, and Southeast Asia in a Global Context* (New York: Oxford University Press, 2021), 177.

33 Erik Rosales, "Immigration: What Does the Bible Say?," *CBN*, March 13, 2018, www1.cbn.com.

34 Roxanne Lynn Doty, *Anti-Immigrantism in Western Democracies: Statecraft, Desire, and the Politics of Exclusion* (New York: Taylor & Francis, 2003), 30.

35 Earl Cox, "Radical Islamic Immigration Strategy," *Christian Coalition*, March 15, 2017, www.cc.org.

36 Hage, *Is Racism an Environmental Threat*, 71.

37 Jeff Sessions and Stephen Miller are two prominent examples. See Elizabeth Cohen, *Illegal: How America's Lawless Immigration Regime Threatens Us All* (New York: Basic Books, 2020), 153.

38 See Jennifer G. Hickey, "Democrats Introduce Bills to Overturn Trump Travel Ban," *FAIR*, April 11, 2019, www.fairus.org; Matt O'Brien, "The European Union to Member States—We Now Control Your Borders," *FAIR*, September 12, 2017, www.fairus.org; and Nayla Rush, "The Global Compact on Refugees: A New Model for International Lawmaking," *Center for Immigration Studies*, October 26, 2018, https://cis.org.

39 Steve Cortes (@CortesSteve), "Raise your hand if you want this plane landing in your town? America paid unimaginable costs in Afghanistan because of uniparty globalists who dominated the Bush & Obama administrations. No more . . ." Twitter, August 17, 2021, 10:47pm, https://twitter.com/CortesSteve/status/1427839604376444929.
40 Anthony Sabatini (@AnthonySabatini), "The #AmericaLast Globalists will now be pushing for 100,000+ Afghanis to be given permanent residency status then citizenship in the United States. I say absolutely NO—we must fight this. No more open-borders and insane immigration policies," Twitter, August 15, 2021, 5:47pm, https://twitter.com/AnthonySabatini/status/1427039393328599045.
41 Sen. John Thune (R-SD), *The Congressional Record*, January 20, 2016, S102.
42 "Executive Order 13888 of September 26, 2019," *The Federal Register*, October 1, 2019.
43 Laura Strickler and Dan De Luce, "Blindsiding Trump, Most Republican Governors Have Agreed to Accept Refugees," *NBC News*, January 10, 2020, www.nbcnews.com.
44 See Robert Shaffer, Lauren E. Pinson, Jonathan A. Chu, and Beth A. Simmons, "Local Elected Officials' Receptivity to Refugee Resettlement in the United States," *PNAS* 117:50 (2020): 31722–31728; Daniel Thompson, "How Partisan Is Local Law Enforcement? Evidence from Sheriff Cooperation with Immigration Authorities," *American Political Science Review* 114:1 (2020): 222–236; Abigail Fisher Williamson, *Welcoming New Americans? Local Government and Immigrant Incorporation* (Chicago: University of Chicago Press, 2018), 15; and Tom K. Wong, S. Deborah Kang, Carolina Valdivia, Josefina Espino, Michelle Gonzalez, and Elia Peralta, "How Interior Immigration Enforcement Affects Trust in Law Enforcement," *Perspectives on Politics* 19:2 (2021): 357–370, 360.
45 Lauren Aratani, "Utah a Not-So-Unlikely Haven for Refugees in the Face of Trump Cuts," *The Guardian*, December 22, 2019, www.theguardian.com.
46 Evyn Lê Espiritu Gandhi, *Archipelago of Resettlement: Vietnamese Refugee Settlers and Decolonization across Guam and Israel-Palestine* (Oakland: University of California Press, 2022), 185.
47 Jeremy Pelzer, "Ohio Will Still Accept Refugees, Gov. Mike DeWine Tells Trump Administration," *Cleveland.com*, December 31, 2019, www.cleveland.com.
48 Scott Bourque, "Gov. Ducey Opts in to Refugee Resettlement in Arizona," *KJZZ*, December 6, 2019, www.kjzz.org.
49 Troy Stolt, "Gov. Mike Parson Says Missouri Will Continue Accepting Refugees," *St. Louis Post-Dispatch*, January 1, 2020, www.stltoday.com.
50 As previously discussed, this bifurcation tends to conflate "illegal" immigrants with southern border crossers, overlooking the diversity of undocumented migrants and prevalence of visa overstays. See Rebecca Hamlin, *Crossing: How We Label and React to People on the Move* (Stanford, CA: Stanford University Press, 2021), 7.
51 Lindsey Erdody, "Holcomb Opts in to Accepting Refugees," *Indianapolis Business Journal*, December 20, 2019, www.ibj.com.
52 Randolph B. Persaud, "Situating Race in International Relations: The Dialectics of Civilizational Security in American Immigration," in Geeta Chowdhry and

Sheila Nair, eds., *Power, Postcolonialism and International Relations: Reading Race, Gender and Class* (New York: Routledge, 2022), 56–81, 59.

53 Nicole Narea, "Texas Just Became the First State to Shut the Door on Refugees," *Vox*, January 10, 2020, www.vox.com.

54 Kevin R. Johnson, Raquel Aldana, Bill Ong Hing, Leticia M. Sucedo, and Enid Trucios-Haynes, eds., *Understanding Immigration Law* (Durham, NC: Carolina Academic Press, 2019), 220.

55 Ilhan Omar (@IlhanMN), "With silent lips. 'Give me your tired, your poor, Your huddled masses yearning to breathe free, The wretched refuse of your teeming shore.' These are the words that welcomed me and millions of refugees. I still believe in those values. We shall overcome," Twitter, January 10, 2020, 6:47pm, https://twitter.com/IlhanMN/status/1215797294206980096.

56 Greg Abbott (@GregAbbott_TX), "The values America needs you to believe in are the: U.S. Constitution & the Declaration of Independence," Twitter, January 11, 2020, 10:00pm, https://twitter.com/GregAbbott_TX/status/1216208315958616064.

57 See W.E.B. Du Bois, "The First Universal Races Congress," in Phil Zuckerman, ed., *The Social Theory of W.E.B. Du Bois* (Thousand Oaks, CA: Sage, 2004), 27.

58 See Geoffrey Cameron and Shauna Labman, "The Dynamics and Divergences of Executive Discretion in Refugee Resettlement," ch. 5 in Kiran Banerjee and Craig Damian Smith, eds., *Migration Governance in North America: Policy, Politics, and Community* (Montreal: McGill-Queen's University Press, 2024), 143–170.

59 Robert Harding, "Katko, Bipartisan House Caucus to Trump: Don't Cut Refugee Cap," *The Auburn Citizen*, September 20, 2018, https://auburnpub.com.

60 Harding, "Katko."

61 Domenico Montanaro, "These Are the 10 Republicans Who Voted to Impeach Trump," *NPR*, January 14, 2021, www.npr.org.

62 "Factbox: U.S. Republican Lawmakers Who Say They Won't Vote for Trump," *Reuters*, August 15, 2016, www.reuters.com.

63 The Republican signatories to the letter are discussed in Lynn Tramonte, "Sixteen House Members Urge Trump Administration to Uphold Refugee Protections," *Interfaith Immigration Coalition*, October 22, 2019, www.interfaithimmigration.org.

64 "Press Release: Congressman Neguse Leads Bipartisan Letter to Oppose Trump Administration Actions Targeting U.S. Refugee Resettlement," *U.S. Congressman Joe Neguse*, August 7, 2019, https://neguse.house.gov.

65 See "2019 Report Cards: All Senators/Ideology Score," *GovTrack*, January 18, 2020, www.govtrack.us.

66 Alexander Barder, *Global Race War: International Politics and Racial Hierarchy* (New York: Oxford University Press, 2021), 202.

67 "Senators Lankford, Coons Lead Letter on Concerns to Eliminate Refugee Cap," *U.S. Senator James Lankford*, August 5, 2019, www.lankford.senate.gov.

68 Tramonte, "Sixteen House Members Urge Trump Administration to Uphold Refugee Protection."

69 "Ken Buck Calls for the United States to Uphold Our Commitment to Refugees Around the World," *U.S. Congressman Ken Buck*, October 18, 2019, https://buck.house.gov.
70 Anugrah Kumar, "Christian Groups Say 15K Cap on Refugee Resettlement for 2021 Is 'Unconscionable,'" *The Christian Post*, October 3, 2020, www.christianpost.com.
71 John Binder, "Soros-Linked Group Gets Six GOP Governors to Resettle More Refugees," *Breitbart*, December 11, 2019, www.breitbart.com.
72 Tara Isabella Burton, "The Centuries-Old History of Jewish 'Puppet Master' Conspiracy Theories," *Vox*, November 2, 2018, www.vox.com.
73 See, for example, Neil Munro, "Foreign Refugee Managers: Keep Americans in the Dark," *Breitbart*, December 18, 2020, www.breitbart.com.
74 "Constituent Survey," *Congressman Glenn Grothman*, 2020. Print campaign mailer.
75 B. S. Chimni, "The Birth of a 'Discipline': From Refugee to Forced Migration Studies," *Journal of Refugee Studies* 22:1 (2009): 11–29, 18.
76 "The Power of America's Example: The Biden Plan for Leading the Democratic World to Meet the Challenges of the 21st Century," *Biden 2020 Campaign Website*, n.d., https://joebiden.com.
77 Joe Biden, "My Statement on World Refugee Day," June 20, 2020, https://medium.com.
78 "Remarks by President Trump at the 2020 Salute to America," *U.S. Embassy in Georgia*, July 4, 2020, https://ge.usembassy.gov.
79 Melissa Quinn and Kathryn Watson, "Trump Accepts GOP Nomination and Says Biden Victory Would Destroy American Way of Life," *CBS News*, August 28, 2020, www.cbsnews.com.
80 "President Trump Campaign Rally in Duluth, Minnesota," *C-SPAN*, September 30, 2020, www.c-span.org.
81 Donald Trump (@realDonaldTrump), "My Administration has suspended the entry of refugees from terror-compromised nations such as Syria, Somalia and Yemen. Biden's plan surges refugees 700% into Minnesota, Michigan & Pennsylvania—burdening schools & hospitals while opening the floodgates to Radical Islamic Terror," Twitter, October 29, 2020, 6:45pm, https://twitter.com/realDonaldTrump/status/1321961340341121025.
82 "Seven Hundred Percent," Donald J. Trump, September 18, 2020, campaign advertisement video, 0:30, www.youtube.com/watch?v=6TQvqk8EqIE.
83 "Trump Administration Sets Record Low Limit for New U.S. Refugees," *Reuters*, October 28, 2020, www.reuters.com.
84 Alexander Mallin, "Feds Arrest Syrian Refugee Accused of Plotting Terrorist Attack on Pittsburgh Church," *ABC News*, June 19, 2019, https://abcnews.go.com.
85 *The Congressional Record*, July 16, 2019, H5830–H5831.
86 See Zoltán Búzás, *Evading International Norms: Race and Rights in the Shadow of Legality* (Philadelphia: University of Pennsylvania Press, 2021), and Alise Coen, "Can't Be Held Responsible: Weak Norms and Refugee Protection Evasion," *International Relations* 35:2 (2021): 341–362.

87 *The Congressional Record*, July 16, 2019, H5830–H5831.
88 "Afghans Living in COVID-19 Saturated Iran Flee Across Border, Headed Home," *Refugee Resettlement Watch*, April 7, 2020, https://refugeeresettlementwatch.org.
89 See "Arizona: Videos Produced in Ten Languages to Teach Refugees COVID Cleanliness Practices," *Refugee Resettlement Watch*, April 27, 2020, https://refugeeresettlementwatch.org; "Changing South Dakota One Slaughterhouse at a Time," *Refugee Resettlement Watch*, April 25, 2020, https://refugeeresettlementwatch.org; and "Ohio: Refugee Agencies Scramble to Get COVID-19 Warnings to Those Who Don't Speak English," *Refugee Resettlement Watch*, March 17, 2020, https://refugeeresettlementwatch.org.
90 James Jay Carafano, "Europe No Longer Welcoming Refugees—Some Likely Carry Coronavirus," *Fox News*, March 5, 2020, www.foxnews.com.
91 Lev Golinkin, "Guests of the Holy Roman Empress Maria Theresa," in Viet Thanh Nguyen, ed., *The Displaced: Refugee Writers on Refugee Lives* (New York: Abrams Press, 2018), 75–80, 77.
92 Jacqueline Alemany, "Power Up: Trump Resists Concession As His Legal Team Plans to Fan Out to Key States," *Washington Post*, November 9, 2020, www.washingtonpost.com.
93 John Bowden, "Retiring GOP Rep: 'I Don't Understand' the 'Hold that President Trump Has Over' Republican Leaders," *The Hill*, November 9, 2020, https://thehill.com.
94 "Hebrew Immigrant Aid Society Salivates Over Prospect of Biden/Harris in White House," *Refugee Resettlement Watch*, November 8, 2020, https://refugeeresettlementwatch.org.
95 The post included a photograph of Somali American Rep. Ilhan Omar (D-MN) wearing her headscarf and speaking into a microphone. "12,924 Somalis and 14,084 Syrians Already in Pipeline to Enter US If Biden Inaugurated," *Refugee Resettlement Watch*, November 7, 2020, https://refugeeresettlementwatch.org.
96 See "Proclamation on Ending Discriminatory Bans on Entry to the United States," *The White House*, January 20, 2021, www.whitehouse.gov, and "Executive Order on Rebuilding and Enhancing Programs to Resettle Refugees and Planning for the Impact of Climate Change on Migration," *The White House*, February 4, 2021, www.whitehouse.gov.
97 Sahar Aziz, "Orientalism, Empire, and *The Racial Muslim*," in Tamara Sonn, ed., *Overcoming Orientalism: Essays in Honor of John L. Esposito* (New York: Oxford University Press, 2021), 221–244, 232.
98 "Congressman Biggs Leads Letter to Biden Administration about Plans to Weaken Immigration Screening and Vetting," *U.S. Congressman Andy Biggs*, February 10, 2021, https://biggs.house.gov.
99 See Jamal Barnes and Samuel M. Makinda, "A Threat to Cosmopolitan Duties? How COVID-19 Has Been Used as a Tool to Undermine Refugee Rights," *International Affairs* 97:6 (2021): 1671–1689.

100 See Alise Coen, "Trump, Biden, and the U.S. Role in the International Refugee Regime," ch. 6 in Banerjee and Smith, eds., *Migration Governance in North America*, 171–206.
101 "U.S. Annual Refugee Resettlement Ceilings and Number of Refugees Admitted, 1980–Present."
102 Rep. Alexandria Ocasio-Cortez (D-NY) (@AOC), "Completely and utterly unacceptable. Biden promised to welcome immigrants, and people voted for him based on that promise. Upholding the xenophobic and racist policies of the Trump admin, incl the historically low + plummeted refugee cap, is flat out wrong. Keep your promise," Twitter, April 16, 2021, 1:09pm, https://twitter.com/AOC/status/1383120325454467072.
103 Rep. Ilhan Omar (D-MN) (@Ilhan), "As a refugee, I know finding a home is a matter of life or death for children around the world. It is shameful that @POTUS is reneging on a key promise to welcome refugees, moments after @RepSchakowsky @RepJayapal, myself and others called on him to increase the refugee cap," Twitter, April 16, 2021, 12:40pm, https://twitter.com/Ilhan/status/1383113038606254084.
104 See Aline Barros, "Biden Administration, in Response to Criticism, Says It Will Lift Refugee Cap Next Month," *Voice of America*, April 17, 2021, www.voanews.com; Charles Davis, "The Catholic Church Is Urging President Biden to Accept a Lot More Refugees," *Business Insider*, April 19, 2021, www.businessinsider.com; "IRC Deeply Disappointed at Biden Administration Decision to Maintain Trump-era Refugee Cap," *International Rescue Committee*, April 16, 2021, www.rescue.org; and "Statement in Response to Biden's Historically Low Refugee Cap," *America's Voice*, April 16, 2021, https://americasvoice.org.
105 Maria Ramirez Uribe, "Joe Biden Welcomed Thousands of Ukrainians; Many Are in Immigration Limbo," *PolitiFact*, February 23, 2023, www.politifact.com.
106 See, for example, statements by Sen. Joni Ernst (R-IA), Sen. Deb Fischer (R-NE), Sen. Jon Tester (D-MT), and Sen. John Thune (R-SD) in Brianne Pfannenstiel, "U.S. Sen. Joni Ernst Pushes for More Aid to Ukraine after Leading Trip to Poland, Germany," *Des Moine Register*, March 21, 2022, www.desmoinesregister.com; "Fischer: 'The Ukraine Crisis Demands We Fundamentally Reevaluate Our Approach to Dealing with Putin,'" *U.S. Senator Deb Fischer*, March 2, 2022, www.fischer.senate.gov; "Tester Statement on Russia's Illegal Acts of War in Ukraine," *U.S. Senator Jon Tester*, Febrary 24, 2022, www.tester.senate.gov; and "Thune: The Free World Stands with Ukraine," *U.S. Senator John Thune*, March 1, 2022, www.thune.senate.gov. See also a similar discussion of ideological narratives in Jonathan Haidt, Jesse Graham, and Craig Joseph, "Above and Below Left-Right: Ideological Narratives and Moral Foundations," *Psychological Inquiry: An International Journal for the Advancement of Psychological Theory* 20:2–3 (2009): 110–119, 115.
107 Barder, *Global Race War*, 3.

108 Joshua Rodriguez and Jeanne Batalova, "Ukrainian Immigrants in the United States," *Migration Policy Institute*, June 20, 2022, www.migrationpolicy.org.
109 See Alise Coen, "Localizing Refugeehood: Norms and the U.S. Resettlement of Afghan Allies," *International Affairs* 98:6 (2022): 2021–2038.
110 Rep. Mo Brooks (R-AL). "U.S. House of Representatives: Morning Hour," *C-SPAN*, March 2, 2022, www.c-span.org.
111 Rep. Tom Reed (R-NY). "Congressman Supports Jamestown Refugee Resettlement Efforts," *Erie News Now*, April 12, 2022, www.erienews.com.
112 Sen. Jim Risch (R-ID). "Ranking Member Risch Opening Statement at Hearing on Russia's Invasion of Ukraine," *Foreign Relations Committee*, March 8, 2022, www.foreign.senate.gov.
113 Sen. Rob Portman (R-OH). "Portman on Senate Floor: We Cannot Continue to Allow the Weak Screening of Afghan Evacuees Endanger Our Communities," *Homeland Security & Government Affairs*, November 4, 2021, www.hsgac.senate.gov.
114 Sen. Rob Portman (R-OH). "Remarks from U.S. Senator Rob Portman," *The City Club of Cleveland*, April 21, 2022, www.cityclub.org.
115 Dylan Smith, "Ducey Wants to Block Syrian Refugees from Arizona," *Tucson Sentinel*, November 16, 2015, www.tucsonsentinel.com.
116 Mark Philips, "Arizona Ready to Welcome Ukrainian Refugees If Needed," *ABC15 Arizona*, March 3, 2022, www.abc15.com.
117 Polling data from 2021, for instance, showed the majority of Democrats expressing support and the majority of Republicans split between expressing disapproval and uncertainty regarding whether "refugees leaving Afghanistan" should be allowed entry. When the survey avoided the term *refugee* and instead asked whether "Afghans who worked with the U.S. military or its allies" should be allowed to come to the United States, Republican respondents became more unified in expressing approval. "Yahoo! News COVID-19/Afghanistan Survey," *YouGov*, September 1, 2021, https://docs.cdn.yougov.com.
118 See "Public Expresses Mixed Views of U.S. Response to Russia's Invasion of Ukraine," *Pew Research Center*, March 15, 2022, www.pewresearch.org.
119 "Chairman Menendez on New 'Uniting for Ukraine' Parole Program for Ukrainian Refugees," *Senate Foreign Relations Committee*, April 21, 2022, www.foreign.senate.gov.
120 "Reps. Lee, Beatty, Meeks, Bass and Paskett Urge Humane and Non-Discriminatory Treatment for People of Color Fleeing Ukraine," *U.S. Congresswoman Barbara Lee*, March 4, 2022, https://lee.house.gov.
121 Rebecca Beitsch, "Critics Decry Double Standard on Migrants Amid Ukraine Crisis," *The Hill*, March 31, 2022, https://thehill.com.
122 See Nathan P. Kalmoe and Lilliana Mason, *Radical American Partisanship: Mapping Violent Hostility, Its Causes, and the Consequences for Democracy* (Chicago: University of Chicago Press, 2022).
123 Vu Tran, "A Refugee Again," in Nguyen, ed., *The Displaced*, 165–171, 169.

124 See Barder, *Global Race War*, 204.
125 It is questionable to what extent such narratives are sustainable among more liberal and decolonizing voices within the Democratic coalition. A 2020 survey found self-identified Democrats far less likely to view the United States as "the greatest country in the world" compared to self-identified Republicans, for example, and exceptionalist claims were scrutinized during pivotal moments of contemplating what America means, such as the January 6, 2021 insurrection. See Hakeem Jefferson, "Storming the U.S. Capitol Was About Maintaining White Power in America," *FiveThirtyEight*, January 8, 2021, https://fivethirtyeight.com; David Paleologos, "Paleologos on the Poll: First We Couldn't Talk Politics at Thanksgiving. Now, the 4th?" *USA Today*, July 2, 2020, www.usatoday.com; and Kelebogile Zvobgo, "'This Is Not Who We Are' Is a Great American Myth," *Foreign Policy*, January 8, 2021.
126 It is noteworthy that trends point toward state and municipal officials—who might have been more supportive of refugees in the past—becoming increasingly polarized as part of the "nationalization" of state and local politics. See Daniel J. Hopkins, *The Increasingly United States: How and Why American Political Behavior Nationalized* (Chicago: University of Chicago Press, 2018); Daniel J. Moskowitz, "Local News, Information, and the Nationalization of U.S. Elections," *American Political Science Review* 115:1 (2021): 114–129; Benjamin Melusky and Jesse Richman, "When the Local Is National—A New High-Water Mark for Nationalization in the 2018 U.S. State Legislative Elections," *Regional & Federal Studies* 30:3 (2020): 441–460; and Aaron Weinschenk et al., "Have Supreme Court Elections Nationalized?," *Justice System Journal* 41:4 (2020): 313–322.
127 "Congressman Biggs Leads Letter to Biden Administration about Plans to Weaken Immigration Screening and Vetting."
128 "2016 Republican Party Platform," *The American Presidency Project*, July 18, 2016, www.presidency.ucsb.edu.
129 Holly Fuong and Geoffrey Skelley, "Do Democrats and Republicans Agree on Anything About Climate Change and Immigration?" *FiveThirtyEight*, September 29, 2022, https://fivethirtyeight.com.
130 See Avi Brisman, Nigel South, and Reece Walters, "Climate Apartheid and Environmental Refugees," in Kerry Carrington et al., eds., *The Palgrave Handbook of Criminology and the Global South* (Cham, CH: Palgrave Macmillan, 2018), 301–321a.

INDEX

1980 Refugee Act, 39, 44, 55, 142
1980 Republican National Convention, 38
9/11 attacks, 33, 44, 52–54, 85–106, 157, 180n237. *See also* September 11 attacks

Abani, Chris, 6. *See also* Nigerian-Biafran War
Abbot, Greg, 141–42
ACT for America (ACT), 64, 66–67
Afghanistan: Biden administration and, 1, 153–54; bipartisanship, 5; Republican opposition to refugees from, 1–2, 5; resettlement, 1, 5, 9, 45, 66, 139, 154–55; Sanders, Bernie and, 115–16; War on Terrorism (WOT), 53–54; withdrawal of US and NATO forces, 1
Afghans: Biden administration and, 1, 153–54; conservative and Republican resistance to resettlement, 1–2, 134, 139, 167; refugees and deservingness of protection, 155, 234n117; resettlement, 1, 5, 9, 45, 66, 139, 154–55, 189n49; "terrorist affiliations" and, 155; Taliban and, 1, 5, 53, 154.
African countries: diaspora and discriminatory treatment, 155; imagery of chaos, 89; Muslim refugees, 67; North Africa, 3, 66, 89; Organization of African Unity Refugee Convention, 166n84; racialization, 66, 148–49; refugee admissions, 8–9, 41, 52, 117, 148; and US exceptionalism, 117
"Afro-Cubans," 47
"Afro-Latinx" racialization, 38

al-Qaeda, 97
America First: Biden administration and, 153; ideology, 118–19, 141, 156; interpretations of national identity, 142; refugee responsibility-sharing and, 146; Trump's 2020 reelection campaign, 138; Trumpism and, 152
American Freedom Law Center (AFLC), 64
Anglo-Saxon/Anglo-Protestant, 21, 39, 70–71, 115, 139
anti-American: Middle East as, 86, 89, 100; refugee resettlement organizations and, 146; religious refugee advocacy and, 146; Syria, 86
anti-Black racism, 47
anti-Christian: agenda, 130; Democratic support for refugee resettlement as, 126, 129–130; nativist logics and bigotry, 79; Obama, Barack as, 129; pro-Muslim/anti-Christian binaries, 33, 108, 127–29, 131; refugee admissions and, 130–32; Syrian refugees, 97; United Nations as, 130; US immigration as, 127; victimhood and, 82. *See also* Christian
anticommunism, 45, 47. *See also* communism
anti-Sharia legislation, 64. *See also* "creeping Sharia;" Sharia
Arendt, Hannah, 10, 167n93, 173n165
Asian refugees: capitalism and, 47; refugee admissions, 9, 40, 46, 148; "model minorities," 39, 47; as "non-Western," 149; Vietnam War and, 55

assimilation, 49, 52, 70–71, 76, 139, 150
asylum: Christians as victims, 79–80; claims, 11; claimants, 8, 153; countries of first origin, 14, 22; criminalization, 7–8; reparations, 15; Republican Party and, 38, 40–41; seekers, 3, 5–6, 8–12, 14, 50, 55, 57, 70, 145, 150–51, 153–54 154, 157
Australia, 25, 45

Baltic, 46, 51
Bhutan, 9, 41
Biden, Joe, 1–4, 9, 16, 34, 134–35, 137, 139, 146–48, 151–54
Bipartisan Congressional Refugee Caucus, 44, 53, 142–43
Black political power/autonomy, 38, 52
border control/security, 35, 56, 87, 107, 122, 145, 149, 157
borders, 6, 8, 10–15, 28, 50, 52, 55, 57, 7–74, 78–79, 122, 133, 138, 141, 149–50, 154
Bosnia: Hemon, Aleksandar, 7; mass atrocities and, 50–51; refugees, 7, 51, 54; "white" and "western," 51
British, 6, 177n209, 177n210
"burden-sharing," 11, 13–16, 28–29, 108, 111. See also "responsibility-sharing"
Bush, George H. W., 42, 50
Bush, George W., 37, 41–44, 50, 52–54, 86, 96, 99, 127
Bush, Jeb, 109–10

Cambodia, 51
Canada, 24–25, 45, 142
capitalism, 47–48
Caribbean refugee admissions, 8–9
Carlson, Tucker, 1
Carter, Jimmy, 49
Catholic: Charities, 124; Democratic Party and, 123–24; migrants, 61; refugees, 51; Relief Services, 124; teachings, 61; US Conference of Catholic Bishops 123–24

Center for Immigration Studies (CIS), 74, 76, 139
Center for Security Policy (CSP), 64–65, 67, 139, 204n68
Central America, 8, 38, 57, 71, 73, 153, 177n206
Central Asia, 66, 87–88, 91, 106, 131, 139, 151, 157
Chinese: Exclusion Act, 61; refugees, 47; "virus," 150
Christian: Coalition, 51, 77–78, 139; discrimination, 126–27, 130; hegemony, 26, 66, 69, 82, 128; liberal, 123–26; migrants, 81–82; Reformed Church, 123; refugees, 9, 79, 81, 127, 130; supremacy, 82, 130, 151; Syrians and, 63, 81, 202n37; victimhood, 4, 32, 81, 96, 126–131, 135, 149, 151. See also anti-Christian
Church of Jesus Christ of Latter-day Saints, 140. See also Mormon
citizenship, 38, 65
civilizational: attributes, 19, 154; crisis, 61; discourse, 87; identity, 85–86; infiltrators, 32, 86, 105; preservation, 82; refugee threat, 59, 82, 96–97, 100, 106; sovereignty, 141; superiority, 83; supremacy, 98; transformation, 59. See also cultural transformation; Western civilization
civil society actors/groups, 18–20, 23–27, 32, 34, 37, 60–63, 74, 75, 82, 134, 146, 150, 152, 156
civil war, 89
climate change, 10, 12, 103, 158
climate refugees, 12, 158. See also environmental refugees
climate-related disasters, 7
Clinton, Bill, 40, 50–51
Clinton, Hillary, 100, 107, 115, 122, 126
Cold War, 27, 32, 35–36, 40, 45–50, 52, 55, 58, 63, 89, 192n88
colonial: assimilation programs, 52; dichotomies, 96; fantasies of America,

36. 140; foundations of the refugee regime, 43; foreign policy accountability and, 98; frameworks, 33; modes of categorizing the world, 6; origins of US state-building, 39; structures encoded in migration and refugee regimes, 58; violence, 38; war on terror and, 87. *See also* colonialism; postcolonial

colonialism, 7, 25, 52, 88. *See also* colonial; postcolonial

communism, 9, 39, 45, 48–49, 99. *See also* anticommunism

Congressional Black Caucus, 155

Congressional Human Rights Caucus/ Commission (CHRC), 50

coronavirus, 34, 135, 149–50. *See also* Covid-19; pandemic; Title 42

COVID-19, 34, 135, 146, 149–50, 153. *See also* coronavirus; pandemic; Title 42

"creeping Sharia," 98. *See also* anti-Sharia legislation; Sharia

crimes against humanity, 14. *See also* mass atrocity crimes; war crimes

criminality/criminalization, 7–8, 11, 49, 107

Cuban refugees: 9, 38, 47–49, 57, 117; 188n33; "Afro-Cubans" versus "white elite Cubans," 47; exceptionalist vision of the United States and, 117.

cultural transformation, 72, 83, 86, 96. *See also* civilizational; ethnocultural

cultural warriors, 33, 108, 112, 119, 121, 126, 131

Deferred Action for Childhood Arrivals (DACA), 57

Democratic Republic of Congo, 9

demographic change/transformation, 1, 59, 62, 70, 73, 77. *See also* cultural transformation

Department of Homeland Security (DHS), 8, 53, 85

deportation, 42–43, 154

detention, 4, 11, 43, 87, 94, 153

deterrence, 6, 25, 35, 50, 58

disease, 149–50

displacement: the environment and, 158; forcible, 7, 21, 37, 39, 136; partisan responses to, 109–10, 147, 156; representational practices, 133; root causes of, 58, 89; security threats and, 157; US contributions and culpability, 24, 33, 37, 42, 88–89, 131

Department of Homeland Security (DHS), 8, 53, 85, 104

Department of State, 8

Director of National Intelligence, 72, 85

divine purpose/plan, 35, 37, 38, 48, 99, 114, 138

Du Bois, W. E. B., 21, 60, 189n48

Egypt, 81, 162n24

Eisenhower, Dwight D., 42, 45

elections: 2015–16 US election cycle, 4, 16–18, 23, 25–26, 31–32, 34, 57, 59–63, 66, 77, 80, 82, 86–87, 96, 105, 108, 111–12, 119, 123, 130, 132, 135, 140, 153; 2016 US elections, 1, 4, 16–18, 23, 26, 32, 35, 66, 70, 107, 112, 133, 140, 146–48, 151; 2019–20 election cycle, 146–47, 152; 2020 US elections, 138, 140, 146–48, 151–52

El Salvador, 7, 38

empire, 7, 50. *See also* imperial/imperialism

environmental degradation, 10, 12

environmental refugees, 7, 158. *See also* climate refugees

Episcopalian, 124

ethnocultural: identity narratives, 32, 60; nativism and, 59, 61–62; preservation, 4, 61, 75, 111, 121. *See also* civilizational; cultural transformation

Europe/European, 17, 24–25, 37, 42, 45–46, 51, 61–62, 65, 71–73, 76, 81, 87, 93, 96–98, 103–4, 106, 115, 138, 150, 154, 190n60

European Union (EU), 24

evangelical, 48–49, 77–78, 124–27, 129, 137–38, 145
Evangelical Immigration Table (EIT), 145–46
Evangelicals for Biblical Immigration (EBI), 77–78
exceptionalist mythologies/visions, 8, 36–37, 42, 45–46, 52, 72, 112–18, 131, 143, 145. *See also* providential exceptionalism
Executive Order 13769, 3, 135. *See also* Travel Ban
Executive Order 13888, 140, 142

"failed states," 53, 55, 66
Family Research Council (FRC), 77, 79–80, 126
FBI, 85, 104, 128, 136, 149
Federation for American Immigration Reform (FAIR), 74–76, 139
feminine: Democrats as, 106; humanitarian protection as, 93. *See also* feminized
feminized: Democrats as, 33, 106, 108, 120; migration as, 93; representations of refugees, 91–94, 105, 120, 122, 157; Syrian men as, 93. *See also* feminine
forced migration, 10, 13, 22, 145
France, 85, 90, 102–3, 173n165
Francis, Pope, 124

Gaza, 3
gendered: binaries, 29, 85–86, 93; Democratic Party and, 33, 105; logics, 26, 33, 105, 108; hierarchies, 17, 31, 91, 93; narratives, 3, 5, 105; norms and Republican Party, 112; objects of humanitarian care, 92–93
genocide, 14, 78, 81, 128–29, 146
Germany/German, 14, 70, 109, 177n209, 183n257
Global Centre for the Responsibility to Protect, 66
Global Compact on Migration, 138

"globalists," 135, 138–39, 146
Global North, 14–15, 22
Global South, 3, 14, 22, 45, 158, 169n114
"good immigrants"/"good migrants," 27, 47, 52, 55–56
Guatemala, 7, 38

Haitians, 38, 47
hate crimes, 102, 137
hate group, 66, 126
Hebrew Immigrant Aid Society, 51, 152
Heritage Foundation, 150
"Hispanic challenge"/"Hispanization," 8, 73
Hmong, 41, 48
Honduras, 7
hospitality, 15, 37, 40, 47, 123, 125, 141, 154
humanitarian/humanitarianism: agenda, 50; aid, 45; assistance to victims in Syria and Iraq, 113; attempts to discredit arguments for, 149; concerns and terrorism, 105; configuration of refugees and, 58; crises, 16; gendered protection and, 91–93; hegemony, 32, 49, 53, 55; hierarchies, 95; human rights and, 58; liberal Christians and, 123; liberal Democrats and, 113; marketplace, 51; migration, 3, 5, 9–10, 13, 22–23, 133–34, 153, 156; narratives of benevolent, 24; needs, 44; NGOs, 20; objects of, 92; parolees, 9, 153; policy and refugee resettlement, 56; protection and race, 155; support to people in refugee camps, 80; US power and, 52
human rights violations, 7, 43, 76, 117, 145, 151, 153
Hungarian refugees, 9, 46

ideology, 3, 10, 23, 27, 30–31, 33, 59, 63, 73, 75, 99, 100, 107–8, 110–11, 115, 118, 123, 130–32, 136, 141, 144, 156, 219n23
illegality/"illegal immigrants," 5, 55–56, 70, 74, 141

imperial/imperialism, 15, 40, 55, 140. *See also* empire
Immigration and Naturalization Service (INS), 52
indigenous/Indigenous, 15, 21, 38–39, 41. *See also* Native Americans
industrious: America as, 8, 32, 36, 47–48, 58, 143; refugees as, 145; refugees and whiteness, 47, 61
infiltrators: Muslim, 129; Muslim Brotherhood, 35; refugees as, 1–2, 4, 26, 31, 79, 92–95, 98–106, 121–22, 133, 136, 148, 154
internment: Nazi, 10; Japanese Americans and, 116
international law, 6, 15, 148–149
International Relations (IR), 4, 10–11, 17, 20, 28–30, 33, 183n260
Iran/Iranian, 5–6, 45, 89, 137, 150, 201n22
Iraq: ISIS and, 80, 121; persecuted Christians in, 81; Iran and, 137; mothers and children in, 124; War, 41, 53–54, 90, 113, 211n25
Iraqi: Christians, 128; interpreters, 41; refugees, 54, 71–72, 85, 89, 94, 97, 105, 113, 115, 121, 125–26, 128, 189n49; US moral leadership and, 123
Irish migrants, 61
irregular entry/irregular migration, 3, 8, 11, 21, 55–57
ISIS, 1–2, 33, 59, 66, 80–81, 85, 89, 93, 96–97, 99, 120–22, 131, 136, 148. *See also* Islamic State
Islamic: enemies, 131; "extremism," 36, 53, 86–87, 99, 152; immigration strategy, 139; law, 64, 67; Revolution, 137; "savage," 102; "supremacism," 64; "terrorists," 95–97, 99, 108–9, 122, 128–29; threat, 120–122, 148; theocracy, 139. *See also* Islamic State; "radical Islam"
Islamic State, 97, 136
Islamophobia, 68, 116, 151
Italian migrants, 61

Japan/Japanese, 62, 85, 116
Jewish: conspiracy, 61, 138, 146; diaspora, 173n165; escapees, 2; halakhah/law, 64; organizations, 124; refugees, 50, 128. *See also* Soros, George
Jews: Christian refugees and, 128; former Soviet Union and, 41; Holocaust and, 116, 128; as "Orientals," 62; persecution of, 38, 48; refugee admissions and, 41, 50, 117; "War on Terror" and, 86. *See also* Jewish
jihad, 95, 98–99, 102, 129. *See also* jihadist
jihadist, 80–81, 87–88, 120–21. *See also* jihad
Johnson, Lyndon B., 43
Jordan: Palestinian refugees in, 3; responsibility-sharing and, 136; Syrian refugee resettlement departures and, 3

Kosovar refugees, 54
Kurds, 41

Laos, 48–49, 51
Latinos: racialization and, 38; paradigms of invasion, 73; Huntington, Samuel and, 70; threat narratives, 8, 71
Lebanon: Palestinian refugees in, 3; responsibility-sharing and, 136
Lutherans, 124
Lutheran Social Services, 146

masculinity: Republicans and, 93, 106, 108, 112, 119, 122–23. *See also* gendered; masculinized
masculinized: imagery and Syrian refugees, 92–93; Republican cultural warriors, 108, 112, 120, 131; threat, 33, 86, 91. *See also* gendered; masculinity; Syrian men
mass atrocity crimes, 2–3, 66, 148. *See also* crimes against humanity; war crimes
media, 18–20, 74, 80, 84, 99, 126, 146, 172n148

Methodists, 124
"methodological nationalism," 29
methodology, 5, 16
Merkel, Angela, 14
Mexico, 8, 50, 57, 71, 73–74, 78, 150, 154
Middle East: anti-Americanism and, 86, 89, 100; assimilation and Syrians from, 71; Christians in, 128; civilizational threat and, 106; European response to refugees from, 72; Muslim refugees from, 67; mischaracterization of refugee admissions, 9; ontologies of, 88–90; orientalist representations of, 33, 62–63, 73, 76, 86–94, 101, 105, 122, 151, 157; US policy and, 53, 131; racialization and refugees from, 66, 149 "radicalized Muslims" and, 82; "radical Islamic immigration strategy" and, 139; refugee camps in, 81–82; refugees from, as coronavirus carriers, 150; safe haven for refugees from, 117; Travel Ban and, 148
"model minorities," 39, 47. *See also* Asian refugees
Mormon, 140. *See also* Church of Jesus Christ of Latter-day Saints
multicausal: drivers of migration, 10; process and reconfiguration of refugees, 105, 111; refugee policy as, 27, 105; refugee representations, 19
multiculturalism, 26, 32, 69–70, 72, 74, 151–52
Muslim Brotherhood, 139
Myanmar, 9, 41, 53

National Origins Act of 1924, 61
National Security-Entry-Exit Registration System (NSEERS), 87
Native Americans, 39, 115. *See also* indigenous
nativism: adaptation, 134, 150; competitive victimhood and, 77; cultural threat, 37, 48–49, 59–84, 86, 97, 104, 106, 121; definition of, 60–61; origin stories and, 41; Trumpism and, 127, 137, 147, 151; early 1900s and, 62
NATO, 1, 5, 154
Nayeri, Dina, 6, 10
Nazi/Nazism, 2, 10, 99, 117
Nicaragua/Nicaraguan, 48, 54
Nigerian-Biafran War, 6. *See also* Abani, Chris
non-refoulement, 11, 153
norm evasion, 12, 145, 149, 151, 153
norms, 11–12, 20, 22–23, 25, 28–30, 43, 51, 83, 108, 111–13, 115, 122–25, 129–33, 139, 158, 183n260
Norway, 45
NumbersUSA, 137, 228n26

Obama, Barack, 2, 36, 44, 56, 73, 78, 93, 107, 109, 120–22, 126–29
Omar, Ilhan, 142, 148, 152, 232n95
Orderly Departure Program, 56
Orientalism: definition of, 62–63; gender and, 91–94; global and transnational discourses, 25; juxtaposition of Western and non-Western, 75; Muslim infiltration and, 61–69, 122, 136, 142, 153; ontologies of the Middle East, 26, 73, 76, 86–90, 100, 105–6, 148, 151, 157

Pakistan, 5, 45
Palestinians, 62, 101; refugees, 3–4, 12. *See also* United Nations Relief and Works Agency for Palestine Refugees (UNRWA)
pandemic, 34, 135–36, 146, 149–50, 153. *See also* coronavirus; CoVID-19; Title 42
Paris attacks, 33, 85–87, 89–90; 93, 97, 101–5, 110
parole power, 9
parolees, 6, 9–10, 27, 134, 153–55, 157
Pelosi, Nancy, 114, 123–124

polarization, 1, 4, 16–17, 23, 26, 30, 33, 56, 107–8, 110–11, 115, 135, 140, 151, 156, 158, 220n29
political correctness, 26, 64, 74, 108, 112, 121–22, 128–32, 135, 151–52
postcolonial, 24, 65. *See also* colonial
Protestant, 21, 61, 70, 72, 115, 137
providential exceptionalism, 32, 35, 37–38, 40, 49, 51, 58, 117–19, 143, 149, 157. *See also* exceptionalist mythologies

racialized/racialization: anticommunism and, 47; Central Americans, 38; foreign policy, 58; "global color line," 31; Muslim refugees and, 59; narratives, 3–5, 16–17, 25–26, 29, 31–35, 105, 133; world order and, 55
racist/racism, 31, 40, 47, 60, 68–69, 73, 84, 100, 116, 130, 137, 152–53, 205n76
"radical Islam," 25–26, 87, 89, 100, 102–8, 112, 121, 128, 132, 147–48, 157. *See also* Islamic
Ray, Robert, 39, 189n36
Reagan, Ronald, 38, 46–47, 50, 57, 177n206
refugee camps/encampment, 3, 13, 55, 80–82, 148, 150
Refugee Convention, 6, 8, 11–12, 14, 42–43
"refugee crisis," 4–5, 25, 32, 34, 57, 60–61, 80, 83, 99, 103, 107, 112, 114, 120, 153, 163n33
"Refugee Day," 42. *See also* World Refugee Day
refugeehood: legal definition of, 6–7, 12; liberal policy values and, 156; feminized accounts of, 105; stories and interpretations of, 6, 9, 19, 21, 29, 31, 57, 133–135, 145, 153, 155, 157; vulnerability and, 92; white settler narratives of, 39, 140
Refugee/migrant binary, 10, 15
Refugee Resettlement Watch (RRW), 67–68, 74, 149–150, 152

Resettlement Accountability National Security Act, 89
Responsibility to Protect (R2P), 14, 66
"responsibility-sharing," 1, 4–6, 11, 13–18, 22–24, 26–35, 37, 40, 44–46, 49, 51, 53–54, 58–60, 77, 80–81, 83, 93–96, 100, 103, 108–10, 113–15, 118, 120, 122, 125, 130–33, 136–39, 140, 142–43, 146, 154, 156–58. *See also* "burden-sharing"
Roosevelt, Franklin D., 85
Russia/Russian, 46, 154–55

SAFE Act (American Security Against Foreign Enemies Act), 33, 85–86, 89–91, 94, 97, 99, 106, 113–14, 116–18, 121–25
"safe haven": faith-based civil society groups and, 37; mythologies, 38–39, 44, 58, 141, 143, 145, 157; America's founding fathers and, 41; communism and, 49; Democratic Party and, 39, 108–9, 112–14, 116–17, 131, 147; United States as, 35, 147;
Salafi, 100, 211n25
Sanders, Bernie, 115
Scott, Rick, 2
September 11 attacks, 35, 86, 89, 101, 103. *See also* 9/11 attacks
Sharia, 64–66; 98, 136, 139, 142. *See also* anti-Sharia legislation; "creeping Sharia"
Shire, Warsan, 6
slaves/slavery, 37–39, 46, 77, 115, 171n139
Somalia/Somali, 6, 41, 49, 52, 66, 142, 148, 152, 162n24, 174n181, 232n95
Soros, George, 146
Southern Poverty Law Center, 66, 74, 126
Soviet Union/Soviet countries, 38, 40–4, 48, 50–51, 57, 117
Special Immigrant Visa (SIV) program, 189n49
Statue of Liberty ethos, 34, 108, 112–13, 115, 131

Sudan, 41, 52–53, 162n24
Sunni Muslim, 80, 127
Sweden, 45, 192n84
Syria Bright Future, 21, 2133n67
Syrian men: Democratic Party and, 93, 105; feminized, 93; manhood, 93; masculinized threat, 91–93; "Muslim-migrant-male" triad and, 93; not deserving resettlement, 93–95, 105, 157; potential combatants, 86, 93–95. *See also* masculinized
Syrian women: "bad victims," 95; Democratic Party and, 33, 91–93, 115; as potential terrorists, 95; objects of humanitarian care, 92–93; "saving" women and children, 53, 86, 91–92; victimhood, 87, 91–92; widows, 95. *See also* "womenandchildren"
Syrian Refugee Verification and Safety Act, 88

Taliban, 1, 5, 53, 154. *See also* Afghans
Title 42, 153–54
torture, 2, 4, 11, 41, 51, 94
tradition, 38, 40, 43, 44, 49, 64, 69, 79, 93, 114, 118–19, 129–30, 141, 147
Tran, Vu, 156
trauma, 7, 18, 21, 101–2
Travel Ban, 3, 16, 34, 86, 132, 135, 137, 139, 147–49, 153–54. *See also* Executive Order 13769
Truman, Harry, 42, 192n88
Trump, Donald, 1–5, 16–18, 24, 26, 34, 59, 64, 72, 75, 78–79, 93, 95, 100, 102, 107, 113, 115–116, 119, 122, 126–127, 129, 132–135, 137–140, 142, 144, 146–148, 151–154
Turkey/Turkish, 62, 171n144, 177n209, 183n257
two-party system, 16, 33, 108, 110

"un-American," 115–116, 131
United Kingdom, 25

United Nations (UN), 25, 32, 55, 81–83, 128, 130
United Nations Refugee Agency (UNHCR), 6–8, 11–12, 14, 22, 35, 42, 44, 56, 130, 136, 190n60
United Nations Relief and Works Agency for Palestine Refugees (UNRWA), 3–4, 12, 16, 22, 153. *See also* Palestinians
Universal Declaration of Human Rights, 50, 190n60
Ukraine, 153–155
Ukrainians, 9, 34, 46, 135, 154–155
USA PATRIOT Act, 87
US Constitution, 64–65, 75, 98, 121, 136, 142
US Refugee Admissions Program (USRAP), 8

Values Voter summits, 80, 126
Venezuelans, 7
Vietnam/Vietnamese, 9, 38–39, 41, 47–49, 51, 53–57, 117, 156, 173n172, 188n24, 189n35
violence: against Christians, 82, 128; associations with Syrian refugees and, 101; colonial, 38; forms of, 7; hate crimes and, 137; indigenous peoples and, 39; military interventionism and, 139; Muslims and associations with, 97, 129; Orientalism and 87, 89; refugee origin countries and, 76; threats by refugees and, 75; Syrian refugees fleeing, 114, 146; Syrian refugee men and 91; "The West" and justifications of, 96
voluntary agencies/resettlement organizations, 78, 146, 161n11, 173n172
"voluntary migrants," 10

war crimes, 14, 76. *See also* crimes against humanity; mass atrocity crimes
War in Afghanistan, 5

Washington, George, 37, 40, 155
Western civilization, 25, 33, 65, 71–72, 86–87, 95, 99, 105, 134, 139, 157. *See also* civilizational
whiteness, 19, 26–27, 31–33, 36, 45–47, 61–62, 72, 82, 98–99, 134
women and children: Syrian and gendered dimensions of refugees, 90–94; Orientalist infantilizing, 91; as innocent, dependent, or helpless, 91–92; US refugee responsibility-sharing and, 91, as deserving resettlement, 94; terrorist threats and, 94
"womenandchildren," 91
World Refugee Day, 52, 147. *See also* "Refugee Day"
World Relief, 146
World War II, 2, 6, 42, 61, 107, 116, 122, 128

Yemen, 66, 148, 162n24

ABOUT THE AUTHOR

ALISE COEN is Associate Professor of Political Science at the University of Wisconsin-Green Bay.

www.ingramcontent.com/pod-product-compliance
Lightning Source LLC
Chambersburg PA
CBHW031146020426
42333CB00013B/529